Rethinking
Relationships

For Ratty.
"He was a good rat" (Gabriel Lawson-Duck, personal
communication)

Rethinking Relationships

Steve Duck
University of Iowa

SAGE

Los Angeles | London | New Delhi
Singapore | Washington DC

For information:

SAGE Publications, Inc.
2455 Teller Road
Thousand Oaks,
   California 91320
E-mail: order@sagepub.com

SAGE Publications Ltd.
1 Oliver's Yard
55 City Road
London EC1Y 1SP
United Kingdom

SAGE Publications India Pvt. Ltd.
B 1/I 1 Mohan Cooperative
   Industrial Area
Mathura Road, New Delhi 110 044
India

SAGE Publications Asia-Pacific Pte. Ltd.
33 Pekin Street #02-01
Far East Square
Singapore 048763

Printed in the United States of America

Library of Congress Cataloging-in-Publication Data

Rethinking relationships / Steve Duck.
    p. cm.
Includes bibliographical references and index.
ISBN 978-1-4129-5876-9 (pbk.)
    1. Interpersonal relations. 2. Interpersonal communication. I. Duck, Steve.

HM1106.R48 2011
302—dc22

This book is printed on acid-free paper.

10   11   12   13   14   10   9   8   7   6   5   4   3   2   1

Acquisitions Editor:	Todd R. Armstrong
Editorial Assistant:	Nathan Davidson
Production Editor:	Libby Larson
Copy Editor:	Liann Lech
Typesetter:	C&M Digitals (P) Ltd.
Proofreader:	Sally Jaskold
Cover Designer:	Gail Buschman
Marketing Manager:	Helen Salmon

Brief Contents

Detailed Contents

Acknowledgments

A lthough I normally enjoy writing, this book has proved particularly difficult to complete, and I have had working drafts of the manuscript around for about 6 years, during which time I have edited or written another six books. For sustaining me through the difficulties, contributing ideas that I have been able to discuss and consider, for criticism and suggestions made in classes I have taught using the ideas now finalized in this script, I would like to acknowledge and thank the following: Seth Bunting, Min Kyong Cho, Jordan Flesch, Ryan Gourley, Dena Huisman, Linda Maxson, David T. McMahan, Sarah Nebel, Kristen Norwood, Ratty, Cara Roberts, Stephanie Rollie, Lee West, Julia T. Wood, and Brendan Young.

I would particularly like to thank those friends and reviewers who read (parts of) the whole manuscript and gave excellent feedback on the many drafts, giving me new insights and approaches to the venture: Mark Fine, Jimmie Manning, Bob Milardo, Marshall Prisbell, Stephanie Rollie, Carla Ross, Pam Secklin, and other anonymous reviewers. All of these reviewers provided encouragement and specific examples, and Pam Secklin was a rock in checking for lunacy and connectedness with the real world. Jimmie Manning in particular was extremely helpful in providing instances of popular culture that supported (or challenged) the arguments of the book, and I am very grateful for his specificity and enlightening comments and examples.

As ever, the support from Sage Editor Todd Armstrong was exemplary, and his skills at balancing demands with understanding are much appreciated, as was the cheerful encouragement and indirect support of Carmel Schrire, at various stages while working on another book. Todd provides the incisive insights and the reality that authors sometimes lack, yet he also appreciates the ways that work best to talk authors out of a funk. Unique among editors in my experience, he clearly takes a genuine interest in the books that he commissions as *books* rather than only as "consumable units," which is not as common as it should be these days.

Steve Duck
University of Iowa

1

Old and New Ways of Seeing Relationships

If this book "works," then by the time you reach the end of it, you will think about relationships in an entirely new way.

That is a very large claim. In order to justify it, I must first prove that I have some idea of what you think about relationships at the moment. Then I need to show how I expect to change it, so that I make it worth your reading further. (I suppose I also have to convince you why my opinion is relevant. This book is not all about me, I assure you, but the publishers asked me to mention that in 1982, I cofounded the first ever international conference on personal relationships; in 1984, I launched the first ever journal on relationships [*Journal of Social and Personal Relationships*] and edited it for 15 years. In 1987, I cofounded an international and a local organization that later became the International Association for Research on Relationships, the only society for the study of relationships. I have published 50 books on relationships, and this one is a sort of legacy volume. Not that any of that matters to you, but I was asked to put it in, and now we have got it out of the way.)

Let me guess that you see relationships as involving social or biological urges, emotions, feelings, self-disclosure, and intimacy; that you talk about people being "in" relationships; that by and large, you see people as having choices about their relationships; that a good relationship is based on "good communication." If this is a more or less accurate guess, it is because it is what my students tell me. They have needs, attractions, physical impulses, or social desires for company, and they fulfill these needs through relationships that they *choose* to enter. They think that romance is good, that similarity of personality attracts (birds of a feather flock together), and that a kiss is either a greeting or a sign of passion. Like them, you probably don't think that people should have sex on the bus, and you would be intrigued enough by the headline to read the rest of the story about a 75-year-old woman marrying a 20-year-old man. You probably believe that your close relationships are more important to your life than are other sorts of distant relationships or general acquaintances. If you are like my students, then you probably believe that your relationships with friends and lovers are created freely, even if the original opportunity arose by chance from circumstances, events, or location; that you can get out of undesired relationships; and that all you need is love.

In this book, all of these assumptions are up for grabs. I want to present material in a way that makes you think either "Yes, I believe that. Is it right or not?" or "I never thought of that. I wonder if it is a good idea?"

Many people accept that a lot of relationship behavior—certainly, romantic behavior—is based on microbiology over which you have very little control—hormones, for example—and on the physical features like your sex and how you are built by genetics. You may feel strong sexual urges, your heart may race in the presence of someone you find attractive, your pupils may dilate (enlarge) when you feel attracted, you may perspire with excitement in a romantic event, and you may feel intense arousal and rage when spurned by a lover. Your body does this to you, willy-nilly. Much important relational research emphasizes the biological forces to which human beings are subject as part of this animal substrate to human nature. For example, you have physical urges, biological needs for sex, and tendencies to react physically and even physiologically to emotions of love or desire. Levels of cortisol or testosterone can even explain some of what goes on in family interaction (Floyd, 2004).

This is not surprising because we all know that human life, even relational life, has an animal, biological basis. But even though it is not surprising, is it a good idea?

> Humans share more than 98% of their DNA with chimpanzees, and you may have met some people who seem to share even more.

Well, here are some of the problems with the idea: Chew over them and see what you think. Even if desire has a physiological basis, it is nevertheless expressed, performed, and understood in a cultural and social context. Accordingly, you probably recognize the social and cultural boundaries that surround your physical enactment of these urges, such that even your animal lusts are expressed in socially or culturally approved ways. Your affections are expressed in a cultural and social environment that restrains or redirects your animal feelings. For example, even though the microbiology of Koreans, Canadians, and Fijians is essentially the same, they have a hugely divergent set of ways of enacting a marriage ceremony to legitimize the expression of the fundamental human urges for sex (Duck, 2007). This is not especially surprising, and we rarely consider it as a problem or something worth thinking about. Culture/society and shared value systems about what is "right" in relationships not only direct relational behaviors, but are so much a part of life that they feel natural or, in other words, are completely taken for granted (TFG).

That is not all. The media, too, shape expressions of feelings and emphasize those cultural norms that are most expected and desired as "reasonable." Social control of relational activities is pervasive and yet often invisible. Nevertheless, you do not kiss everyone you desire whenever you feel like it, because social rules forbid it; you do not marry a sibling because your society does not regard that as an acceptable form of marriage. The media and other people whom you meet in everyday life help you to see that there are good, bad, appropriate, inappropriate, and even forbidden ways to do love or friendship or even liking (adultery is bad, friendship is good).

The tensions between the biological ways to do relationships and the social constraints on such expression are often quite strong, and, by and large, it is very likely that you follow the social guidelines that exist in your own society. There are social forces that prevent pedophiles, for example, from making love to children, and also proscribe public sex or people demonstrating their deeply felt hatred of one another by stabbing them in public without consequences of law.

There is more, then, to relationships than the simple enactment of desires or choice. We must consider other factors than the ones you may have immediately thought to be relevant to desires for relationship, including the cultural context in which your

---

Open Question to Ask Your Friends

Ask yourself and your friends which of these ideas seem to be obvious. (Note that some are contradictory, yet are also common sense.)

- Love is created by similarity (birds of a feather flock together)
- Opposites attract
- I could never date anyone I would not marry
- Love at first sight is not only possible but magical
- Beauty is in the eye of the beholder
- Distance lends enchantment to the view
- Absence makes the heart grow fonder
- Out of sight, out of mind
- True love is always founded on true friendship first
- It is quite reasonable to feel jealousy if your partner is flirting with someone else
- Someone who commits a crime in the heat of passion should be excused

beliefs about relationships are developed and enacted. All experiences of relationships are located in the more general set of cultural romantic beliefs and expectations.

This is both a reason why people see relationships as based on choice, emotion, similarity, and all the other items listed earlier, but also—more subtly—the reason why research keeps finding results consistent with those beliefs. Everyday folks think about relationships in the ways that are both taken for granted and reinforced by the culture in which people—and the scientific enterprises that seek to explain relationships—are based, and hence scientific research rests on the same assumptions. This is why, naturally enough—or so it seems to most people—the science tends to confirm and also conform with their (cultural) beliefs about the nature of relationships.

A key point I will highlight in this book is both obvious and overlooked. Language itself—the very way you talk about relationships and enforce the rules that surround them—is not a neutral medium, but affects discussion of relationships and also shapes them. If you talk about love, then it is judged to be good; try talking about incest, and you will find that society thinks that it is not a great idea. Your relational activity is done in talk with other people who share your relational assumptions because they are from the same society. That, in part, is what "culture" means: a *shared* set of assumptions that is freely bandied about and reinforced in your chatter with other people. You express love, liking, and desire, not only with hugs and kisses, but also through verbal discourse that your culture recognizes ("I love you"; "honey"; "darling").

In order to understand relationships properly, we must understand the roles that society, language, those taken-for-granted assumptions, and other people who share those assumptions play in the conduct of relationships. In social context, your own personal ideas won't mean much to anyone else unless the society at large "speaks the same language" about such relationships, because it is not (I will argue) all about you and your feelings for your partner; society steps into the picture as well. Everyone knows what you are talking about when you refer to adultery, friendship, Valentine's Day, relationship success, relationship breakup, and the rest. You take for granted what other people know in a particular society.

Think about what is taken for granted when you read "Pope Breathing Without Assistance"—a headline from the BBC in March 2005. You have to know what a pope is, why you would expect him to need assistance to breathe, and why that would be important enough for a major news source to tell you about it. My neighbor is breathing without assistance right now, and there is no newspaper headline about it. In fact, a pope is a key figure in the world, and a lot of people cared about what was happening to this particular pope. In fact, he was dying, and the headline updated you on that state of affairs.

But see this in another light and you will recognize that relationships not only are conducted in a social context of shared beliefs, but occur in a society that *judges* the performance according to that set of beliefs and assumptions about what is allowed and what is prohibited or proscribed. You can therefore bring all these ideas a bit closer to home: The other people who influence you are not just distant members of society, but people you know personally and talk to in your everyday chitchat.

Our culture does not stress the role of parents in marriage partner choices, but in other cultures, they have the decisive voice. Members of those cultures believe as firmly as you do that their way is natural and right and reflects reality. Because you have been encouraged to think of abstractions like "society" and "culture" as precisely that—abstractions—you fail to recognize that these concepts work on the ground at the interpersonal level with one person talking to another. Therefore, you often fail to make explicit the ways in which your culture works through "secret agents"—all the people you know personally. Your talk with them subtly directs and sustains your beliefs about the ways in which relationships are supposed to happen.

DISCUSSION QUESTION

The divorce rate in India, where many marriages are arranged, is around 1%. In the United States, where people express their own free choice, it is about 50%. Why do you think this is so?

Perhaps without recognizing it as such, you nevertheless feel the force of distant societal beliefs right at home, when you might, for instance, argue with your parents that you have individual rights to make your own choices. You might criticize or advise a friend about his or her relational behaviors, or you or the media feel free to disparage a celebrity for behaving inappropriately in a relationship—let's say adopting a baby from Somalia, or being a president of a bank who breaks rules to do favors for his girlfriend. When these events happen, there is critical, judgmental society at work right in your face (if you are watching the media) or your ear (if you are talking with a friend). Your relationships, then, somewhat surprisingly, are not just yours but society's.

What Do Relationships Do for You?

If you are part of a society that has rules and boundaries about particular relationship types, does that mean that human beings have no *general* needs for relationships? Probably not the case. Work by sociologists suggests that there are common requirements for relationships, but within such common needs, a society steers its members toward particular types of fulfillment. However, it is worth spending a short time exploring the broad value of relationships to people in general so that I can advance a more specific approach on top of that.

Given that I am explaining 21st-century relationships from a Western point of view, note that the very idea that humans get into relationships to fulfill personal (especially psychological) needs is a new idea. Seven hundred years ago, the needs of relationships would not involve psychological intimacy so much as the simple need to cooperate in order to stay alive. Modern Western culture has largely overcome the problems of sustaining life that may have driven the social needs of 700 years ago. In 1300 AD, people in the West bonded together to produce food, procreate, and prepare themselves for death. For the average person who actually made it to adulthood, death would arrive about the age of 32 years, and for most people alive in the middle of that century, it would take the devastating form of the Black Death that wiped out between 25% and 40% of the population of Europe (Gottfried, 1985). For such folk, relationships were not about a mushy sort of intimacy, full of flowers, sunsets, and self-disclosure, or even love. Everyone was striving to stay alive, reproduce, and save his or her soul, with little time or regard for the finer points of romance.

Nowadays, you expect a little more. People tend to presume that relationships are about fulfillment, love, companionship, and personal satisfaction and gratification. You have a choice, and you expect this because other, more basic needs for survival are taken care of. Upon what basis, then, are such choices made? Let's start to answer that by looking at general human needs, which can be brought down to the individual preferences that may be credited with influencing your relationship choices.

GENERAL REASONS FOR RELATING:
THE SEVEN PROVISIONS OF RELATIONSHIPS

Alas, the idea of freedom of choice over relationships may be viewed with suspicion, given that researchers have routinely shown the ways in which choices are actually restricted by social and demographic forces (Kerckhoff, 1974). Demographers can easily demonstrate that there is a naggingly high relationship between the social class, religion, and racial background of people who marry each other, suggesting that the freedom of choice that we had imagined to exist may not be as great as assumed.

Sociologist and relational scholar Robert Weiss (1974) looked for some general features of human relating. From careful analysis of bunches of different reports, he identified seven "provisions" of relationships, starting with some that are based on physical-social needs and moving on to the deeply psychological. Again, keep in mind that this approach is a strictly Western one and a psychological one, too, that takes little account of structural factors and culture, such as the historical needs that previously guided relational form.

The seven provisions are distilled from consideration of many different reports, stories about relationships, and even cultural stories (like fairy tales) that seem to show seven different, but equally important, benefits that make it attractive to be in relationships with other people. They summarize general human needs to be connected, as well as drawing on specific needs and desires that all humans have. Let's look at them one by one, then discuss the whole idea of whether (and how) such general needs would steer us to connect with other human beings.

1. Belonging and a Sense of Reliable Alliance

This provision is, in essence, a desire for acceptance and inclusion by other people, but also a strong need to see them as "there" for you. Weiss (1974) saw this as a major—perhaps the major—human requirement and one that has lasted from earlier times in history.

Note the ways that advertisers play to this desire: "Membership has its privileges" is a familiar reminder of the fact that inclusion is agreeable and that exclusion is undesirable. Many different attempts to be included also imply that a person is *preferred,* largely through the explicit exclusion of others who do not qualify for preferred membership. The underlying idea is that a decent social life—indeed, a major human goal—depends on acceptance by others. By being accepted and included by other people, you are explicitly being approved for who you are and what you represent, what you believe, the ideas that you hold, and the qualities that you exemplify. You are granted status as an "acceptable" person. Other people recognize and accept your very essence, and in doing so, they ratify your personal order. Advertisers try to sell relationship or "membership of a community of owners" in order to get people to buy products. They also stress reliable alliance: They are on your side, you can trust them to be there for you when you need them; they want to be with you and they want to help you. (Even those annoying "on hold" messages that claim that "Your call is important to us" play up to this theme of belonging and reliable alliance.)

2. Emotional Integration and Stability

This proposal is fundamental to human experience, and Weiss (1974) notes that a social world is virtually impossible without some benchmark against which a person can assess the appropriateness and validity of experiences and emotions. For example, displays of grief are culturally guided so that other members of the society recognize the feelings that the person is express-ing. So if you feel grief, then your performance of it is culturally influenced. (In some Middle Eastern cultures, grief is demonstrated by violent hurling of the body to the ground and rolling in the dust, whereas in Britain, grief is supposed to be dealt with in a restrained manner and a "stiff upper lip.") Your emotional expression, in short, has to be accepted by others as meaningful and is not simply something that you feel inside alone. On top of your personal feelings, your expression of the emotion must be understandable to others and accepted by those others as a proper and *appropriate* way to express and feel.

For example, if the spouse of a murder victim does not show any emotion when told about the victim's death, the police often treat that lack of emotion as suspicious. The media are forever reporting that someone showed no emotion when pronounced guilty by a jury, as if that person's stillness confirms his or her guilt by its inappropriateness to the situation (as expected by the culture or society). You know how to express your emotional experiences in a form that other people can interpret correctly, but—here's a key point—you *ask* other people. "This guy dumped me and I feel really bad. What should I do about it?" "My neighbor said this to me. Should I have been offended?" "Should I feel this bad about my job? Is it a normal way to feel?" Teenagers tend to do this quite a bit when it comes to dealing with romantic relationships and how they should be handled (Baxter, Dun, & Sahlstein, 2001). They refer their experiences to other teenagers for comment and advice. They learn by comparing their experiences with their friends' experiences and finding out how other people deal with life.

In short, your daily relationships provide a stable and meaningful way of seeing the world "out there," and this way of seeing is relational and based on communication rather than just being an individual experience. Even if you feel the emotion *personally*, all the same, the way in which you express it is shaped by the culture or the society to which you belong. Again, then, your per-sonal feelings are expressed within a set of social expectations, and this helps you to feel integrated and stable.

3. Opportunities for Communication About Ourselves

Weiss (1974) represented this as a fundamental provision of relationships, and indeed, there are many examples of cases in which people deprived of opportunities for communication about self readily unload themselves upon the nearest available victim, whether this be representatives of shower-curtain ring companies on planes or the traditional "strangers on the train" who talk your ear off about their own lives. Basically, we all like to talk about ourselves, and lots of "conversation" is basically people talking just about themselves to someone else ("Yes, that's interesting that it happened to you, because it hap-pened to me too. I . . . [goes on for 20 minutes]").

This need for communication about ourselves is fundamental and depends entirely on one's acceptance of the idea that social interaction itself pre-requires the listening presence of others who will share, accept, or at least listen politely to one's view of the world. So it means again that you are aware of the need to shape your personal reports into a form that other people can at least tolerate, but preferably accept. The new point that I'm making here is quite a simple one. Communication about yourself in everyday life also serves to assist you in satisfying your other needs, such as membership or acceptance of your personal reports. Although you have a need to communicate, then, that need is based on a deeper basic need, a pack mentality: a need for the acceptance of your way of looking at the world and inclusion in a group of other people who find it acceptable.

4. Provision of Assistance and Physical Support

Another obvious benefit that friends provide for one another is to help each other physically, although this is not evident in all relationships and can be done differently in different sorts of relationships (for example, relationships with one's elderly parents may require more demonstration of physical support than one's relationships with same-age peers). However, a general likelihood of being called upon to help friends, relations, and lovers is presumed when you enter such relationships.

Physical assistance is often provided by others for tasks that require more than one actor (like moving furniture too heavy for one person), and it is well-known that friends or relations can be called upon for physical help when other people would not be asked to do so (e.g., looking after cats, rats, and other pets during a person's absence; collecting the mail; driving one to the mall; and so forth).

But take a deeper look. Help giving, rather like the sending and receiving of birthday cards, is really about the honoring of the relationship and not about the monetary or physical value of the help or the gift—a story I will cover in much more depth in a later chapter. In short, *help is symbolic.* In other words, if you value the opinions of other people, then you accept the symbolic actions by which they indicate your value to them. As a matter of fact, this happens in the development of friendship, too: As you get to know and like someone more, you are opened to his or her influence in offering you new insights and attitudes about the world. You expect that he or she will help you and you will help him or her, even when it is inconvenient to do so. It is all part of the connecting bond that there is also a restricting bind (Wiseman, 1986). Think about the symbolism that is involved in doing favors for people. When you do something for someone else, it shows how much you value him or her as a person. You acknowledge the person's effort to be nice, even if you don't like the gift itself, because "it's the thought that counts." This is such a significant topic that I will devote a chapter to it later in the book.

5. Reassurance of Your Worth and Value

Weiss (1974) separated this provision from others, but it seems to me to be a version of the fundamental driver of interpersonal communication, namely, the need for emotional integration and stability (confirmation of your personal perspective), of which the reassurance of one's worth is merely one example. In other words, if you need to be accepted, then other people's opinions about your worth are counted as valuable. However, for most people in Western society, it is also important to be recognized as an individual, and this recognition is about more than emotional integration (Provision 2). It is important recognition of a person as an individual who has rights and privileges. The importance of being seen as an autonomous individual with freedom of choice about many issues is a fundamental element of the social order of modern Western society.

The other side of choice—being chosen by other people—also helps to reinforce your value as people. Accordingly, it is important to people to *demonstrate* that you have friendships, and indeed, Facebook explicitly allows people to show and tell how many friends they have (with pictures!). Similarly, award plaques and birthday cards are not hidden away in drawers (because *you* know you got them) but instead are openly displayed so that *others* can see that you received them.

Advertisers also like to show the users of their products as popular and valued people. Just look at all those photos of happy groups of people laughing with one another and hence showing closeness, membership, and acceptance of one another as they use the product. This, too, plays into the human need to be made to feel good.

The importance of Weiss's observation is that this happens through acceptance of you as a person—or in my terms, acceptance as a person who has a reasonable, socially acceptable, personal perspective. Because personal perspectives are personal, it is important that in a competitive world with different sets of personal perspectives available, your own personal version is evaluated and judged acceptable by others. Obviously, this connects to the idea that people are motivated to be in relationships because of their similarity to one another, an idea that we will revisit in several different ways in the rest of the book.

6. Opportunity to Help Others

Most people enjoy the chance to show that they are decent, honorable people who are valuable to others. If someone else falls over in the street, many would just keep on walking, but you would probably feel a lot better about yourself if you were to stop and help. Then you would feel good about yourself for acting as a decent human being. This provision of relationships is about acceptance of a worldview in which you play a leading role. By helping others, a person not only establishes his or her own worth to others but also shows, on the basis of this implicit dependency of others, a further indication of the value of self in relation to other people ("I'm a Good Samaritan").

7. Personality Support

You probably choose to hang out with people who think and value the same things you think and value. It is unsettling to hang out with people who always disagree with everything you say. Note that today you have more options about choices of who to hang out with than people may have had in the past, when a village was small and you knew everyone there personally, like it or not, and couldn't just get in your car and drive off somewhere else. The luxury of seeking intimate personality support is quite likely a recent development that stems from greater freedom and choice. Intimacy now has something to do with sharing secrets and facts about one's inner self that may not have been true a long time ago, and so this way of thinking about intimacy is itself, in the broader historical context, a relatively recent one.

All of these provisions of relationships seem to represent general human needs, yet they are specific to a historical time, as I noted at the start of this section. They seem quite natural to us these days because our culture places a lot of stress on individual choices and rights to satisfy individual needs. Therefore, because you are a member who subscribes to that social viewpoint, the above list seems natural and perhaps even obvious—but open your questioning mind.

The way culture recognizes relationships seems to be natural not only to you as an individual in your own world but also to those researchers from your own culture. They create that reality to you in their scientific enterprises drawn from a Western culture that emphasizes choice, science, and biology. Research on relationships tends to support cultural views, often without acknowledging the fact that the research is carried out in a particular culture that has sets of beliefs that might influence the results. Research participants who are asked to report about their relationships naturally enough do so within the framework of beliefs that they hold to be normal and natural, just as you would do. Likewise, researchers rarely challenge this underlying set of frameworks because it is a set to which they themselves subscribe and in which they are naturally engulfed.

I will occasionally refer to this set of assumptions as The Old Way: Relationships are important; they are based on feelings, choice, enjoyment, and intimacy; and they may even be the result of some hardwired human biological or physiological drives and yet are contained within some sense of public decency and norms of behavior. This way of thinking about relationships probably feels so natural that it doesn't appear to reflect any biases, but merely indicates the way the world actually is. Indeed, you will see that much research takes this view and sees its job as simply uncovering the kinds of attitudes and personality styles that help people to make their choices of partners, render people attractive to others, and predict relationship success (usually measured in terms of relational length and the partners' satisfaction levels). All the same, there are biological, social, and cultural influences on the ways in which relationships happen. The Old Way, just described, is actually reinforced by such relational enterprises as speed dating, online dating, and the people around you. People accept as natural the idea that similarity underlies attraction, acquaintance, and relational success.

A Brisk Look at Research and Assumptions

Given that, let's take a brisk look at research on relationships—simply a high-level map at this stage, a sketch only—and then go on to indicate what is different about my angle on it all. I will base my approach on talk and the fact that we are materially embodied beings—that is, people with a physical shape and structure that may be judged by others. This book takes a close look at the subtleties that underlie elements of real life, and I will challenge common beliefs about relationships that you may presently take for granted as I explore these implications.

I will be swimming against the tide of the sea of research in relationships, and so at this point, it makes sense to give a brief summary of what this research says and then go on to indicate new ways of understanding such research and beliefs. As you read the rest of this book, you should keep remembering the way in which research tends to reinforce the values of the society that generates it, something to which I will return many times. As you go along, remember just how much research plays into this Western narrative, studying freedom of choice, love and romance, and showing a mild surprise when it turns out that social class, religion, and education levels actually predict marriage patterns pretty well (Kerckhoff, 1974). In short, all that freedom of choice actually steers people into very predictable groupings anyway.

DISCUSSION QUESTION

Should marriages be arranged by parents? Should they be approved by parents? How much freedom of choice do you think you had in your romantic choices? How different are you and your partner in terms of race, religion, socioeconomic standing, education, locale of origin—and what is the longest distance you had ever lived apart before meeting?

RESEARCH ON RELATIONSHIPS: A SKETCH MAP

My main purpose in this chapter at this point of the book is only to point out some key features represented in the huge amount of research on relationships and against that to sketch an alternative and unique way of understanding relationships. Therefore, rather than summarizing this research, except in the broadest possible way, here I intend to introduce it only; then, as we go along, I will expand on it as I put it into the new framework that I offer. However, this research will largely confirm the ways of thinking about relationships I outlined just now as The Old Way. That is, it assumes that relationships are about emotions and positive attitudes toward other people, are based on choice, and very often happen in stages of development, from initial attraction to deep and long-lasting personal attachments. When you feel close to somebody, it is because you like them, and you like them because *they are like you.*

A brief and encapsulated review of all this research on human relationships would go something like what follows (and a fuller review can be found in Duck, 2007). Since the study of attraction first became marked by the publication of a book on interpersonal attraction by Berscheid and Walster (1969), there has been at first a steady, and then a sudden, growth in research on interpersonal attraction and relationships. Attraction was regarded in these books as an attitude (Berscheid & Walster, 1969)—not a physical response; not a calculated, rational decision; not the response of loins; not anything performed (enacted, carried out, done) in the real world, but an attitude—a mental, internal, psychological state. According to this approach, I could be attracted to you as one brain or adding machine may be attracted to another. Not very exciting, and not at all connected to the real world of experience outside of the experimental laboratory.

In the early days, those who studied attraction were divided between those attending to initial attraction (Berscheid & Walster, 1969) and those who saw attraction as a longer term process (e.g., Levinger, 1974). Reviews of the research in any decade since the 1960s in psychology alone ran to several dozen pages, and yet there are now at least four handbooks about real relationships (Duck, Dindia, Ickes, Milardo, Mills, & Sarason, 1997; Duck, Hay, Hobfoll, Ickes, & Montgomery, 1988; Hendrick & Hendrick, 2000; Vangelisti & Perlman, 2006). There are also two major flourishing multidisciplinary journals about relationships that specifically publish almost monthly volumes of several hundred pages per year on the new and exciting research being done on real-world relationships more broadly (*Journal of Social and Personal Relationships* and *Personal Relationships*), and a number of other journals in specific disciplines such as psychology, communication, sociology, and family studies that also publish research on relationships.

While acknowledging the impossibility of a full review here, I can identify a number of important points:

1. Most research on relationships focuses on *voluntary relationships,* and generalizations about them are made from that basis without recognizing some of the limits of doing so (for example, that you tend to have relationships with people from the same socioeconomic status, religious background, race, neighborhood, and so forth). The fact is that, given a choice, the influences on those choices may be different from those that, absent choice, affect relationships (for example, think about the ease of sustaining relationships with people whom you meet frequently, as opposed to those you meet only rarely).

2. Most research on relationships is done with *young subjects,* usually of college age, because they are really easy to persuade to do experiments for course instructors, even though this represents a segment of about 5% of the life span, and in demographic terms is clearly educationally, economically, and racially biased.

DISCUSSION QUESTION

What, if anything, is wrong with using college-age students in research about romantic relationships?

3. The research tends to emphasize the *freedom, advantages, and positive aspects of relationships* to the neglect of the dark side (Cupach & Spitzberg, 1994). More important, the research tends to split life into light and dark rather than explaining the ways in which people manage the two together (Wood & Duck, 1995). Yet in everyday life, you are constantly confronted with the fact that you cannot actually do whatever you want. In fact, you are constantly influenced by the opinions of other people, or media that both promote certain sorts of relationships (for example, marriage) and criticize others (for example, adultery and pedophilia). Life is not a glossy set of simple black-and-white attitudes or straightforward choices but a largely complex and confusing array of dilemmas. When people tell stories about their relationships, they often dress up events as simpler, more linear, and perhaps even more logical than the way in which they are actually experienced. and so too, perhaps, do the researchers. At any rate, the nature of storytelling and narrative will become an important part of the way in which I unfold my view of relationships.

SOME MAJOR THREADS OF RELATIONSHIP RESEARCH

Likewise, one can summarize and simplify the main threads of this research. Of course, it is only a sketch, and fuller details can be found in the cited sources.

First, a major element involves the study of *initial attraction between strangers,* mostly between people of college age. It is based largely on the assumption that similarity of attitudes (Byrne, 1997) causes conditioned responses or that similarity of personality characteristics (Levinger, 1974) or that ingrained personality dynamics make people physically or psychologically attracted to some specific people as distinct from different other people.

Second, a major aspect of relationship research is based on *attachment styles,* which are the attitudes toward relationships that are formed in infancy in connection with caretakers of the infant (Hazan & Shaver, 1987). Huge amounts of research have been done since 1987 that demonstrate that a person's attachment style—his or her way of relating learned in infancy—tends to predispose the person toward certain kinds of relationships later in life. Those people who feel secure in relationships develop longer and more satisfying relationships than those who are anxious or avoidant of other people. We will consider and reinterpret this line of research in Chapter 3.

A third style of research pays attention to the *communication influences* on the way in which relationships are conducted. For example, relationships are based on disclosure of intimate information to other people as you become closer and more intimate with them (Petronio, 2002). Other research focuses on individuals' management of the difficulties and tensions of relationships that arise in their communication with other individuals (Baxter, 2010). This research looks at the ways in which you conduct relationships in the face of competing demands on your time or dilemmas between your desire for autonomy and your need for connection, for example. Should you spend time with a lover at the expense of time with friends? What about your desires to be an autonomous, free, and independent individual, as compared to your desires to be connected with someone else—a fact that necessarily constrains your independence? You are prepared to enter relationships knowing that you must give up some independence in order to spend time with others who want to share your time and attention.

What about the fact that you want to be open and honest in relationships and yet retain some control over the privacy of your own life, thoughts, feelings, and personality? What are the boundaries of privacy when close relationships demand that you reveal information to intimates that may not be made available to just anybody? This line of research explores such factors as the disclosure of personal information in a variety of circumstances; the tendency to feel more comfortable and to be more intimate with those about whom one knows more in detail and depth; and the fact that in everyday conversation, individuals balance their needs for privacy with their desire for intimacy (Baxter, 2010; Baxter & Braithwaite, 2008; Baxter & Montgomery, 1996; Petronio, 2002).

As relationships develop, individuals disclose more about their personal inner experience, and yet they do so in ways that require careful management such that neither too much nor too little is revealed. Individuals desire personal autonomy but are willing to give up some of this autonomy in order to become connected with other individuals. For example, I may wish to be an independent human being with my own personal secrets and concerns, but I recognize that in order to become intimate with somebody else, I must be willing to disclose and share, honestly and openly, certain aspects of myself that are not made available to everyone at large.

A fourth and equally important area of research in personal relationships demonstrates the strategies that people use in order to *maintain relationships* that have reached a particular level of intimacy ("relational maintenance") (Canary & Stafford, 1994). Indeed, it is expected that you continually practice certain sorts of disclosure and some ritual forms of attachment as part of the nature of belonging to such a relationship. These may be routine meetings or offers of tokens of commitment and love, such as gifts, cards, or favors for friends that may be burdensome—for example, giving up time to drive friends to the airport—that demand the relinquishment of your personal time in order to keep the relationship going.

Fifth, there is broad awareness that the *social networks* within which people operate as a dyad or pair or couple have a large influence on the way in which their relationship is experienced. Partners are often introduced to one another in the first place through third parties or are influenced by their social networks in decisions about the nature of relationships and what counts as satisfactory performance there (Parks, 2006). People are sensitive to the norms of society that dictate how relationships are "done" or must be managed, particularly when under strain. Much research is now done on the influence on personal relationships exercised by the family as a whole (Floyd, 2004) and on the dark side of relationships, which involves conflict, difficulty, and stress (Kirkpatrick, Duck, & Foley, 2006; Spitzberg & Cupach, 1998). After all, relationships are not easy and often require work. You take that for granted because society tells you it is true and important that you must be prepared to work on relationships. Initial choice (all that naïve early work on "attraction") now turns out in real life to require the hard work of dedication, exclusivity, and commitment rather than just having an attitude about someone.

Sixth, research has focused on the *narratives* that people tell about relationships: You do not just have them, you perform and talk about them. For one thing, you talk to your partners about how you feel and they may like what you say. Families also have stories about what is important to them

(Huisman, 2008; Koenig Kellas, 2007). In telling the stories, relating to others, performing socially accepted rituals of relationships, and maintaining both your relationships and your personal freedom, you are not simply expressing personal choice or reacting to your own internal emotions. You are molding your behavior and your relationships to forms imposed by a society outside of yourself. See how free choice may not be so free after all?

A Different Approach

Relationships are talked into being (Chapter 7) and are about knowledge as we experience it in a material world. So let me start to contrast the previous hasty sketch with my own approach in this book by drawing attention to the glaringly obvious fact that when you relate to other people, you usually do so through everyday communication. Any underlying basis of emotional attachment is essentially expressed through the sending of messages that indicate emotion in everyday talk. This book emphasizes and reevaluates this important fact. I will be trying to demonstrate that many of the elements that you regard as central to relating are actually based on the fact that your communication with other people does more than simply declare or express the inner worlds of your psychological essence, or bring about results of your own thoughtful choices and actions. Life is more complicated and messy.

Relationships are based specifically on *transacted communication,* a form of communication that creates more than it appears to do on its face. For example, a handshake can *transact* a contract; saying the words "I do" can *transact* a wedding; and the response of your partner to a text can *transact* love and trust between you, even if the message itself just says "OK, see you tonight."

The way you talk or think about something—whether relationships or anything else—is tightly bound up in the larger worldview that you adopt as a member of a particular culture, and "does" or transacts that membership for you by connecting you to others' TFG assumptions. A relationship is not simply the waving in other people's faces of your attitudes, beliefs, or personality, to which they respond with either positive or negative affection. Indeed, the very way you now talk and think about relationships is connected tightly to your larger belief system about the nature of relationships. Therefore, I am going to introduce two unfamiliar ideas: *the presentational nature of communication* and *rhetorical vision.*

THE PRESENTATIONAL VIEW OF COMMUNICATION

Most people see communication as *representational:* that is, it reports facts, describes objects, declares states of affairs, discloses one's heart, and represents the outside world or your inner personal feelings in a more or less accurate, if personally selective, way. On the other hand, many researchers in communication studies recognize that communication is always *presentational* (i.e., it is a spin on the facts) or *performative,* an act, in a theatrical sense, that does the drama of relating.

I am not saying that people *can* spin the facts, I'm saying that all relating is about spin and performance—about doing relationships rather than just having them, and presenting something rhetorical. It is all that you do. Even choice of what to reveal about yourself to someone is strategic and therefore "spin" to suit the circumstances. Communication is always spin; always persuasive; always an attempt to persuade; always rhetorical, argumentative, and position-oriented. Carl and Duck (2004) conceived of talk and relationships as inherently connected to interpersonal influence, tying together the rhetorical and interpersonal aspects of relating. They claim that "talk is inherently rhetorical in that it implicitly offers a persuasive account of a view and hence is an effort to attempt to persuade others to support said view of the world or of self" (p. 7).

DISCUSSION QUESTION

Have you ever presented a relationship as if it were fair when you kind of knew that it wasn't?

RHETORICAL VISION

Every time you speak or act, you present your perspective, your own personal view, your "take" on events, which in large part will be positioned within the framework that your culture accepts as the normal and taken-for-granted way in which relationships should be done. As such, talk always presents the speaker's *rhetorical vision*: A rhetorical vision is a depiction of values, preferences, and opinions, whether explicit or implicit. In the explicit case, rhetorical visions are presented whenever you take a position in an open discussion, debate, dispute, or battle of ideas over a contentious issue.

In the implicit cases, which are much more frequent, a person's values, judgments, preferences, and opinions are bound up in the topics chosen or avoided in everyday conversation, the ideas or other people held up to criticism, the endorsement or approval of ideas and statements. Even the choice to wear a Cubs T-shirt is an expression of a rhetorical vision—that sports matter, that people can legitimately express preferences for teams. Every phrase that you utter has some set of values, assumptions, and preferences (and therefore, by definition, some rejection and disapproval of other values, etc.) built into it.

The Language of Relationships

All through life, you go around offering these rhetorical visions to people, and the visions are central to the understanding of relationships. In fact, you cannot think of relationships without buying into a rhetorical vision (usually one endorsed by your culture) about them. That is why it is important to begin by inspecting and assessing the kinds of hidden assumptions that lay beneath the open beliefs that you now make about the way in which relationships work. For example, it is a rhetorical vision that friendship is good and desirable (which is why Twitter is so popular) and that isolation, loneliness, or unwillingness to enter relationships is a bad thing.

> ### Listen in on Your Own Life
>
> Look around you. In what ways are your associates depicting and presenting their rhetorical visions? Consider T-shirts, clothing styles, and dress as part of someone's rhetorical vision, but don't stop there. What is conveyed about their rhetorical vision by hairstyle, jewelry, body posture, way of walking, use (or not) of makeup, tone of voice, size of car, place of living, ownership of pets, ways of spending Friday night, and so on? Keep on making the list, and then ask, "What is the message?"

Sometimes, you may be aware of the existence in your culture of these social beliefs about relationships that affect what you do. The norms and social constraints within a rhetorical vision may be more apparent when you realize that you care what the neighbors think about the way you conduct your relationships, and that a lot of relationships happen in a set of social structures that influences relational performance. For example, you have colleagues at work (a social and organizational structure), and the organization may have fierce rules about the relationships you may and may not have with coworkers. These may range from rules that you cannot spend all day chatting cheerfully with pals at work instead of spending time serving customers, right through to a ban on sexual relationships between a boss and employees.

Some of these rules in your closest relationships are also almost inescapable. As every teenager has at one time observed, you cannot choose your parents, and in fact, the same basic point is true for neighbors, classmates, coworkers, and the people on your holiday tour bus. You are stuck with them, and have to have relationships with them whether you want to or not. In fact, you don't see it as a restriction on you yet, but you do probably have a vision of relationships as containers in which you are held ("*in* a relationship") or states that you have entered ("*in* love") or stable elements of your life and circumstances ("I *am* friends with . . .," "I *am* married to . . .").

Materiality and Relationships

Other long-term constraints on your relationships are provided by your biological age and your sex, the definition and the limits or expectations imposed on you by your social gender ("he-man," "femininity"), or your sexual orientation. All of this affects the way in which other people treat you and you treat them. Also, in their own ways, they limit, focus, or restrict the range of relational possibilities. All three of them—the biological, the social, and the orientational influences—affect your expectations and beliefs about relationships and the ways in which other people make relational demands or grant relational benefits to you. It is possible, for example, that other people will comment on whether you are behaving appropriately in relationships, as compared to the expectations surrounding your sex ("Guys can't say that to guys") (Burleson, Holmstrom, & Gilstrap, 2005).

So where did choice in relationships (that was part of your original rhetorical vision of relationships) go, before you ever realized that it is a rhetorical vision to think of relationships as being based on choice? Does it matter that a lot of your relational time is actually spent with people you did not choose, and that you are necessarily, even if sometimes unwittingly, acting within the constraints imposed by social expectations about your culture, your race, your gender, or your sexual orientation? Yes, all this matters if you assume, as I do, that relationships, whether chosen or enforced, are actually formative—that is, they do something to contribute to your identity and make you who you are.

Now, you probably believe right now that your identity is prior to relationships (by which I mean that you, as the person you already are, go into relationships rather than relationships being processes that make you the person you are). Of course, you can see that relationships are so important to you that in some ways, you would be a different person without your loved ones, but you don't see them as making you who you are, especially the ones that you do not choose or react against. People like to believe these don't influence or shape identity, but you might change your mind about that as we go along.

Do Relationships Make You Who You Are?

This book invites you to reflect on and perhaps rethink some of your assumptions and beliefs about relationships. An easy place to start to drive the wedge is with the earlier assumptions about the permanence of relationships as states ("I *am* friends with . . ."). You have probably ended friendships, lost lovers, had rough patches with the family, and argued with coworkers in ways that actually point to another way of seeing relationships, one based on *insta-bility* and *un*certainty. This will lead me to characterize relationships as always *incomplete* and never really ending—unfinished business. You can still be seri-ously affected by previous relationships even after it seems that they have ended: They can affect your sense of self even though they do not continue. They are ongoing, they are unfinished business, they always have surprises in store (Duck, 1990), and you can still be upset by a whiff of the fragrance that reminds you of a past love.

Relationships are *not* containers you are in or belong to, or states you have entered, or stable elements of life in any simple way. On the contrary, the sense of stability is one that you impose through a rhetorical vision that promotes the idea of stability: It helps you to make sense out of continuity, change, and chaos. It therefore serves as a mechanism to help you deal with change not only in relationships, but also in your sense of self and way of life. So the choices in relationships are, in fact, choices about the way in which you "spin" your talk about relationships, and perhaps are not the same as freedom of choice.

All the same, your sense of self and relationships can be influenced by the actions and behaviors of other people—which points again to the idea that relationships are formative, and that your identity may not be prior to relationships.

RELATIONSHIPS AND SENSE OF SELF

Consider a scene in the movie *Love Actually* in which Emma Thompson's char-acter confronts her husband (played by Alan Rickman) about her suspicions that he is having an affair. He admits to being "a classic fool," and she responds that he has not made just a fool of himself but also a fool of her and, more important, of *her whole way of life*. In other words, his relational actions reflect not only on their relationship as a married couple, but on her way of being in the world and her sense of identity as a loyal wife and mother.

Another, even more compelling example is provided by this note written by a recently widowed woman.

> There is the question of identity, or self, or "Who the hell am I now?" I know that my life is a bigger set than the part of it I spent with Pete, but quite frankly, I didn't like my life much before then and felt myself to be flounder-ing before I met him. Now I am fearful of being pulled out to sea by the rip-tide, to take a metaphor too far. I think one of my (far too many) challenges right now is to claim or keep what I received from him (safety, love, respect, positive regard, trust, a sense of myself as a capable and strong and worthy woman). He provided such a foundation for me that I could go out into the world without fear, as long as I knew I could come back home to him and be

understood, cared about, listened to, and encouraged. It is that foundation that is missing, and I have no idea how to create it for myself. And now, once again, I am fearful about being in the world. I know that part of this journey of grief is to create a new life, a new identity, a new sense of self. I would just rather have the old one back.

These examples outline the main claim of this book that relationships are part of how you understand the world: Relationships are ways of knowing, and they influence the ways you know the world, what you know, and how you know it. Ways of being with a specific person activate a part of self that no one else activates in the same way. The character making a fool of another person in a role (as wife) makes a fool of her choices, her way of life, her whole way of being.

More than this, a person's whole sense of self comes from a primary relationship. The widow saw a primary sense of herself coming from her previous relationship with her husband, and how he knew her and helped her to understand the world. She felt able to cope with the world because he was there, but what he provided was beyond a sense of just coping—it was a way of seeing herself and a way of being. She wonders, "What will I do now that he is not here? How can I be the person he made me when he is not here anymore as a guide?" She wants to know what or who will give her that sense of knowing and what or who will offer her a way of being.

She is aware that others help you to cope with the world. She means that other people—especially close, loved other people—provide a sense of how to deal with the world, how to understand its ways of working, how to minimize the threats that she feels it has in store for her. She is expressing the same view as Weiss (1974), but in a different way: Emotional integration can mean that if you don't know how to cope, then others will help tell you how to relate to the world. They will provide both the physical and the emotional means to give you a grasp on the world, a world that would otherwise be chaos.

This even works for negative relationships as long as we start to see them as more than "attitudes" and instead as unfolding behavior, performance, everyday life, and transactional communication between living people who are themselves relatively likely to change over time. Most people live their lives in the everyday world that is quite dissimilar from the environment in which subjects in psychological experiments are asked to report what they believe about imagined scenarios.

SENSE OF SELF AND RELATIONAL ABUSE

Pam Secklin is a researcher on relationships who had a personal experience relevant to the above idea that relationships reinforce the view of self.

Secklin (2001) reports on her experience in an abusive relationship that became so much a part of the very way she saw herself, so inextricably tied up with her sense of worthlessness in the eyes of someone who, at the time, mattered to her, that at first she tried to make it work by pleasing him. She played a submissive role up to a point where a particular event (her husband's giving away her pet dog without her permission) forced her to recognize that she was being not supported, but annihilated. That event and her final meeting with her dog, now owned by someone else, gave her the courage to end the abusive relationship and so reassert her identity as the person *she* wanted to be rather than the one *he* wanted her to be. This report is particularly important not just because it emphasizes how a person can be manhandled to become a different person from the one she wants to be, but also because in this case, the person was a relationship researcher who knew how to write a research report on the problem and how to change things.

At this point, all of these considerations should be making you think much more carefully about whether relationships are about simple choices, basic emotion, and taken-for-granteds. They have a complex connection to your sense of self and the way in which it is presented through talk. Creeping into the material I have presented so far is not only the idea that society, other people, and even close relatives can shape the way in which we experience ourselves, but also the idea that the *presentation* of self through talk is a big part of relating.

Relationships are more than emotional attachments; they tell you, guide you, and show you how to understand and deal with what is going on. The widow does not believe that she can create it for herself, that she can be herself without the specific help of someone else. Secklin (2001) had to experience a deeply hurtful personal trauma concerning a pet in order to realize how her self, her view of the world, her rhetorical vision was being essentially negated in the relationship as it previously existed. In both cases, each woman felt that she could not be herself without specific other people to activate the parts that make her feel whole. In Secklin's case, it took a key catalytic event to say "Enough!" and allow her to accept that the other person was abusive and that she needed to get out of the relationship, not just out of an emotional bond, but out of a way of seeing and knowing herself.

A Preview of the Book

All the above sets up a contrast between The Old Way and some new ideas for looking at relationships. I will be introducing traditional research and theory about relationships from the point of view of interpersonal communication, psychology, family studies, and sociology, which have all contributed to the understanding of relationships. I will also be encouraging you to reflect on your own personal experiences of relationships not only from this research perspective, but also in your own daily experience of the world as it leads you to think about relationships. This includes not only your relational experiences in daily life, but also the ways in which other experiences in the world influence relationships in particular cultural frameworks for understanding.

These influences can be songs you hear or what other people say to you about relationships, the way relationships are reported in the news or on TV shows, the effects of friends and neighbors discussing what you do, and what is acceptable relational behavior. You can even count the fact that greeting card companies offer us ways to celebrate the nature of relationships from Mother's Day to birthday to anniversary cards (for romance, but not for friendship) and that Facebook and Twitter essentially advertise the importance of huge numbers of "friends" as a measure of your own worth in society. They are ways in which other people and "society at large" influence what you believe about relationships and the effects of being in a society that instructs you about the sorts of relationships that are acceptable and those that are forbidden.

The book also shows how relationships are the synapses between self and society, miniature forms of connection of the human solo subject with an abstraction such as "society." The first purpose of the book is to rethink the role of relationships and how they work. A second purpose is to show the centrality of relationships in our very experience of the world as forces for influencing our thoughts.

I will start the contrast by focusing on the role of communication in relationships, particularly the way in which it helps to order our world and create meaning. Communication is an often-reported source of success or failure in relationships, but equally, the term is used by people at large and in some research paradigms with different meanings. Research and ideas about communication can actually be at odds when researchers mistakenly believe that use of the same term means that they are talking about the same thing. I will introduce the notion of the *epistemic*—the way in which we know and are aware of experiences in the world—and relationships as persuasion (*rhetoric*), because it is clearly the case that we will do favors for friends that we would not do for other people. Therefore, I will spend some time proposing that relationships are inherently persuasive backgrounds.

In Chapter 3, I will reconsider the nature of personality and reframe it away from a set of values or beliefs and into a set of experiences and reactions by other people, starting in childhood, which themselves influence our likelihood of relating to others in ways based on our sense of knowing who we are.

Chapter 4 will focus on the bodily materiality of relating and the way in which our selves are material, embodied, and physical. This will lead to consideration of the way in which our material selves influence our relationships. As part of this consideration, I will look at the way in which we tend to see ourselves as objects in the eyes of others.

Chapter 5 will reconsider the nature of sex and society, and in particular, the relationship between sexual activity and our knowledge of the world. It will present three different series of sexual epistemics that, in themselves, either conform with or are morally rejected by society as a whole. Other aspects of our material world are considered in Chapter 6, whether these are material historical forces with which we contend in our particular circumstances of life or the material gifts that are used to serve symbolic functions in creating knowledge about and commitment to or rejection of relationships. In Chapter 7, I will consider the ways in which relationships are talked into being by the nature of conversation, context, the rhetorical situation, and our abilities to interpret one another's worlds of meaning. Chapter 8 will show why this rethinking matters.

PEDAGOGICAL ISSUES

ETHICAL ISSUES

Is it ever right to date two people at the same time?

Is relational jealousy ever justified?

Why should/should not romantic relationships be based on the notion of exclusivity?

MEDIA ISSUES

Find three different sources in the media that represent relationships in different ways.

Check a recent issue of *Cosmopolitan*, count the number of articles that concern relationships, and fill out at least one questionnaire that compares whether you are doing things "correctly" or as successfully as other people. Make sure that the questionnaire gives you a score that interprets your skill in relationships at some level. Keep the results and the magazine for later.

References

Baxter, L. A. (2010). *Voicing relationships: A dialogic perspective.* Thousand Oaks, CA: Sage.

Baxter, L. A., & Braithwaite, D. O. (2008). Relational dialectics theory: Crafting meaning from competing discourses. In L. A. Baxter & D. O. Braithwaite (Eds.), *Engaging theories in interpersonal communication* (pp. 349–361). Thousand Oaks, CA: Sage.

Baxter, L. A., Dun, T. D., & Sahlstein, E. M. (2001). Rules for relating communicated among social network members. *Journal of Social and Personal Relationships, 18,* 173–200.

Baxter, L. A., & Montgomery, B. M. (1996). *Relating: Dialogs and dialectics.* New York: Guilford.

Berscheid, E., & Walster, H. E. (1969). *Interpersonal attraction.* Reading, MA: Addison-Wesley.

Burleson, B. R., Holmstrom, A. J., & Gilstrap, C. (2005). "Guys can't say that to guys": Four experiments assessing the normative motivation account for deficiencies in the emotional support provided by men. *Communication Monographs, 72*(4), 468–501.

Byrne, D. (1997). An overview (and underview) of research and theory within the attraction paradigm. *Journal of Social and Personal Relationships, 14,* 417–431.

Canary, D. J., & Stafford, L. (Eds.). (1994). *Communication and relationship maintenance.* New York: Academic Press.

Carl, W. J., & Duck, S. W. (2004). How to do things with relationships. In P. Kalbfleisch (Ed.), *Communication yearbook 28* (pp. 1–35). Thousand Oaks, CA: Sage.

Cupach, W. R., & Spitzberg, B. H. (Eds.). (1994). *The dark side of interpersonal communication.* Hillsdale, NJ: Lawrence Erlbaum.

Duck, S. W. (1990). Relationships as unfinished business: Out of the frying pan and into the 1990s. *Journal of Social and Personal Relationships, 7,* 5–29.

Duck, S. W. (2007). *Human relationships* (4th ed.). London: Sage.

Duck, S. W., Dindia, K., Ickes, W., Milardo, R. M., Mills, R. S. L., & Sarason, B. (Eds.). (1997). *Handbook of personal relationships* (2nd ed.). Chichester, UK: Wiley.

Duck, S. W., Hay, D. F., Hobfoll, S. E., Ickes, W., & Montgomery, B. (Eds.). (1988). *Handbook of personal relationships.* Chichester, UK: Wiley.

Floyd, K. (2004). Introduction to the uses and potential uses of physiological measurement in the study of family communication. *Journal of Family Communication, 4*(3,4), 295–317.

Gottfried, R. S. (1985). *The Black Death: Natural and human disaster in medieval Europe.* Boston: Free Press.

Hazan, C., & Shaver, P. (1987). Romantic love conceptualized as an attachment process. *Journal of Personality and Social Psychology, 52,* 511–524.

Hendrick, C., & Hendrick, S. S. (Eds.). (2000). *Close relationships: A sourcebook.* Thousand Oaks, CA: Sage.

Huisman, D. (2008). *Intergenerational family storytelling.* Iowa City: University of Iowa Press.

Kerckhoff, A. C. (1974). The social context of interpersonal attraction. In T. L. Huston (Ed.), *Foundations of interpersonal attraction* (pp. 61–77). New York: Academic Press.

Kirkpatrick, C. D., Duck , S. W., & Foley, M. K. (Eds.). (2006). *Relating difficulty: The processes of constructing and managing difficult interaction.* Mahwah, NJ: Lawrence Erlbaum.

Koenig Kellas, J. (2007). Narrative theories: Making sense of interpersonal communication. In L. A. Baxter & D. O. Braithwaite (Eds.), *Engaging theories in interpersonal communication* (pp. 241–254). Thousand Oaks, CA: Sage.

Levinger, G. (1974). A three-level approach to attraction: Toward an understanding of pair relatedness. In T. L. Huston (Ed.), *Foundations of interpersonal attraction* (pp. 99–120). New York: Academic Press.

Parks, M. (2006). *Communication and social networks.* Mahwah, NJ: Lawrence Erlbaum.

Petronio, S. (2002). *Boundaries of privacy.* Albany: SUNY Press.

Secklin, P. L. (2001). Losing Sammy: A catalyst for exiting an abusive relationship. *Journal of Loss and Trauma, 6*(1), 65–74.

Spitzberg, B. H., & Cupach, W. R. (Eds.). (1998). *The dark side of close relationships.* Mahwah, NJ: Lawrence Erlbaum.

Vangelisti, A., & Perlman, D. (2006). *Handbook on personal relationships.* Cambridge, UK: Cambridge University Press.

Weiss, R. S. (1974). The provisions of social relationships. In Z. Rubin (Ed.), *Doing unto others* (pp. 17–26). Englewood Cliffs, NJ: Prentice-Hall.

Wiseman, J. P. (1986). Friendship: Bonds and binds in a voluntary relationship. *Journal of Social and Personal Relationships, 3,* 191–211.

Wood, J. T., & Duck, S. W. (1995). Off the beaten track: New shores for relationship research. In J. T. Wood & S. W. Duck (Eds.), *Understudied relationships: Off the beaten track* (pp. 1–21). Thousand Oaks, CA: Sage.

2

Personal and Social Orders

Relating, Meaning, and Talking

Chapter 1 proposed a new view of the role that relationships with other people have in creating your own identity and creating or fixing the stabilities in your lives. The central question of the book is "How do relationships with others introduce us to society; shape and sustain our beliefs, and even our identities; and influence our knowledge habits in the future—not just about relationships but about everything?"

You will soon find that relaters talk about matters other than relationships: Relaters discuss the world about them, and so relationships influence knowledge and assessment of the world. Relationships are not just pretty, emotional parties, they are fundamental to the way you think about yourself and the rest of your experience of the world.

Two Important Ideas: Social and Personal Orders of the World

Two ideas fill this all out. I shall write about *social orders* and *personal orders,* and it is important for you to grasp these notions before I introduce the material, such as the ways in which we talk our relationships into being, against the cultural context (social order) and individual preferences, comparisons, and experiences (personal order).

SOCIAL ORDERS

Social order refers to the structuring of society, its power functions, and its organizational rules. All societies have rules about the conduct of relationships.

Some of them are stated quite explicitly in religious guidelines ("Honor thy father and thy mother"; "Thou shalt not covet thy neighbor's wife [or his ox or his ass]"). However, these rules are stated more simply by other means, too. For example, "Friends don't let friends drive drunk," "You can't treat people like that," and "One for all and all for one" are all examples of the direct expression of a social order about relationships.

Rules and orders about relationships have always been celebrated in songs and stories that reinforce the norms for relating in a particular society. Older folk songs told of how "a lover and his lass" should conduct themselves. Nowadays, tune into any iPod or music video or scan YouTube and there will be current versions of the social order about relationships represented too. Some of them are in conflict with one another (for example, Christian ethics compared to some of those stated in emo music).

Media and the Social Order of Relationships

To test this hypothesis for science, I sat in a bar in Amsterdam and wrote down the title of every song that played on the jukebox over a 2-hour period, something you could do in any café, bar, or social space yourself. I found that 90% of all songs played were about relationships (and, more important, how relationships should be done), ranging from the good old oldies like "You Can't Hurry Love" (indicating right and wrong ways to "do love") and "People Who Need People . . . Are the Luckiest People in the World" (social membership or contact is the perfectly endorsed and most desirable goal) to "Love Is All You Need" (relationships are more

---

Two different approaches to relationships and what people want to get from them:

1. *Christina Aguilera (Get Mine, Get Yours)*
Now I don't mind us bein' some kinda casual thing. Listen all I want to do for now is have you come and take all of me. Can you put your hands on my waistline? Want your skin up against mine. Move my hips to the baseline. Let me get mine and you get yours.

2. *Black Eyed Peas (My Humps)*
I drive these brothers crazy, I do it on the daily. They treat me really nicely, they buy me all these ices. Dolce & Gabbana, Fendi and NaDonna Karan, They be sharin' all their money got me wearin' fly. Brother I ain't askin. They say they love my ass 'n, Seven Jeans, True Religion's. I say no, but they keep givin,' so I keep on takin' and no I ain't taken. We can keep on datin'; I keep on demonstrating.

My love (love), my love, my love, my love (love). You love my lady lumps (love), my hump, my hump, my hump (love). My humps they got you.

Sources: Christina Aguilera, "Get Mine, Get Yours" from the album *Stripped*, RCA Records, © 2002. Black Eyed Peas, "My Humps" from the album *Monkey Business*, A&M/Universal Records, ©2005.

important than other personal goals) to several more recent songs by Christina Aguilera or even Black Eyed Peas.

If you reflect on the advice that "all you need is love," then you might note that the more recent sentiments (Black Eyed Peas and Aguilera), even though nearly 10 years old, are stressing what can be *gotten* from relationships and are deromanticizing intimacy in popular culture. This is something perhaps reflecting the sexual pressures now felt by today's students and connected to the increase in hookups on campus and elsewhere (Paul, 2006).

Cultures and Relating

Furthermore, the idea that all you need is love as a basis for marriage or courtship or long-term relationships is a strictly Western narrative (at least if love is defined not as a version of loyal duty—as in the love of one's country—but as a somewhat irrational passion that overwhelms thoughtful consideration and judgment). In many countries in the East, it is considered downright stupid to base lifelong decisions, such as marriage choices, on the casual whims of emotional preference. It is seen as far more sensible to pay attention to the wise guidance offered by parents, who can arrange it for you, on the basis of more thoughtful reflection and consideration of the best interests of the families and partners involved.

The above evidence from your everyday life (however innocently it infiltrates your beliefs about relationships) indicates a subtle way in which societies not only organize and distinguish relationships but reinforce the "correct" ways of doing their performance. Societies in these forms reinforce some sorts of relationships that they accept and those they don't, and some that they forbid (for example, in our society, romance is good, rape is bad, and incest is forbidden) (Duck & VanderVoort, 2002). Even the songs that you hear in elevators are telling you something about the way in which relationships are preferably done, and so contribute to definitions of the way in which your culture understands relationships and relationship performance. Some cultures regard the relationships between cousins or between a woman and her aunt's children as particularly important, whereas others do not; some see "blood brotherhood" between adult males as basic to society, whereas others do not.

A social order, then, is a set of beliefs reinforced in various ways, from religious doctrines and explicitly stated cultural maxims and ideas, to children's stories, to elevator music through which your society tells you about relationships and about the sexes (biological), genders (social roles), and romance. Social order helps you to know what relationships are like, how to do them, what they are, and which ones deserve to be marked and celebrated (or else will be fleshed out, as it were, in later chapters, the links between the terms that we use—such as *girlfriend*—and the embodied performances that we expect from someone given that label [Butler, 2004].

Listen in on Your Own Life

Pick any popular magazine, such as *Cosmopolitan,* and notice the ways in which its features and quizzes reinforce beliefs about how relationships *should* be done. Just reading the front cover for the main stories is often enough to get the point that such magazines serve to set standards by which people judge their relationships.

In simpler language, what this means is that the terms we use to describe others within a social order for relationships results in their performance of the role in the predetermined kinds of ways. If you and a female partner agree that she is a "girlfriend," then she is strongly influenced to perform the role in a way that is implied by the term. "Girlfriends" *behave* in particular ways).

Social Order and Relational Appropriateness

Of course, there is also a social order in another sense, too—namely, that you are reinforced for doing relationships "properly," politely, and in ways that respect other people's needs not to be insulted. These rules of social order apply also to the ways in which you handle undesired relationships—those where someone gets too close or where you want less involvement than he or she seems to want (Hess, 2000). You rarely tell people simply to "bug off," and you have elaborate formulas for declining relationship involvement ("I'm washing my hair tonight," "Got to go, I have a call on the other line") that are intended to get you out of an obligation without directly offending the other person. Because of this, there are elaborate social orders and practices for ending relationships or for declining to be involved in relationships that are all based on the recognition that the open statements of some opinions are discouraged ("I don't like you," "You are ugly," "You stink," "You are nuts") if there is a polite alternative ("Not tonight, Josephine").

Social orders are general societal rules and preferences about the styles, forms, and practices for relationships, and they may be reinforced and upheld by a variety of social mechanisms, including laws, politeness rules, proverbs, folk stories, and popular music. Social orders essentially make your familiar ways of doing relationships appear to be so normal and obvious that you do not question them. I identified some of these assumptions from a Western society at the start of the book, when I guessed at the way in which you see relationships. Social orders thus represent society's understanding of what relationships are and how they work best.

PERSONAL ORDERS

Personal order, in contrast with social order, refers to the ways in which an individual structures an understanding of the world and represents that through behavior and speech. A personal order is something like "personality," which I will cover in more detail in Chapter 3, but goes beyond that notion. Each person has a set of values and priorities that you typically think of as indicators of his or her personality. For example, you might think it is very important to be loyal to friends or that you cannot have a marriage without love. Such personally ordered priorities can also be preferences for a particular sort of music, a belief in the enduring values of martyrdom, or a fear of open places. Such personal values represent the ways in which you order your life. For example, the places you go, the habits you have, the items you buy, and the places where you buy them are of interest to market demographers because these features reveal to them what it is that particular sorts of people prefer.

Personal values also influence the ways in which you approach situations or relationships with other people—with confidence or fear, for example, or with liking or hostility. You can probably see clearly that personal order is easily attached to the idea of rhetorical vision that I discussed earlier. In a personal rhetorical vision, people present their own personal order; their set of inclinations, beliefs, and values; and their preferred ways of thinking about the world. In other words, an individual's rhetorical vision presents that person's personal order in his or her speech.

DISCUSSION QUESTION

Draw up a list of all the ways in which your personal visions and values may be presented to other people through means that do not involve speech, and then through means that do. Is it possible that some of these ways of presenting yourself to others are in conflict, and that this presents you to others as a person with double standards or uncertainty about yourself?

Personal orders map onto social orders, and this is precisely why personal relationships bring society to life, where the rubber of personal order hits the road of social order. I mean that people have their own personal desires and preferences about relationships, their own needs to fulfill, and their own hopes and dreams. But you have to enact relationships in the eyes of society at large and need to be aware of (even if you react against) social rules and norms in your society. In addition to earlier examples about public sex, incest, and adultery, you are strongly steered by society to be heterosexual, monogamous, and childbearing.

In short, social order tells you what a good relationship is like in your society; personal order is your understanding of how your own relationships should work to be good for you personally, within that broad field. Communicative and social forces act on your conduct of relationships, and these can structure how you act. For example, you speak more informally with a friend than with a stranger, and you listen thoughtfully to the advice offered by your friends about how relationships should work (Baxter, Dun, & Sahlstein, 2001), often getting information from them about good and bad ways to do relationships.

The TFG in Relationships

That may seem terribly obvious because you have been making such distinctions since childhood and performing them daily. Although you probably do not start out thinking that such a small difference either matters much or tells you much about relationships, the taken-for-granted (TFG) differences in style are more important than they seem. For example, since childhood any emotions that you have about a friend or stranger are channeled into particular and accepted ways of expression (or performances) that are not of your choosing. You know how to do intimacy or how to do "stranger-hood" because your social order taught you how intimacy and nonintimacy work. You also learned how to talk intimately and to speak to people you do not know, thus connecting your personal order to the speech formats that go with each style of relationship.

Only within those guidelines are you relatively free to choose a personal way to show it. However, if you walk down the street holding hands with your same-sex friend in a Western culture, you would be doing something odd; in an Eastern culture, it would not be so odd. In the Eastern cultures, that is one way in which same-sex friends "do" intimacy. In the United States, you can go on dates without seeking your parents' approval first; in Spain, people don't go on dates at all (at least they do not call it that) (Chornet-Roses, 2006); and in some other cultures, you might be killed for dishonoring your family if you did go on a date. In modern student life, many personal orders now include such relationships as hookups (Paul, 2006), friends with benefits, or random play, and as more individuals accept such relationships and broadcast their involvement on Facebook, the growth of many personal orders can change the social order.

Putting this another way, your choices of ways to "do" intimacy are channeled by your societal and experiential backgrounds rather than just by your personal emotions alone. That's why most married people do not go out on dates with other people they like, and why the fact that you love someone is not in itself a good enough

> Most societies condemn adultery and promiscuity, particularly between married adults. Against this background, how do you explain the rise in college experiences of hookups and "random play"? You could even ask the larger question of the relationship of sexual behavior to society at large and the way in which personal orders are supposed to reflect the social order in this respect. Does a revolution in personal sexual behavior threaten the social order? (Then see Chapter 5.)

reason to make love to them (e.g., if it would count as adultery). If you accept this point, then you are already some way forward in a new way of thinking about relationships.

UNDERSTANDING OTHER PEOPLE'S ORDERS OF THE WORLD

Personal Orders and Relational Appropriateness

Consider the above point from another angle and see why it can run deeper. The fact that you express your emotions in a particular way that fits and is understood in your society indicates something important. Whatever you feel inside, you know something about how your feelings should be expressed outwardly to other people. For example, violently throwing your body to the ground and rolling in the dust is an acceptable way of expressing grief in some cultures; yet in England, all the newspapers wrote about it as significant when Queen Elizabeth II simply bowed her head as Princess Diana's coffin rolled past, because the Queen normally shows almost no signs of emotion at all and maintains a dignified protocol at all times! (Rent *The Queen* on DVD to see this at work.)

Another way to think about this is that your personal feelings have to be expressed/performed "appropriately." What that means is that you have to express/perform your feelings in a way that other people will judge as being OK. In other words, you do not just feel something personal, but also reflect on its appropriate expression before you express it.

To put this a third way, your feelings are expressed in a form that puts you into an "attitude of reflection" first—you think about how it will look to other people; you see yourself in their mirror, as it were. That is, your outward behavior requires that you have first thought—even for a microsecond—about how it will look to other people who live and relate and act within the same overarching social order. You probably guess how other people will read it, or to put it yet another way, you know how it *should* look in order to be meaningful to other people in your vicinity. You can't just make up how to "be happy" or how to "look sad"; other people have some preconceived ideas about how you should look when you are happy or sad, and you play out your emotions in a way that reflects that. Thus, your personal order is expressed in terms of the social order to other people, too.

Of course, I am not suggesting that all behavior is fully thought through or carefully calculated, but the point is that you know not only how to interpret other people's behavior but also how they might read yours. Such a presumption depends on you knowing or guessing reasonably accurately what they know, knowing what is meaningful to them, and hence knowing something about the social and personal orders that they use.

Not everyone is capable of doing this at all (some people with mental disorders, younger children, and schizophrenics). Other adults possess different levels of ability to make empathic assessments of other people, some of them being good at reading other people, and some less good. Nevertheless, your ability to read what other people know will affect the appropriateness of the fit of your relational behavior, even your stories about relationships and your performance of relationships. Your personal order must fit within the social order or you will be judged odd or even mentally disturbed.

Reading Others' Personal Orders: Symbols, Action, and Motion

There is a subtle and important point here, a very fundamental one for understanding relationships. In order to behave in a way that other people understand, you have to be capable of knowing something about their thoughts. That is the simple and obvious way of putting it. A more complicated and interesting way of expressing it depends on what it means: what lies beneath the process of knowing someone else's thoughts. First, you conduct your relationships in ways that other people recognize, so you "do intimacy/ relationships" in ways that other people recognize as doing intimacy/ relationships—including performing and speaking them correctly, using appropriate forms of language in different types of relationships (for example, a romantic partner may touch you in an intimate way, and so may a physician, but one is intimate and one is not because of other cues in the circumstances). You have to know what other people will recognize as "doing intimacy." Second, you must know something about their personal order so that you can connect to it when you talk with them.

Kenneth Burke (1966), a rhetorical, social, sociological, political, and literary theorist, saw something quite interesting in this. His emphasis fell on the forms of knowledge that must be present for you to understand another person's thoughts. He realized the importance of a cultural basis of consciousness and how experience itself attains shape and content. That is, he recognized that to understand someone else's thoughts, you must first operate within a similar social order, but, more than this, you must first see him or her as the sort of being who has thoughts. You must be able to consider, treat, and acknowledge other people as thinking beings who act within the same basic social order that you use. He argued that you do this recognition through the use of symbols that they share with you, and that symbol usage itself shapes and steers your ways of seeing the world, making it more possible that people who share the same symbols will think the same way. For example, if I give you a gift, I do it in part because I know you'll see it as a "friendly" thing to do and you will realize that I want to be your friend.

To make this argument, Burke first made a distinction between action and motion. *Motion* is what animals and humans do when they aren't really thinking about it. You present them with a stimulus, and they react to it by performing certain outward behaviors. Motion is simply movement as a direct response to stimuli. A knee-jerk reflex is a good example of that idea: If a doctor hits my knee with her little hammer, my leg will jerk forward without me even thinking about it. *Action,* on the other hand, is thought-ful. It requires an assessment of the situation, a reflection about one's interests and purposes. Action requires awareness, a purpose, a goal, and motivation. I give you a gift because I am aware that you will see it as "friendly" and that is what I want you to think. Action is based on assessment, awareness, and representation of the world by symbolic means. The world becomes mean-ingful to symbol users within the whole context of judgment. Situations take their character from the entire framework by which you judge them. So, you might like someone yet also know that you may not simply go up and kiss him or her; you have to take account of his or her feelings, and a number of other questions of "appropriateness." This is one reason why you think twice before, as the Beatles indicated, you ask yourself, "Why don't we do it in the road?" Thus, for you to carry out an action, you have to reflect on the situation somewhat first. Any planned and purposive action is an example of that, such as going shopping together or arranging a date with someone.

DISCUSSION QUESTION

What is wrong with public displays of affection when they are regarded as the highest and most noble form of intimacy when conducted in private? What is it about publicizing love or affection that changes its nature in the public mind?

Knowing What Other People Think: Symbols

The important next step in the argument is that your own ability to reflect on and assess situations includes an ability to reflect on and assess other people, including *their* assessments and reflections. This requires a language of motives, and Burke's idea was that a motive is not (as you normally think of it) a source of behavior so much as a concept used by people to make other people's (and your own) actions understandable. In other words, people don't *have* motives, but the term helps you to understand them better if you act as if they do, and we talk about others' motives all the time, especially as we build relationships with people.

Burke went on to argue that motivational language has a grammar (i.e., a particular structure for explaining motives—"He did this *because* he is shy") and a rhetoric (i.e., there are some ways to explain other people's behavior that are persuasive in a given society and some that are not. If I say you acted from guilt, I am more likely to be believed than if I say you acted as a result of green goblins whispering in your ear. We both share the social order that tells us that guilt explains behavior and that green goblins do not).

Such use of language pre-requires that you are users of symbols (defined as representations of other objects or ideas). Symbols stand in for something that may or may not be present at the time or something so abstract that it is not ever present in the physical sense and is not visible. For example, the Stars and Stripes flag is a symbol of "America," a wedding ring is a symbol of marriage, and a flashy car is a symbol for a man's hope that his sex life will pick up a bit sometime soon.

As another example, you can think about "my friendship with Krissy" both when Krissy is not present and when Krissy is present, but you cannot actually see the friendship in either case (because "friendship" is an abstract concept in the first place). When Krissy is present, then you can see the friendship being performed, but you still have to work out from behavior that it is, in fact, a friendship that is being performed rather than some other kind of relationship. On the other hand, you can think about objects or people when they are not there only through uses of symbols—which includes words, photographs of loved ones, and wedding rings. Humans take meanings from events because we are capable of using such symbols and abstractions; for example, you can think abstractly about past and future or "the person I would like to be."

Language and Relationships

Burke's important observation is based on the idea that language itself is a symbol system. When you use language, you are using symbols that have some distance from the objects or ideas that you use language to represent. The word *table* does not look or sound like a table, but it represents to English speakers an object that we all know about. The word *wine* does not taste of anything, but it represents to you symbolically something that does have a taste and is also more sophisticated than beer.

Why does this matter here? It matters because the ways in which you use language (and, as a body that learns language, perform the relationships that you have) also carry symbolic overtones. For example, the word *relationship* has some important overtones as well as literal meaning. The meanings that are added are important in understanding how people have relationships. If I say that "you and I have a relationship," I am claiming something about how well you and I get along, and that claim is more than a simple description. Thus, your use of language is symbolic and acts a bit like hypertext does on screen. I can write a sentence that says something about relationships, and you can read that as a grammatically sensible statement. However, you could also challenge the words *sentence* and *relationship* with a sort of conversational mouse-click ("Just exactly what sort of relationship do you think we have, then?"). This would reveal that there are pages hyperlinked and concealed behind the grammatical sentence and that I have a lot more to say about sentences and relationships ("I think we are falling in love with one another").

In everyday conversation, your discourse is riddled with symbolic hypertext, so that I could say something that refers hypertextually to the hidden context shared by both myself and you. For example, I could say "9/11" and it would refer to so much more than just numbers, or even a date on the calendar (and even to see it as indicating a date at all, you would have to do some hypertextual jumping anyway, wouldn't you? The form of the numbers and the "/" give you a clue). You would immediately be triggered to search your memory of experiences for a lot of symbols associated with the term "9/11." Relationship partners have hypertext that the relationship has built as collective memories and shared histories. The more personal the relationship, the more personal the hypertext and the more private it is from other people in a way that 9/11 is not. So, if you know about "Percy the Lady Bird," I know exactly to which set of four people you belong because they play games hiding a stuffed toy in unlikely places!

Language as Symbolic Action

In a similar way, Burke says that language is a form of symbolic action: Language operates by symbols. Language is the primary aspect of life through which events are thoughtfully perceived and assessed. That sounds strange, because at first glance, you don't imagine that even representational language is a way of perceiving so much as a way of describing. As you go further into this book, you will come to see language differently and recognize that it really does affect perception and presents your rhetorical vision.

Actually, you may already know intuitively that language and perception are determined and interconnected. You have all heard the urban myth that the Eskimos have many words for snow (it turns out to be not quite accurate, but it helps make the point). It suggests that one word ("snow") works for us, but in a land where there is not much else but snow, people become capable of differentiating types of snow—wet snow, dry snow, snow that is heavy, snow that is light, snow that is dusty, snow that means the coming of a huge storm, snow that looks like it is coming to an end, snow that heralds the onset of spring and warmer weather, and so on.

Indeed, there is even a hypothesis (the Sapir-Whorf hypothesis) that claims that you are what you speak, or, to put it another way, the language distinctions that you are capable of making affect the ways in which you perceive the world. If your language is capable of distinguishing several types of snow, then you begin to be able to differentiate them as you learn the language. You see the world in terms of the words that you use to depict that world.

Language is therefore action, not merely a means of conveying information to other people, but it is also a thoughtful and intentional way of separating your experiences into meaningful categories. Talk makes distinctions between categories, and so different relationship types are done in different language formats. (For example, informal relationships are talked into being through informal styles of language use, whereas hierarchical and pompous relationships are talked into being through the use of more technical and complex language. There is an important difference between the kind of relationship implied by "Hey, wassup?" and "Good morning, Madam President. I trust that you are well.") Experience is filtered through terms in the language, but also enhanced by terms insofar as they sensitize you to the categorical distinctions that your social order makes in the environment. In its own ways, then, your language—and your use of your language—frames your thinking in a way that fits and serves to reinforce social order and also influences the presentational aspects of its use in declaring your personal order.

DISCUSSION QUESTION

If experience is filtered through language and language gives us the basis for our thinking processes, then why do we have a name for the front of the hand (palm)—which is physically quite a distinct surface—but have no name for the back of the hand?

The Social Order and the Language of Relationships

In the context of relationships, if you have words that make distinctions between types of relationships and for degrees within the same type (e.g., words such as *acquaintance, best friend, close relationship, social relationship*), then you are capable of distinguishing those sorts of relationships and degrees. You know what they look like and how they are different. In a culture where it is important to know whether someone comes from one's own tribe or not, then there may be special words for "husband of my cousin" or "person from outside the tribe." These words might be used to describe relationships, so that a friendship with the husband of my cousin might require a different word from the friendship that I have with a person outside the tribe. In some cultures/social orders, relationships are more important than other matters. For example, in some

Arab, Mediterranean, and African cultures, there is nothing immoral or unethical about favoring your cousin when awarding a contract. Relationships are more important than other factors, so of course you will give the contract to your cousin rather than to some stranger who merely "makes the best offer." In that culture, relationships are marked as central to the decision-making process and not as something to be disregarded or given second place to a notion of "fairness" (Duck & McMahan, 2010).

In Japan, there are more than 200 different terms for the relationship between a speaker and the person to whom he or she is speaking, which suggests that the culture is one that is extremely sensitive to both status and relational differences between people. In the West, differentiations of relationships are much less sophisticated. In other words, you know fewer ways of differentiating relationships, and you act within the limits of your knowledge when relating to people. Such a difference in cultures has made it hard for Westerners (who distinguish only friend, acquaintance, stranger) to deal with the subtleties of Japanese culture (who can distinguish . . . 196 . . . 197 . . . 198 . . .).

Language and Social Order

Overall these examples show that what you know about relationships is tied to distinctions you make linguistically between objects in the world as you experience it using language and symbols for relationships. The ways in which you conceive of the operation of relationships on other matters (must be irrelevant to the award of contracts vs. must be considered in the award of contracts) and in which you conceive them to work internally (whether through freedom of choice or as a pre-existing set of obligations to cousins, for example) naturally—or so you think—affect the way in which you give precedence to relationships (or not) in making other sorts of decisions (for example, about the awarding of contracts). Your social orders make it so.

> There are many references in Shakespeare's works to other people as "cousin," but in fact, at the time Shakespeare was writing, this did not signify a particular biological relationship (common grandparents) but *any* person who belonged to the same family or clan as the speaker, or in some cases, merely that the person was of the same noble rank as the speaker.

Even in the West, there are subtle differences that, without going in for 200 distinctions, people can recognize as meaningfully different. People can differentiate a date from merely "going out" with someone, for example, and in the United States, "going out" is seen as longer term, and also "dating" is different from "a date." People also now discuss whether they should "go Facebook" and admit to the world that they are now a couple.

There are subtle meanings to "seeing someone" that do not apply to "dating someone." "What do you mean, this is a date?" can be a question that challenges whether the two people doing what they are doing are doing it on the same set of assumptions (Mongeau & Kendall, 1996). In the same way, being "a friend" is different from being someone who is just pretending to be only a friend but who really wants a romance and is just waiting patiently for that to happen. Think about what the "just" means in "just friends."

Language as a Screen

Let's go a bit deeper into this, though. By making distinctions for us like this, language acts as a filter and screen. As Burke (1935) put it, "Every way of seeing is also a way of *not* seeing" (p. 70). If you see this as "only a friendship," then you don't see it as "a romance," or at least you cannot act as if you do. Burke introduced the term *terministic screen* to describe something important about language. Your terms, the words you use, act as screens. That is, they screen out certain ideas at the very moment when you say something. There is always something left out of someone's presentation of a situation. Language screens out particular ways of looking at events and ideas. (If this is a ball, then it is not square; if this is a date, then it is not platonic; if this is love, then it should be playful, enjoyable, smooth, and fantastic. It should certainly *not* involve a lot of work, although people often talk about "working on a relationship" when it is not going as hoped/expected.) Obviously, our social order prefers certain kinds of relationships to others, so the distinction made by language connects to the social order, and when we talk about somebody as "a *loyal* friend," we are supporting the social order about the nature of friendship relationships and expectations about them.

In the context of relationships, the way you conduct a relationship leaves out (or, more accurately, actually prevents) other ways of conducting it. One way of describing or relating or seeing something screens out other ways. If you define the relationship as "not a date," then you'll be surprised and even shocked if your partner, acting under a different set of assumptions, starts coming on to you. Any symbol thus acts as a filter for the world that you look at and reduces the number of elements that you perceive.

For Burke, an analysis of a culture is an analysis of its linguistic frameworks and the symbols that it uses, especially in a context of polysemy (i.e., where something might carry several possible meanings at once; for example, where a wide-eyed stare can mean surprise, longing love, or resentful hostility) where people need help deciding what is meant on a given occasion. Some cultural symbols help you to understand the context (for example, when you observe someone waving a national flag during a song, then that might help you to understand that the song being sung is patriotic). Some contexts help you to understand symbols (for example, if you saw a lot of Chinese people dressed in white and following a coffin, you might realize that white is a symbol for mourning in China).

Thus, your cultural ideology screens you out from seeing marriage, say, as a strictly instrumental relationship that will last only as long as the partners want it to last. Marriage is something that your culture says is "Till death us do part" and should not be entered into lightly, wantonly, or for only short periods. For us, marriage is a serious, long-term, irrevocable (except with difficulty) relationship, although the divorce rate is running at 50% (Barber & Demo, 2006)!

Romans, on the other hand, recognized several forms of marriage, one of which was "usus" (pronounced *yoo-soos*) (instrumental). It came into effect only after a year's cohabitation—basically what we would call a "common-law marriage" today. It lasted only as long as the partners wanted it to last, having been entered into expressly on that understanding—a kind of "married friend with benefits"—and if the "wife" stayed away for three nights in a row each year, this specifically prevented the wife or her property from becoming the property of the husband. She was still regarded as the property of her father or family under these conditions.

Other Roman forms of marriage were more along the lines of traditional political alliances between families, which were contracted monogamously for life and resemble the present-day version of arranged marriages. In these cases, the wife became the property of the husband and was removed from her house of origin. Such marriages required paternal consent, rather than just the consent of bride and groom. Several other forms of Roman marriage were based on fine distinctions about who "owned" the wife, and in some cases, a couple could be married on the understanding that the wife remained the property of her father. The Romans felt no particular compunction or guilt about these kinds of arrangements, and it was simply part of their cultural ideology that women were pawns in men's political power games.

DISCUSSION QUESTION

In what ways do "hookups" get described in popular songs of recent memory? Do you find that they are the subject of more songs by males or females? When females sing about them, what sort of personal order are they recommending? Control? Power? Liberation? Dependency? Neediness? Ability to satisfy? What is the role of women as represented in such songs? Compare and contrast your answers with those derived from such songs sung by males.

RELATIONSHIPS AS WAYS OF KNOWING (EPISTEMIC)

I have now reached a key point. Relationships are epistemic, a word derived from the Greek word for "to know." To say that relationships are epistemic is to say that they are ways that you understand, ways in which you order the world, ways in which society orders the world, ways that assume that particular behaviors are "natural" or seen as "normal" ways to act. The ways in which you conduct relationships affect your sense of how the world is, who should have power over others, and who has rights and who does not. Remember the widow in Chapter 1? She knew the world differently when her husband was alive and supporting her sense of self; now she fears she does not know how to be herself without the relationship with him.

Consider what you know. For example, you all know that parents are able to take their children where they want (within reason), and that an infant should not be given any say about when to end a visit or where to go on vacation. You also know that women and men are equal, that no human being should be a slave, and that you can vote whether or not you are rich. In the past, by contrast, people *knew* that men owning property should be the ones to make decisions—not women, not slaves, not children, not people without property. They *knew* that slaves were not smart enough to vote, even though you know differently now. However, you might want to spend some time reflecting on this. How does the way in which you relate to other people affect the way you know, and vice versa? Why did it seem right in 1850 to most Americans that there should be slaves and that slaves should not vote? That women were relational and otherwise inferiors of men? Why do *you* think that children should not vote and that they are essentially parental property? Why do you believe that if the parents decide that the family will go to Florida on vacation, then the children have no choice but to go along?

RELATIONSHIPS AS PERSUASION (RHETORIC)

Relationships are not only epistemic, but also rhetorical and performative. That is, the nature of a relationship requires you to perform it in particular ways that are persuasive and accepted in a given society and that play into a social order. You can't just make up a way to do marriage and simply declare that you are now married and expect anyone to accept your word for it. A legal ceremony—itself a performance of legal, state approval and social order recognition—is required. Others in society are not persuaded that the relationship is okay unless it is performed in a way that suits the social order. Correct performance presents a relationship in its accepted way to others in that society.

In a comparable way, language about relationships persuades people as well, not only by reinforcing the social order but also by presenting your view of the relationship. The fact that you use language affects what you experience and what you do with other people. You have already learned that language provides for a reflective capacity, and language is a presentational form of action, not just a description of reality. Language is a form of reflection and assessment. It is not merely a way of describing or representing reality (the *representational function of language*).

Putting a subtly different spin on this, you are instead presenting to others your way of understanding situations (the *presentational function of language*). Thus, whenever I say something like "Pat and I have a relationship" (which assumes love, not just friendship), I am presenting to my audience the fact that I am referring to what they know the word/symbol "relationship" to mean. I am claiming that Pat and I have one.

In a given culture, the word *relationship* will carry meanings and overtones that are specific to that culture, because the word represents something to those people and means something to them within their social order. So, what I am presenting to them is the idea that the connection between Pat and me satisfies the personal and social orders of the term *relationship*. I assume that people recognize that claim and know what it implies about the way we interact with one another, the expectations that we have about exclusivity in sexual behavior, and the manner in which we will conduct ourselves in public as well as in private.

RELATIONSHIPS ARE DONE IN TALK

Apart from the claim of emotional attachment, what else is it that you do in relationships? When you are "in" relationships, you talk; indeed, a distinguishing feature of human relationships is precisely the fact that you depend very heavily on language and conversation. You spend a great deal of your relationship time with other people talking with them. What do you talk about? Well, disappointingly perhaps, quite a lot of it is very ordinary and pedestrian (stuff about clothes, the weather, what you did last night, what you thought about a TV show or music video, and so on).

However, your social order still clings to the belief that intimacy is created only when the talk goes deeper and exposes the self (self-disclosure and revelation of intimate private thoughts, feelings, or secrets). By and large, you talk about what you know, and you assume that you share other codes of knowledge (usually, at least a language). If you have ever tried to converse with someone in a foreign language, you will know exactly why that assumption of sharing is important and helps to make life easier.

The more you get to know someone, the more you come to understand what you can say to them without explanation, what the partner means, and what the partner knows. Part of getting to know someone is getting to know how they think, feel, and experience the world. You find that out by talking with them. Language that you use in relationships is therefore not just a way of presenting events to people, but also a way of showing others how you think (your personal order) and a way of finding out what they think and representing that symbolically (social order meets the personal order).

Now let's take that a step further and claim that when you present your way of knowing (your personal order) to others, and vice versa, it is because you think your view is correct and you want them to accept that. When you talk with someone else, each person is offering a view of the world, a way of knowing, and at the same time is, as it were, standing behind it and offering it up as a *good* way to understand the world, "good" or "right" according to their personal order. I don't mean just that this is what people do when they are arguing and trying to persuade (although of course I do believe that).

DISCUSSION QUESTION

Do you prefer to talk with people who have the same sorts of views of life as you do? What happens when you do not share the same perspective on life?

Whenever people speak, they are offering a way of seeing/knowing/ understanding the world in the expectation or hope that the audience will accept and endorse it. Such a presentation does not have to be obvious, and the person may not even be fully aware of it—it is his or her personal order spoken out loud, but the person may take so much for granted that it is not treated as such. An example is provided by an acquaintance of mine who seems to suffer more misfortune than anyone else. Every disease hits her hard, every mischance comes her way, no accident goes unexperienced, and so forth. It has dawned on me over the years that this acquaintance sees herself as life's victim, and the desired response from me is "Oh, how awful that you have to suffer so much more than everyone else." She tells me this stuff because she wants to persuade me that she is right to see herself as a victim and invites me to acknowledge and endorse her personal order view of herself as someone suffering unreasonable slings and arrows of a fortune that is more outrageous to her than to everyone else. If she feels comfort from my responses, then we have successfully worked out good ways to form our mutual understanding. In short, her description of her life is presentational and reflects a rhetorical vision that presents her personal order as contrasted with the social order.

The lesson that I draw from this observation is that everyday speech—the basis of relationships—is about the ways in which people interact with, and know, the world, and that everyday chatter is a symbolic way of presenting a "way of knowing" to other people for endorsement. I see this symbolic action of language as part of the greater commerce of personal orders that make up much of social discourse. When you dress a particular way (for business meetings, as a student, as a woman or man), you are *presenting* and *performing* a way of being. Also, you are acknowledging that you endorse that way of being (or want to portray yourself as endorsing it), while also inviting other people to accept you in that role (for example, they may see your dress as appropriate to the situation in which you find yourselves—that is, you try to conform to the social order).

All that you know about nonverbal communication is relevant here too, then. When you adopt a closed posture (arms folded, legs held in tight under your seat, performing a postural message that says "keep out"), you are endorsing the view that "You are threatening me and you should not do that. I don't like to feel this way." All of your symbolic actions, including dress, speech, and nonverbal behavior, present messages to the outside world about your feelings, thoughts, and understandings of situations. They also attempt by their very existence to persuade other people to accept your presentation. Goffman (1959) noted that a presentation of a Self is an attempt to get people to buy into the image that you are trying to present.

People are out to persuade others rhetorically in speech and performance. For example, you are out to persuade your relational partner that you are still a good and presentable relational partner, that you are credible, that you are nice and decent, and that you are still the partner of their labors. Rhetoric is ever present in social action, and you all use persuasion attempts often without realizing you are doing it. Your symbolic actions are not always obvious and on the surface; sometimes they, too, are hypertext (Duck, 2002)—that is, like blue text on a website, they can be read as part of a normal sentence or else the viewer/listener may "click" on the blue text/conversational hidden meaning and be taken to pages/explanations of deeper meaning that lie behind the obvious superficial meaning of the word. All the same, every action has a rhetorical/persuasive element—even if it is hypertext—whether it is clothing, style, form of language, or relationships.

Questions to Ask Your Friends

What sorts of behaviors do you expect friends to perform with one another that indicate that they are friends? Can people tell from the behaviors that are exhibited to the public whether people are friends with one another? When you have gathered your information from these questions, connect it to the performance element of relationships discussed below.

LANGUAGE IS ALSO PERFORMATIVE
AS WELL AS RHETORICALLY PERSUASIVE

As well as being epistemic and rhetorical, relationships have one more feature of language that you need to connect to the above: Relationships are *performative*. You don't just *have* a relationship; you *do* a relationship, and even one that is clandestine for whatever reason is done in a clandestine way. You carry out behavior that other people will recognize as indicative of the relationship. Thus, although you may feel that relational behavior is actually an expression of some inner feeling or emotion of love or liking, there is actually a lot to be gained by seeing relationships largely in terms of the behavior that is "performed" as relating. ("Love" is a verb as well as a noun, and society has expectations about the right way to demonstrate it or act it out.)

Embodiment of Relationships

A friend of mine reported that when she was called by the Immigration and Naturalization Service (INS) to prove that she was really married to her Eastern European husband, who was now seeking a green card, they asked her to provide evidence of the existence of their relationship over a 2-year period. The INS would not accept single photos, only series of photos, preferably dated and certainly extended through the whole period, indicating that the couple had been together the whole time, done what couples do (such as go on vacation together), and attended events as couples (such as other people's weddings). She was also asked to bring other evidence: letters, bills addressed to both of them together at the same address, jointly filed tax returns, and so on. She was not asked about an emotional basis for the relationship—not asked, for example, to declare merely that the two of them loved each other. She was required to demonstrate that the relationship was *performed*—and performed in public and in ways that conformed to or could be recognized within the prevailing social order. At a later interview with the INS, the couple was taken to separate rooms and interviewed one at a time about the routines of the relationship: Do you sleep in on Sundays? Who mows the lawn? Who irons the clothes? Where do you go out for special meals? Who collects your daughter (yep, the daughter was not, on her own, acceptable proof of relationship!) from daycare? What TV programs do you regularly watch together?

Importantly, this line of questioning recognizes not only that relationships are performed but also that they are part and parcel of the rest of life. The ways in which you conduct life represent and incorporate your thinking and your beliefs, so that all processes are ways of knowing (epistemic). Not only your uses of language but also your conduct of relationships themselves involve epistemics, and in the case of relationships, these take the shape of formalities and routines, whether performed openly or secretly. Relationships involve symbols and are a performance, not just a result of emotion.

Let's call these "processes of embodiment" (a concept introduced by Judith Butler, 2004, and about which I will write more in Chapter 4). What this means is that they give physical (embodied) form to symbols and actions, and this idea will be one that guides much of the rest of the book. I will look at the ways in which relationships are knowledge, persuasion, and performance; the ways in which they are guided by the social, personal, and material circumstances of your living; and how they are about the performance of the actors in specific settings.

Relationships as Unfinished Business

Two final points need to be made about relationships: First, if relationships are not segmented from the rest of life, then they affect the rest of life and the rest of life affects them. This is true in the sense that people bring problems from work home to the family and can act angrily toward a spouse when really they feel the anger toward a workmate (Crouter & Helms-Erikson, 2000). Another example is that when people do something like ending a relationship, they do not suddenly switch from one sort of process (normal living) to another, disconnected set of processes (ending a relationship). Rather, they carry their human nature into the other process. The processes of relationship breakdown are similar to, rather than different from, other normal, everyday processes.

Second, as I noted before, relationships are perpetually incomplete, unfinished, and open-ended. The problem with seeing relationships as containers you are "in" is that doing so symbolically represents them as fixed and bounded entities, rather than as incomplete, open-ended processes. Yet you know from being in relationships that change and variety are their two certain properties. Whether people grow together or apart in a relationship, they are changing—and the relationship is changing with them. Marriages last over a long period of time or may deteriorate, but they are not the same through the whole of their existence. Children who loved their parents can grow to dislike or resent them (especially when the children become adolescents!), and spouses can experience fluctuation in their feelings for each other. It is a very rare couple indeed that has had absolutely no difficult times. (In the UK village of Great Dunmow in Essex, there is a four-yearly prize of a side of bacon [a flitch] that is awarded to the couples who can show they have gone a year and a day without any argument or regret of their marriage. The award of the Dunmow Flitch is mentioned in Chaucer and therefore is a well-established tradition over 700 years, although there have been many times when it could not be honestly awarded.)

There is nothing certain about relationships except that they can never be pinned down: Even a proposal of marriage changes something in the relationship, whether the proposal is accepted or rejected. Relationships evolve, grow, wither, and go through ups and downs. Even when they appear to stay the same, it can take work to make that happen. One common way of seeing relationships is as a journey of discovery (Baxter, 1992), and when people sense that the relationship is not going anywhere, they believe it is time to end it, not time to celebrate its constancy and utter predictability or boring stability.

Taking this emphasis on change seriously, you end up seeing relationships as unfinished business and not as fenced in by closure. Even relationships that appear to be over can still have effects on the way we feel. Almost all relationships are perpetually incomplete in this way, and even some broken relationships live on in people's memories in quite significant and influential ways that affect their egos and sense of competence or attractiveness. As a result, much more weight falls on their everyday performance and on the processes by which people continually enable, enact, symbolize, and form expectations or memories about them. If relationships are open-ended, then their existence depends heavily on what is happening in them right now or in the near future or recent past.

In fact, there is some research by Dorothy Miell (1987) that shows that the memory of the past 3 days of a relationship is more influential on people's expectations about a relationship (and their descriptions of its present quality) than a previous history in the relationship going back several years! Actually, if you think about that fact—which appears on the face of it to be somewhat surprising—something like this *has* to be true or it would always be impossible to get out of long-lasting relationships; otherwise, they would be continued because the weight of their history would give them continuous and irreversible momentum. Yet even long-term relationships can be ended.

Fundamental shifts follow from the view that I am developing here. If you believe that open-endedness and a constant "emergence" of relationships characterizes their course, then you need to focus not on emotions in relationships but on the form of relationships. That is, you must attend to the manner in which the relationship is performed and enacted day-to-day because those ongoing and incomplete experiences will direct and maintain the partners' present sense of the state of the relationship. Along with the unfolding and emergence of the incomplete relationship goes an equal unfolding and emergence of knowledge and interpretation. Acceptance of the unfoldingness of relationships means that you have to at least consider the extra idea that the two partners can also see the world very differently, and might make different choices about the flow of experience and how to understand it. For example, one of them might feel that because they have been seriously dating for 2 years they should get engaged, whereas the other of them might feel that because they have been seriously dating for 2 years, it is time for a change of partner.

DISCUSSION QUESTION

What kinds of examples can you come up with about the things you do or say that recognize the essence of your relationship during periods of absence? (Putting photographs of your loved ones on your desk is one example but you should think of others.)

If you focus on the incomplete "developing-ness" of knowledge and interpretation, on unfinished business, on the importance of the representation of relationships to an audience, then no relationship is just a private connection based on two sets of emotions, but involves both talk ("the discursive," as communication scholars call it) and action ("the performative"). The open-endedness of relationships is actually important in the context of the performative and epistemic: As relationships unfold and you see new behaviors from partners as well as perform new behaviors yourself, then you and your partners both face new and unfolding interpretive dilemmas.

Each partner is faced with a central set of questions: Is this new behavior typical and informative about the underlying personal order of my partner, or is it coincidence or casual and unimportant or uninformative? Does this behavior represent a change in the person, and if so, is it a change that also changes the relationship? How does this behavior fit in with what I know about the person, the relationship, my self, and the world? How do you think, feel, react, and behave when it does not fit at all (i.e., surprising, negative behaviors that, for example, change one's view of a friendship)? The answer is that your epistemic about the other person changes, and this affects your personal order as well as the relationship.

Maintenance of intimacy is not, then, just a set of stages of growth but a set of tensions, a dialectic; that is, it is a transformation of meanings that is involved during change of the ways in which people manage the balance between old stabilities and new growth. Accordingly, because this applies also to you as I attempt to persuade you to see relationships in a different light, the rest of the book lives its own message in that it offers—and attempts to persuade you to accept—a way of seeing all aspects of relationships as ways of performing and ways of knowing, not merely feelings based on emotion and choice but on knowledge: the epistemic.

EXERCISES

This chapter has focused on the role of knowledge in relationships and the way in which relationships are performed. Before you read the rest of the book, write down a list of possible influences on your relationships that you have not previously considered as possible factors in your performance and knowledge about relating. Contrast these with the influence of emotion on relating.

ETHICAL ISSUES

You are an inmate in a concentration camp. A sadistic guard is about to hang your son, who tried to escape. The guard wants you to pull the chair from underneath your son. He says that if you do not do so, he will kill not only your son but some other random innocent inmate as well. You have no doubt that he means what he says. Consider how you perform the role of parent against other moral demands in society. What should you do? (Taken in modified form from "Some moral dilemmas": http://www.friesian.com/valley/dilemmas.htm.)

MEDIA ISSUES

How do media reflect the social order of your society? Watch a TV news broadcast, keeping a list of the topics discussed and in what order. Then check out http://news.BBC.co.uk and make a list of the top stories there. Compare the lists.

Do you have a preferred TV news channel? If not, is that because you don't follow the news or because you think they are all the same? If you do have one, then consider what aspects of it connect your personal order to the social order represented in the channel.

References

Barber, B. L., & Demo, D. H. (2006). The kids are alright (at least most of them): Links between divorce and dissolution and child well-being. In M. A. Fine & J. H. Harvey (Eds.), *Handbook of divorce and relationship dissolution* (pp. 289–311). Mahwah, NJ: Lawrence Erlbaum.

Baxter, L. A. (1992). Root metaphors in accounts of developing romantic relationships. *Journal of Social and Personal Relationships, 9,* 253–275.

Baxter, L. A., Dun, T. D., & Sahlstein, E. M. (2001). Rules for relating communicated among social network members. *Journal of Social and Personal Relationships, 18,* 173–200.

Burke, K. (1935). *Permanence and change: An anatomy of purpose.* New York: New Republic.

Burke, K. (1966). *Language as symbolic action: Essays on life, literature and method.* Berkeley: University of California Press.

Butler, J. (2004). *Undoing gender.* New York: Routledge.

Chornet-Roses, D. (2006). *"I could say I am 'dating' but that could mean a lot of different things": Dating in the U.S. as dialogical relational process.* Unpublished doctoral dissertation, University of Iowa, Iowa City.

Crouter, A., & Helms-Erikson, H. (2000). Work and family from a dyadic perspective: Variations in inequality. In R. M. Milardo & S. W. Duck (Eds.), *Families as relationships* (pp. 99–115). Chichester, UK: Wiley.

Duck, S. W. (2002). Hypertext in the key of G: Three types of "history" as influences on conversational structure and flow. *Communication Theory, 12*(1), 41–62.

Duck, S. W., & McMahan, D. T. (2010). *Communication in everyday life.* Thousand Oaks, CA: Sage.

Duck, S. W., & VanderVoort, L. A. (2002). Scarlet letters and whited sepulchres: The social marking of relationships as "inappropriate." In R. Goodwin & D. Cramer (Eds.), *Inappropriate relationships: The unconventional, the disapproved, and the forbidden* (pp. 3–24). Mahwah, NJ: Lawrence Erlbaum.

Goffman, E. (1959). *Behaviour in public places.* Harmondsworth, UK: Penguin.

Hess, J. A. (2000). Maintaining a nonvoluntary relationship with disliked partners: An investigation into the use of distancing behaviors. *Human Communication Research, 26,* 458–488.

Miell, D. E. (1987). Remembering relationship development: Constructing a context for interactions. In R. Burnett, J. McPhee, & D. D. Clarke (Eds.), *Accounting for relationships* (pp. 60–73). London: Methuen.

Mongeau, P. A., & Kendall, J. A. (1996). *"What do you mean this is a date?": Differentiating a date from going out with friends.* Paper presented at the conference of the International Network on Personal Relationships, Seattle, WA.

Paul, E. L. (2006). Beer goggles, catching feelings and the walk of shame: The myths and realities of the hookup experience. In C. D. Kirkpatrick, S. W. Duck, & M. K. Foley (Eds.), *Relating difficulty: Processes of constructing and managing difficult interaction* (pp. 141–160). Mahwah, NJ: Lawrence Erlbaum.

3

What Has Personality Got to Do With Relationships?

People seem not to see that their opinion of the world is also a confession of their character.

—Ralph Waldo Emerson (1803–1882)

There's nowt so quare as folk.

—(Yorkshire saying) [translation:
"There is nothing quite so odd or unpredictable as people."]

Given what I have proposed as a new way to look at relationships—as connected to social order, as based in language and performance, as connected with identity and the persuasion of others, as about the presentation of preferred ways of looking at the world as a whole in the hope of having other people accept those views, as a form of action based on symbols—then several key issues arise. First, what happens to the view that relationships are based on similarity of personality? What is personality, and how does personality influence choice of friends or romantic partner? Second, given that a lot of the research reviewed briefly so far considers the influence of self, attitudes, personality, and disclosure of one's inner being and private thoughts, how does the new way connect to such a concept as personality? Third, given that many of us believe that our personality is formed to a large extent in childhood, how do our early experiences influence later—apparently free—choices in relationships?

What Is Personality Anyway?

I am not going to spend very long demonstrating that certain types of personality are just more attractive in a given society/social order than others are.

That really is something that common sense gets right. Your society tends to value sociable, outgoing personalities, and people are appreciated for being friendly, affable, agreeable, smiley, approachable, open, happy, and gregarious. Shy, hostile, withdrawn, pugnacious, aggressive, unfriendly, sad, depressed, lonely Scrooges need not apply. It's just obvious to you that society prefers outgoing types, unless you happen to be a shy or withdrawn person who appreciates a bit of peace and quiet most of the time, and finds the noise and hurly-burly of an outgoing style too much to handle much of the time. Some people might typically seek out other quiet folks who will not overload your social experience, although you might like the occasional party with an outgoing, loud friend so that you can get some "secondhand sociability" once in a while; you let him or her do most of the entertaining and loud socializing. You can enjoy being part of it without having to do a whole lot to make it continue or develop. Also, you know that he or she can be counted on to fill awkward silences. So, the shy person is satisfying some human social needs but keeps a bit of a lid on it. Although most human beings like some contact with other people from time to time, some people like more of it more of the time with more people than others do (Bradshaw, 2006). And that brings us to another set of related thoughts about personality and relationships.

If some people are shy and don't generate lots of social interaction or busy social lives, then this is another way of saying that personality might affect the numbers of people that they find attractive in the first place. It also states the obvious, that your personality affects the kinds of people you like. For example, if you are a secure, trusting, and outgoing person, then you will find almost anybody attractive—or at least worth a second look. If you are a nervous sort of person, then you might be attracted only to transparently trustworthy and upright people or may distrust most people and be wary and vigilant in company.

Personality and Connection to Others

Rephrased, this means that your personality affects your ability to connect and also the range of people with whom you can connect. Many people would like to end up with a partner who is at least as socially capable and outgoing as they are (or perhaps a little more so, for shy people). Even so, you tend to see human personality as made up of not just general human needs (Weiss's "provisions," as discussed in Chapter 1) (Weiss, 1974) but also the "spin" given to that by your own personal experiences in life. So if all human beings have needs to connect with other people and personality support is one such need, then you each need some general and some specific support.

In other words, you might get together with other people in order to have your personality shored up and confirmed in *both* a general human way *and* in ways specific to your own experience and way of viewing in the world. Personality is social and personal, and it creates specific relational needs.

DISCUSSION QUESTION

Take a look at TV shows such as MTV's *Parental Control* and write down the ways in which personality of the candidates is viewed as likely to influence relationship success or acceptance. Why does our culture—hint, a Western culture—emphasize the importance of personality in relationships?

In Chapter 2, I pointed out that personal orders, relationships, and the world at large are open-ended experiences, unfinished business. What that means is that one of the main problems for us all as human beings who have to interact with other human beings, then, is how to keep understanding others' behavior and how to respond appropriately in light of what turns out in the future. As your experience develops, and as your partners and your relationships unfold, so you know the world differently in these open-ended adventures that affect what you know and how you know it.

Because relationships are unfinished business, no one knows for sure how things will ultimately pan out, and you do not know what conclusive or final sense to make of a partner's behavior at a given time, so you keep talking and trying to uphold a way of seeing the world. It takes time to make sense of people, and you can change your mind about people, fall out of love or fall into reconciliation and forgiveness, come to admire someone you disliked or become bitter enemies with a previously close friend.

Personality Types. Really?

Hold those thoughts and I will connect them to what I have covered in the preceding chapter. Chapter 2 showed you that relationships are ways of knowing the world and that you filter your knowledge through the contacts that you have with other people, connecting your personal order to the social order. The chapter also set up the next step by saying that personality is a way of knowing (that is, a personal order), a way of seeing and simultaneously a way of *not* seeing. A person with paranoid tendencies, for example, sees people and events in a way that is different from the way in which others see them. Paranoids suspect others' motives and see people as threats; extraverts love being with other people and see them as fun and not as threats. In other words, a person who is an extravert knows and experiences the world in a way different from the way a paranoid knows and experiences the world. One way of seeing (the world) is not the other way of seeing (the world).

"Extravert" and "paranoid" are only two sorts of overlay on personality. You have many other overlays, some focusing on how someone behaves (outgoing, reserved); some on how someone feels about other people (friendly, shy);

some on someone's needs (dependent, submissive); and some on someone's general psychology (neurotic, obsessive). Because you use lots of different ways to see or represent a person's layers of personality, any answer to the opening question about personality and relationships therefore has to take a look at these different ways to see what personality is so that you can connect it to relationships.

PERSONALITY AS A GHOST IN THE MACHINE

Philosopher Gilbert Ryle (1949) famously attacked Descartes's belief that each person consisted of a body and a mind, creating a dualism that made people into something parallel to a ghost in a machine. If we see "personality" as something separate from the body in which it exists, then we are making the same mistake. Let's see why.

Are you tense, nervous, quiet, ambitious, lazy, pessimistic, weak, sympathetic, agreeable, confident, strong, adventurous, or self-reliant? When you think of "personality," it is most likely to be in terms of answers to such questions. You may expect to answer yes or no to each possible label and that someone will add up your answers at the end and say "You are an extravert." They might offer some insight into the traits that you possess, indicating that you have certain personality properties or tendencies revealed by the test.

In short, you commonly think about personality as a compilation of sets of characteristics that people have. For example, you know you are thinking about personality when you ask whether someone is optimistic, introverted, or reliable. You also assume that a set of personality characteristics makes the person what she or he is—that it depicts his or her identity. Also, you make judgments about the sort of personality that somebody has, preferring some types to others ("happy" is better than "whiny"!). You also tend to make evaluations of the acceptability of these personality characteristics and use them to decide whether you like the person or not and would like to date or befriend them.

SO WHAT IS PERSONALITY?

People have been trying to work this out for hundreds of years and have come up with lots of different answers. The topic represents a whole field in psychology, so what I say here is necessarily a caricature. But bear with me for a while, because a discussion of the issues helps to change the way you think of personality in relationships.

There have been many ways of looking at personality, and an early observation by Gordon Allport, a key figure in the field, was that "personality is less a finished product than a transitory process. While it has some stable features, it is at the same time continually undergoing change" (Allport, 1955, p. 19).

An important point that this suggests is that the many ways of looking at personality are not necessarily exclusive. In much the same way that you can describe a house as "contemporary" or "ranch style" and also as "facing south" or "well-maintained," so you can describe a personality in terms of needs, behaviors, ways of thought, or emotional tendencies. You can also see it as an open-ended work in progress for each person.

In broad terms, personality is usually seen by psychologists as a constellation of behaviors and attitudes that are characteristic of a particular individual. Other people see personality as simply an extremely handy way of describing apparent consistency in a person's behavior—a way for an outsider to see a person as consistent and predictable. In other words (remember Burke's view of motives from Chapter 2), it is a linguistic tool for observers rather than a wired-in feature of persons being described. So personality is not understood this way as a set of features that a person *has* or the way he or she *is,* so much as a way for outsiders to describe the perceived underlying consistencies in someone's behavior. Indeed, research (Heider, 1958; Ross, 1977) often shows that you tend to describe others' behavior in terms of their personality ("She did that because she is just a mean person"), but you are willing to describe your own behavior in terms of situational factors ("I behaved carefully over money in that situation, not because I am an essentially stingy or avaricious person but because I know that my bank balance is low at the moment").

So, in the modern world, you usually see personality as some sort of ghost that operates your body. When you look shy, it is because the little rabbit inside your head makes you feel insecure; when you are dominant, there is a personality inside of you that operates the switches in a way that makes you masterful, or a "firefighter" part that gets activated to deal with emergencies that you see as threatening.

PERSONALITY AND BODY TYPE

It was not always like this, and in the early 1800s, "character" was thought to be so fixed that it could be easily detected from a person's physical characteristics. Ancient Greeks and Romans thought that personality came from your stomach or from the various liquids that make up your body—your "humors" ("melancholy" translates as "black bile," for example). In the early 1800s, Francis Gall presented an atlas of the head, indicating his belief that the development of a person's brain was the seat of his or her personality and that such development could be detected in the bumps in the shape of his or her skull. This technique (phrenology) supposed that it was possible to detect a person's degree of, say, ambition by feeling the relevant area of the skull; the bump of ambition would be detected by those skilled in the art of reading such bumps.

The degree of development of the bump and its prominence relative to other areas of the skull alerted the skilled observer to the relevance of ambition to the overall character of the person whose skull was being assessed. Don't laugh. You can still buy phrenology maps and busts on eBay™.

In a somewhat similar idea, Lombroso (1918) supposed that criminal skulls were deformed in ways that indicated a criminal mind. In particular, criminal character was physically represented, Lombroso suggested, by the shape of the skull, beetling brows, length of forehead, and so on. In a modern version of a related idea, people still subscribe to similar beliefs that the face tells you a lot about a person's internal character, a notion that assumes a relationship between mental/behavioral inclinations and physical ones. Lombroso thought that the shape of people's heads and physical characteristics would tell you whether they were criminals; the characteristics that make people criminals would show up on their faces. Think about today's police bulletins and you'll see that unusual facial features (such as scars or deformities) are most often identified when the police are looking for a suspect. When people are armed and dangerous, you expect them to *look* armed and dangerous. When people who looked quiet and placid beforehand carry out violent acts, then you are apparently more shocked than when violent-looking people do them. So if looks could kill, they probably do!

> ## Listen in on Your Own Life
>
> Listen for police descriptions of wanted suspects. How far do they confirm or challenge the idea that physical features are connected to criminality?

So you still accept the broad idea that physical characteristics might represent the personality inside. Every time you make a judgment that somebody who looks good on the outside might have a good personality and be an interesting and likable person, then you are also making the same kind of judgments about personality that Lombroso did. So, again, don't laugh. The idea is one you still use in modified form.

We could also interpret some of Lombroso's approach in a different way from the point of view of this book. Perhaps if someone has a certain set of physical characteristics, then the person may experience the world in a particular way. For example, if a man has a scowling face, then other people may respond to him on the basis of his facial appearance and the fact that he looks hostile and aggressive. Such men may therefore end up being treated as aggressive even if they are actually kind and gentle people. In other words, their facial appearance may lead to particular ways in which they get treated by others, and this may feed back to affect the way in which they actually experience themselves. Perhaps they get used to being treated by other people as if they were aggressive and so the way in which they move about the world may bring about a self-fulfilling prophecy. Responses from other people based on their facial appearance may lead to persons seeing themselves in a particular way. Of course, this would be an example of what was discussed in Chapter 1, namely, that a person's way of being in the world influences his or her way of knowing and vice versa.

The Body and the Ghost Inside

Personality has also been linked to whole body type beyond the shape of the head alone. In such approaches to personality, it is presumed that personality is related to overall bodily structure and that collections of personality characteristics go with and are connected to physical form. A variety of these techniques was available in the work of such theorists as Kretschmer (1931) and Sheldon (1940). Before I describe these approaches, first briefly think whether you would classify yourself as (a) thin, tall, and fragile; (b) soft, round, and fat; or (c) muscular and athletic in build. Now indicate whether you are also (a) nervous, tense, and quiet; (b) dependent, agreeable, and sympathetic; or (c) strong, adventurous, and self-reliant.

Sheldon (1940) came up with an approach to personality that was called **somatotypes**, or body types. The body types corresponded to three predominant types of personality character: *ectomorph* (thin, tall, fragile—seen as tense, nervous, quiet, ambitious, pessimistic); *endomorph* (soft, round, fat— seen as lazy, weak, sympathetic, agreeable, and dependent); and *mesomorph* (muscular and athletic—seen as strong, adventurous, and self-reliant). Sheldon's work linked body type with characteristics of personality, but did this directly and in a deterministic way. That is, he supposed that body shapes linked directly and inescapably to personality. If Sheldon had read Chapter 1 here, then he might consider the possibility that bodily physique affects the ways in which you experience and know the world instead of it determining what people are like. For example, a muscular person can afford to encounter the world in an adventurous and self-reliant way that tall, skinny, fragile people may not be able to do.

Although Sheldon's approach to personality as a physically based feature of persons has few supporters nowadays, stereotypes about it are broadly accepted even today. When you read in William Shakespeare's *Julius Caesar* that "Yon Cassius has a lean and hungry look; such men are dangerous" (*Julius Caesar*, Act 1,

> Think about your favorite movies and novels. Write down the names of these favorites and then read on. Have you ever thought about the way in which the leading characters in novels and movies are characterized? Start listing the number of such leading characters who are fat or ugly.

Scene 2, 193–196), you perhaps do not read it immediately as an endorsement of Sheldon's stereotypes, nor do you ascribe the view that "fat people are jolly" to the same source, but the underlying stereotype is nonetheless connected. As you shall see later in the book, there is an assumption that personality has some connection to physique, even if it is not an overridingly strong one. For example, people still describe an authoritarian boss as "a *little* Hitler," making the connection between small stature and an urge to dominate. (In fact, Adolf Hitler was somewhat above average in height, as is evident from contemporary photographs. It was the French Emperor and General Napoleon Bonaparte who was both short and aggressive, and equally unpleasant.)

You also (perhaps too easily) assume that, for example, physically attractive people will have very nice personalities (that they'll be socially outgoing, lively, fun, and pleasant, for example). There are also negative contrary stereotypes that claim that if someone is too attractive, then she must be "a bitch" or he must be "a player" (Norwood, 2007).

Thus, although many of you would reject the idea that physique *determines* personality, you might still be willing to endorse the idea that physical characteristics have some bearing on how a person behaves—which, after all, is what personality is about. Personality is something that you *do,* and this connects to the idea of performance, which was introduced in Chapter 2. It might also be about how people communicate and about how you know and deal with the world. For example, a simple way of knowing the world ("I can beat it") might simultaneously lead you to be self-confident and also to work out and develop strong muscles. From that, you would, in fact, physically become a mesomorph with those personality traits and behavioral or performative characteristics.

Is Personality a Way of Knowing?

Let's take the example of the mesomorphs, connect it to the discussion about personality and the themes in Chapter 1, and try to see how physical shape could connect to a way of seeing and not seeing ("a way of knowing"). Another way of thinking about it is that if you are muscular and strong, perhaps people treat you with a bit more respect than if you are thin, feeble, or delicate. Putting this into the terms introduced in this book, mesomorphs may be more adventurous because that's the way they get treated by other people—as the sort of muscular persons who will take risks because if other people get in the way, they're able to brush them aside.

On the other hand, the thin, weak, nerdy people get more experience being disrespected and treated badly by others and therefore become more suspicious of them and reserved in their company. Napoleon Dynamite was a good example. Lacking a strong physical presence, he tended to be an outcast at school and one who was bullied and treated disrespectfully—vote for Pedro! Many people resonate with this experience, and it would not be surprising that ectomorphs would behave in these ways that reflect not only their physical structure but the way in which they get treated by other people who do not fear them but regard them as odd and feeble. It is a short step to suggest that ectomorphs are lacking in confidence and social power because that's the way other people have treated them when they lack a powerful physical presence. They come to see the world in a particular way because that's how the world treats them.

BODY OF KNOWLEDGE?

Even if there is a physical basis to personality, then, I reinterpret this by suggesting that physical characteristics actually affect the way in which other people treat you. Therefore, the ways in which you feel and act—and hence the way your personality comes across to others—are part of the ways of knowing the world based on your physical embodiment, your physical experience, and the way your social order interprets the personality that lies behind a particular physical frame. Of course, cultures differ in the way in which they treat people's physical appearance, but, interestingly, they also differ in the way in which they attribute personality characteristics to the physique. In particular, cultures differ in their interpretation of whether somebody is attractive or not, and the way in which they get treated as attractive may lead to them behaving in attractive ways. For example, in India, a woman with a roll of fat around her middle is seen as more attractive than a skinny woman, because she's healthy and wealthy enough to become fat, a fact emphasized by traditional Indian dress for women that exposes the midriff and so makes beauty and wealth physically visible.

Physical Structure and Social Orders of Attractiveness

Even within cultures, beliefs about attractiveness can change. Look back at the ways in which film stars from the 1940s and 1950s were seen as attractive, and yet their physical characteristics are different from the ones you would regard as attractive today—women were plumper and men were weathered and had slicked down, greasy hair. Ideal women's sizes in magazines change over time, but the point remains the same: being seen as attractive in a culture leads to a way of knowing the world.

Physical build affects the way the person approaches life and sees and understands it and justifies a whole chapter (Chapter 4) to fill out the detail. Thus, the factors also affect the way the person approaches other people in life and the relationships that can be had with them. It is therefore an example of personal order of the kind noted in Chapter 2 and its direct connection to relationships. So, even if you see personality in physical terms, personality actually works in the same way as the personal orders that I described in Chapter 2. Physical features are influences on the ways in which you know, experience, and live in the world—the way you understand and perform your self.

Instead of seeing personality as physical or as a bunch of motives or needs or quirky ways of acting, I suggest seeing it as *an expression of what you know.* How a person acts is based on what the person knows as a human being in general and as a person with a background of particular experiences in childhood and beyond. This also affects the way you live in the world. Personality, then, can be seen as a way of knowing and being in the world. This raises two questions: Where do these views come from? and How do they affect our choices?

The Early Years: Formation of Personality and Relationship Style

The physical elements of personality are not the only part of personality relevant to relationships, and a huge influence on your personal order, on your *epistemic,* comes from what you expect other people to be like. This is, of course, something that you learn from interacting with them. Particularly important are your experiences with other people when you were a child.

WHAT CHILDREN LEARN ABOUT OTHER PEOPLE AND THEMSELVES

Another way of looking at personality is in terms of the personal orders that you form on the basis of your early experiences in childhood, first with your parents (or "caretakers").

Early Life and Later Life Approaches to Relationships: Attachment

Psychologist John Bowlby (1951, 1969/1982) noticed that children brought in as "infant problems" to the hospital tended to react in several different ways to their caretakers. He also observed that the way in which their caretakers treated them was connected with anxiety levels. Most children, especially very young children, usually got distressed if the caretaker went away, although some were completely indifferent. Likewise, they were different in their reactions when the caretaker came back. Some reacted very positively to the reappearance of the caretaker and some were quite indifferent to it.

Children showed different kinds of distress patterns when the caretaker reappeared, some responding positively and some responding negatively or indifferently. Bowlby's insight was to suggest that there were different attachment styles (i.e., different ways of connecting to other people) that infants learned from interactions with their caretakers.

The importance of the idea comes when it is suggested that these early learned behaviors transfer to later life and to relationships with other people even as adults (Hazan & Shaver, 1987). In short, the way in which children were treated by their caretakers leads to them expecting to be treated the same way by other people later in life when they have adult relationships.

What this comes down to is the idea that some children trust their caretakers and some do not, and that this is based on the way in which the parents have treated them as young children. In time, their personal order for seeing other people is based on how their caretakers treated them, because the caretakers represent the child's first experience of other people, of course. Secure and confident children know that when a caretaker goes away, the absence is temporary, and as soon as the caretaker comes back, he or she will be glad to see the child and will be supportive and loving. This feeling of security about the caretaker specifically tends to promote a broad confidence about the nature of relationships with other people when the child matures and launches out into a larger social context.

Other children may be more anxious about their parent's likely responses. The anxious-ambivalent ones tended to be more uncertain about whether the caretaker would return. They also seemed uncertain regarding what their parent would do when he or she returned, and the children seemed to be in doubt whether they would be treated lovingly. Hence, these children tended to become anxious and tense, and did not respond positively when the caretaker reappeared. They seemed uncertain about whether the parent would treat them well upon return, and they had a much greater level of anxiety about whether the parent's return would provide a warm and loving experience. These kinds of children appeared to have developed a sense of anxious concern about the unreliability and unpredictability of their caretakers. Unfortunately, it seems that they then became inherently suspicious about all sorts of relationships, even later in life.

Early Experiences as Terministic Screens

You do not enter adult relationships as open events; rather, you do so having been shaped by your previous experiences based on childhood. Do I hear "terministic screens" from Chapter 2? I hope so. You should be thinking about the way you have learned to understand other people through the terministic screens provided by this past experience. Your ways of seeing people have also become ways of *not* seeing them (e.g., seeing them as unreliable and *not* seeing them as unconditionally loving).

If you start out learning that you can trust that when parents go away they will come back and be loving and kind to you, then you form a much stronger impression about the likelihood of other people as a whole being trustworthy, and this carries over to later life relationships. If the romantic partner of a secure person goes away for a weekend, then the secure person doesn't worry much and is secure and will not be worried about whether the partner will come back. Secure folks just assume the partner will come back and will not have spent a weekend getting up to no good.

On the other hand, if you are an anxious type, then you may be less secure about the reappearance and may experience intense relational anxiety not only with parents in childhood but also with other adults later in life. One type (secure) feels safe in relationships and trusts partners quite easily, but the other two (anxious) types find it much harder. The anxious ones experience concern, distrust, and suspicion about their partners.

When Two Personal Orders Interact

Note also the interaction effects that go on here. If a secure person is with an anxious one or an anxious avoidant, then the same person—secure in all other relations—can be nervous with the anxious or anxious avoidant person because he or she becomes more aware of how he or she behaves and the way in which it may trigger anxious responses in the partner. Hopefully, the opposite is also true, that the anxious ambivalent person gets more secure with a secure partner. Often, in therapy, it becomes clear that anxious avoidant partners are paired with anxious ambivalent partners, and this creates stress in the relationship.

So, the first point that Bowlby established is that there are differences in infant responses to separation and that these appear to be lasting responses.

DISCUSSION QUESTION

Collect people's earliest memories. How many of them would you say are connected to themes of acceptance, rejection, comfort, and insecurity?

PARENTAL BEHAVIOR AND LATER RELATIONSHIPS

As a second point, Bowlby discovered that the parents of these children actually do behave in different ways, and that these differences in behavior could be the important force that led to the different outcomes in the children's behaviors. Bowlby discovered a connection between the way the parents treated their children and the way the children formed expectations about their relationships. In other words, you could read the parents' behavior as something that made the children secure or anxious—or, in my terms, created in them a personal order about their value to other people at large.

Parental Behaviors and Infants' Personal Orders

The parents of the anxious children behaved in ways that might make people feel anxious—for example, treating the children unpredictably and inconsistently, one minute being warm and loving and the next being distant and cold. The caretakers of the anxious children tended to be rejecting and would leave the children alone when they cried. They avoided physical contact, did not pick the children up, would not cuddle or hold them or investigate the children's needs, or correct any problems. In other words, they tended to be distant and also tended to be the ones who were more rigid and unresponsive to particular circumstances.

Parents of secure children, on the other hand, tended to be very responsive and adaptable, got deeply involved in play with the children, and responded to them appropriately as required by circumstances.

> **Question to Ask Your Friends**
>
> Can you connect your friends' experiences of childhood to the way in which they see and experience adult relationships?

They were predominantly positive in a way that led the parents to be reliably engaged and helped the child to develop a sense of being loved and cared for. Secure caretakers tended to be more flexible in the way they dealt with the children's needs but always with an underlying message of caring and supportiveness.

In both cases, the children got treated in ways that modified their experience of the parents/caretakers and led to an extension beyond that to any relationships with other people, as the children developed a personal order about other people. They started to form also a personal order about their own value to other people and a terministic screen for relationships based on the lens offered by that personal order.

Parental Behaviors and Their Personal Orders

Bowlby managed to identify not only different ways in which babies were treated by their caretakers, but also three different personality styles that were connected with that treatment. His main insight was to recognize the very strong relationship between the behavior of the parent and the responses of the children, and to draw out the implication to the ways in which the children came to see themselves in the long term. In my terms, Bowlby discovered a fundamental element of an individual's epistemic about relationships—the person's way of knowing other people in close relationships.

Bowlby assumed that what was happening was that the children developed a working model of relationships based on their relationship with the caretaker. The children began to notice a pattern in the way they were treated, and they took that pattern into themselves and saw themselves as the kinds of people who create that kind of response in parents. They developed a working model of themselves and their value to other people one way or another. Secure children learn that they will be protected and cared for. When they go out into the world later in life, they expect that to be what happens to them, and lo and behold, they find that it is. In other words, their epistemic about their value to other people influences the way in which they are treated by other people in the future, because they have formed particular expectations and they evoke relevant responses in others.

Anxious people assume that they will be treated with disrespect by other people, and in later life, this leads them to believe that romantic partners could leave at any moment. Their underlying sense (epistemic) of insecurity develops into a comprehensive style of relationship behavior that leads to them treating and expecting relationships to be of unstable sorts later in life. Ultimately, Bowlby presents the proposition that relationships with people later in life are preconfigured by early experiences to a very large extent. In my terms, a personal order about what to expect is created in early life and remains as the basis of the personal order of expectation about what all relationships will be like.

EARLY ATTACHMENT AND LATER ATTACHMENT

A later psychologist, Kim Bartholomew (1990), pointed out that Bowlby is actually noticing *two* different points when he's talking about the working models: First of all, you have a model of self for other people, that is, you have a model of what other people think about you. Second, you also have a model of what other people are like (see Figure 3.1).

Your Model of Self and of Others

You have a model of yourself as a valuable being or not, and this value extends to your expectations about the way in which you will be treated by others. Your view of yourself as a worthy person depends on the way you feel that you have been treated by other people in the past. Your "model of self" is a model of your value to other people and is represented in the columns of the figure—positive view of self on the left and negative view on the right. The second part of the model is your assumptions about the trustworthiness of other people, your "model of other." These are the rows in the figure, positive on the top and negative on the bottom. By working out how these two different models intersect, you end up in a particular square, with one of the four possible types of attachment that Bartholomew identifies.

It is important to understand that these ways of knowing/being self and knowing others are independent: Your sense of your value to other people does not depend on your model of their trustworthiness, and likewise, your sense of the trustworthiness of other people does not depend on your sense of your own value. Therefore, you end up with four types based on the two different assessments.

Effects of These Models

On this system, then, there are two views that a person can take of self (the columns in Figure 3.1) and two views of other people (the rows in Figure 3.1). In my terms, this approach indicates that a person's way of knowing the world (specifically, the part of the world that deals with relationships with other people) depends on ways of seeing self as a social object in the eyes of other people and also of seeing other people as emotional resources for oneself. As can be seen from Figure 3.1, a person with a positive view of self and a positive

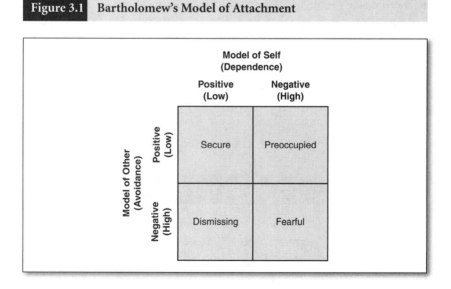

Figure 3.1   Bartholomew's Model of Attachment

Source: Adapted from Bartholomew, K. (1990). Avoidance of intimacy: An attachment perspective. *Journal of Social and Personal Relationships, 7,* 147–178.

view of others will be secure and self-sufficient in relationships. The person has had no formative experiences that lead to a belief that one is *not* a valuable/valued social object and likewise has had no experience of others as being nonaccepting (it makes you sick, doesn't it?). Hence, the person sees self as valuable and also sees others as welcoming, and so the person approaches all relationships with confidence (security).

In contrast, the person with a negative view of self and a negative view of others has learned both that self is not valued and also that self derives its value only from the reactions of other people, who are regarded as largely hostile and unstable or disapproving in their judgments. Hence, this person views relationships with extreme distrust and negativity, preferring to avoid them if possible because they have only proved to be hurtful and threatening experiences in the past.

This person has a dilemma, in that self is undervalued and the person does not trust his or her own assessment of self. Hence, the person needs the judgments, preferably the positive judgments, of other people in order to establish self-worth (i.e., the person is highly dependent on other people for self-concept), needing to approach the very source that has produced only negative experiences in the past. These people (fearful avoidant) are in big trouble in the social world and can be expected to be suspicious yet dependent, and hence insecure and volatile in relationships. Ever met any? Perhaps now you can understand them a little better and be a little more forgiving. Their personal order sees relationships as threatening and of little value.

Emotion and interaction styles are both presumed to be affected by such epistemics/ways of knowing and so result in particular affiliative behaviors or tendencies in relationships. Dismissive and fearful people will avoid contact with others for the most part, although fearful people are torn. According to Bartholomew, these personality styles are directly related to the ways you interact with others and how they have interacted with you in the past. Your reactions are based on the ways you expect/know that others will respond to you.

DISCUSSION QUESTION

Do you think it is reasonable to assume that experiences in infancy determine later relationships? Are we prisoners of our past, or can we make changes and reject our past, turn over a new leaf, and adopt a new style of relating? If attachment theory is right, should all of our experiences in relationships of the same type always be the same kind of experiences? In your own life, have all your romantic attachments been the same?

A REINTERPRETATION OF ATTACHMENT

We can put Bartholomew's system into the framework proposed in Chapters 1 and 2. In Chapter 2, I drew a distinction between action and motion: The way you behave toward others in relationships is a reflection of your ways of understanding them and the world. As such, your actions (which require thought and a framing exercise where you actually think about what is going on) are reactions to the beliefs that you have about what the world has in store for us. Hence, your performance of relating is a reflection of your knowledge and understanding of the world of relating and other people. See? Your performance depends on your assessments of others as welcoming or not. Therefore, an attachment style can be reconstrued as a form of *action* of the sort described in Chapter 1, rather than as simple reaction/motion.

Attachment as Unfinished Business

In this way, then, and starting only from the idea that personality is relevant to the ways in which we perform relationships, attachment styles are means of relating your own and also others' ways of thinking (i.e., a meshing of personal orders), and also fitting one's relational behavior into socially accepted formats (performing relationships within a social order). Any personality style is a mixture of performance and knowledge that frames and drives the performance, and so it involves particular communication styles as well. When you note that extraverts are loud and active and that introverts are sheepish and mellow, then you can recognize that the performance of these two styles of communication is, in fact, based on different understandings of the world of other people and how you should move around in it.

In short, you can reinterpret the attachment approach—and other forms of personality description—as being about ways of knowing the world. One's expectations of others are based on what one knows or has learned from experiences in the past. Thus, one's personality can be seen as a way of knowing and a way of representing the world (to others as well as to oneself). Which one are you? Actually, it is probably better for you to think about other people you know and where to categorize them or else you can go crazy trying to categorize yourself and live with the result. You can probably think of someone that you know who fits into these categories one by one. Secure people do not seem to worry about relationships, and mostly they are people who are happy with all the relationships they have got and so forth.

Attachment as a Personal Order

What does this have to do with the previous chapter and action versus motion? *Motion* is just the movements/behaviors of people, and *action* requires that meaning is given to behaviors so that they are seen as having purpose or thought behind them. Well, you can see attachment style as a form of action. You could see personality just as motion (the instinctive way people act), and just notice that someone is muscular—or you could see it as action. It's the *meaning* that they put on being thin, being fat, being muscular, being rejected by other people, or being confident about their own value that makes the difference about how they experience the world epistemically. Also, you might think these could be healthier and more self-preserving choices that many may make. Attachment research suggests otherwise: that your reactions to relationships are *motion*, internalized reflex responses created by early experience.

In my approach, however, attachment style becomes an action and a way in which you understand how the world is. If people treat you in a dismissive kind of way, why not treat them in a dismissive way? If you feel confident that you're OK and people can't see it, well, screw them! So you become dismissive, and if you dismiss them, they dismiss you. Therefore, it becomes a way of action and a way of thinking and an epistemic in a way that compiles your personality. In short, it becomes something that is a way of thinking and a way of seeing and being in the world.

Of course, the way that you know about people's style is to listen carefully to what they say about life, relationships, and everything. When people tell you stories where everything comes out for the best or everything is a kind of fairy tale where those who go through hardships come out well in the end, you can be confident that you are listening to a secure person, where fantasy matches reality. On the other hand, the friend I mentioned before who keeps on telling me about all her problems in life, all the misfortunes that happen, seems to represent life as rejecting her and the world as a fearful place to be. Her account of being in the world is a fearful one, and it represents her personal order.

ARE CHOICES DRIVEN BY PERSONALITY?

Remember that one of the common beliefs that I used to open Chapter 1 is that people choose one another as partners on the basis of personality similarity (something also derived from Weiss's provisions)? Let's try to connect the previous sections to this idea by asking the question that titles this chapter. If we can reconceive personality as an embodied set of experiences (personal orders that are performed in everyday life) from childhood and later experiences, then does this revise our view of how choices are driven by personality?

Personality as a Personal Order

Personality is less a collection of traits than a personal order or way of knowing. In that case, personality and relationships are both about the major need to establish the validity to others of one's rhetorical vision (personal order) of the world.

Given that there are general ways of thinking about relationships that satisfy broad human needs of both assistance and emotionality, what directs you toward particular other people with whom to form close attachments?

Interesting how something so common can also be complex and unfamiliar when seen in new ways! You have different multiplex relationships, but there is always uncertainty and ambiguity about them in some ways because of their open-endedness. There is continual tension between desire for inclusion and membership, on one hand (Weiss's provisions in Chapter 1), and a desire for autonomy and freedom on the other, both a need to be helped and the need to help without losing independence as a result of either process. You want and need other people, but you have a personal identity that you don't want cramped. There is a neat, impenetrable connection between the way you see yourself as a separate being and the way other people make you who you are. Both the "separate being" and the "who you are" are other ways of thinking about the notion of personality. What you need now, then, is a way to explore the role of personality in relationships. You *know* that personality is connected to relationships, so how does it work?

Personality in a Social Order

In a Western world, you are quite used to the idea that individuals are egos inside a bag of skin and that these egos are a personality that goes out into the world in search of "growth" and "self-development," and to better the world also through connection with other people (or personality support in Weiss's views, Chapter 1). The main challenges for people are to make sense of the world, better themselves, and connect with other people in the process, or, indeed, as a major part of those other two processes. It is generally assumed, then, that you start with a personality that develops and is improved by other people, and in turn can, through connection, serve the purpose of helping others to improve themselves as well.

Although people often break down in French cafés in an agony of existential angst and worry about who they really are, the notion of personality is clearly one that involves a consistency of *behavior* as well as of thoughts, expectations, and personal orders. Its ability to help you connect to other people also depends on the performance of characteristics that others will like.

Obviously, in contrast to my suggestion that life and relationships are both unfinished business, this view presumes that you are relatively stable in some ways and that you both possess and can let other people know that you possess likable traits such as a sense of humor, loyalty, or capacity for loving. In terms

> Personality has not always been the basis for selection of friends and companions. In the agricultural economies of 400 years ago, people could be friends because they helped one another and not simply because they liked one another's personality.

of what I wrote in Chapter 1, that would be stability in terms of the way you know the world, present yourself to the world, and assume stability in others, even the weird ones. On this basis of optimism and stability, you set out on your journey of discovery of lovely partners. Common sense tells you that you will do it on the same basis—the basis of their personality.

Common sense is clear that there is some connection between personalities and relational success, but it bets both ways (for example, "birds of a feather flock together" says one piece of common sense, but "opposites attract" says something contrary). What sorts of "relationships" do you mean, anyway (romances, friendships, brothers, sisters, bosses, co-workers, in-laws)? Are you assuming that *all* kinds of relationships are influenced by personality in exactly the same way? Common sense does not tell us.

How Does Personality Connect to Relationships?

Even if you focus on personality in close relationships only, then obviously you have a lot of scope about types of relationships to think about because there are so many sorts of close attachments, such as parent-child attachments, romantic attachments, and friendship. In each of these, you need to think about possible stages of relationships as they progress and endure: starting, middle, and later stages or simply steady changes over the lifetime of the relationship. First dates, long-term dating, and marriage may all be stages in the same relationship, and you probably expect at least *some* different influences to be important at each stage. The sorts of personality characteristics that make someone an attractive date (lively, fun, gregarious) might be less important when it comes to marriage when you want someone who is basically reliable, supportive, and practical, and who could make a good, solid, reliable, devoted, involved parent.

ROMANCE AND ATTRACTION

Let's start with romance and attraction. If you think that personality can be relevant to the attraction stage of relationships at all, it is partly because few people nowadays would have much trouble believing it—even though some other societies (social orders) do not allow individual choice of romantic relationships and a partner's personality is less important than, say, status or duty to parents, or religious or tribal or group membership. But limiting discussion to societies where freedom of choice is the basis for relationships, then you can look at ways in which such choice might be based on personality.

How Romance Is Kindled

Romance can serve as a working example to help you think through the way relationships start. You naturally tend to think that romance has a cause, such as physical attraction or personality or attitude similarity. If you look at the dating agencies, then many of these characteristics get emphasized in the profiles that people fill out in order to become members of the dating group. You think nothing of listing your favorite music, food, or films; your religious beliefs; your physical characteristics; your social preferences; and a number of other features that may display your personality and that you think may make you more attractive to someone else or help you to match them.

DISCUSSION QUESTION

How do you feel about the personality of Dr. Gregory House on the TV show *House*? He is obviously a grouchy, insecure, arrogant, insensitive person, but also a very gifted physician with some great one-liners. If he is such a bad person, then why do people watch the show?

Such features might include "lively" or "outgoing" or "happy" or certain kinds of attitudes and preferences that display your nature (conservative, religious, freewheeling, vegetarian). Physical characteristics often get mentioned, too, but mostly it's about the sort of profile of your personality or personal preferences (personal orders). You would not feel surprised if people said that they make romantic or friendship choices on the basis of the other person's personality characteristics, some of them stated directly (introvert) or some inferred from other activities that get identified ("likes quiet walks in the forest"). In life's mating game, such personality characteristics are often offered as the basis for your choices ("We share the same values"). Much research, going back decades, supports the idea that some types of personality characteristics are attractive in general, particularly outgoing good humor (Hendrick & Brown, 1971), or that similarity of personality predicts long-term stability of relationships (Levinger, 1964). eHarmony™ and other dating agencies use the matching of personality characteristics and values as the basis for pairing with potential partners and you just *know* it works. You talk of good matches and bad matches, and a bad match is with very dissimilar people.

Relationships Other Than Romance

You can see that this doesn't necessarily apply to family as compared to romance, where life's lottery just *gives* you the family members with whom you have to associate. In fact, you often don't have choices at all about family members. Although you can massage the depth of the relationship with them and whether it is close or not, you cannot alter whether you have a relationship with your parents in the first place. You show up and they are parents. End of story. All you can influence is the depth of affection that characterizes the relationship and the way in which it is performed. Personality might be relevant to that: for example, parents can be loving or distant, harsh or kind, authoritarian or permissive, and children can be obedient, aggressive, truculent teenagers. All of these adjectives are pretty handy descriptions of personality characteristics. But the personality characteristics that make someone a desirable date may not be the same personality characteristics that make him or her a good parent or an appealing family member (Hendrick & Hendrick, 2006).

I was recently appointed to the Iowa Johnson County Livable Community and Successful Aging Advisory Committee, and we talked about ways to help older people stay connected. One obvious way that came up in the course of the conversation was to set up a virtual community where members could communicate with one another over the computer/Internet. Can you guess the crucial point that did not strike us until quite late in the conversation? What a TFG! Many people in their 70s and older *never learned to type* and so cannot easily or usefully employ a computer to communicate with others. Most men of that generation gave typing work to (female) secretaries, but most women of that generation did not work outside the home in the first place or at least did not work in offices. The assumption that everyone can type because *we* have always been used to typing is a TFG built into the use of computers and the assumption that communication over computers is available to everyone.

LIFESPAN CHANGES

A related question about change in relationships is the fact that personal needs can alter over the life span (Blieszner, 2006). Even if personality got you into a particular relationship in the first place, some of these needs that are satisfied by relationships are not just about personality (as you saw in differentiating close attachments and instrumental affiliations). The person's ability to meet those can be modified by the process of aging. For example, physical needs and service needs change with age: Babies need a lot of physical care, whereas adults need less of that sort of "service" until they become sick or very old and then might need it again. Friendships can also be based on the circumstantial needs of the times, so, for example, when people have children, they tend to become friends with the parents of their own child's playmates (Reisman, 1981). Of course, this can help two sets of parents to share child management, for example, by baby-sitting for one another or taking the other couple's child for a sleepover when that couple needs to go out of town for a night, but beyond this instrumental purpose, the friendship may also be based on other factors.

Changing Needs Over the Life Cycle

People change their needs and the kinds of companionship that they seek as they age, even if their choice of target relationships at any of these times is still particular rather than general. Teenagers want dates, old people want help, new parents often need physical assistance and advice from friends who are dealing with comparable issues about children, retirees need a new community to replace work companions, and so on.

So the expectations that you have about relationships are subject to change over the course of life and in the way you live in it—or daily reality. The subtle point that you can think about for later is that these changes in needs can be seen as changes in personal orders, that is, changes in ways of knowing the world. Teenagers looking for sex really do know the world in a different way from the way they knew it as a hormonally unstimulated child; old people who cannot do what they used to do really well now know the world differently; the widow from Chapter 1 really does know the world differently now that she is alone. Of course, it is not just the past tense that matters, and much of an epistemic is about the way you know the world at present or expect it to turn out in the future.

Relationships and Personal Orders Again

On the other hand, although your general personal needs may change like this, they are not all that makes you choose particular partners. Pam hangs out with Gordana (who has no kids) rather than with Stella (who does) and with Rachel, rather than other possible choices in the same environment. Some of the choices made in the environment are based on personal preferences connected to personal order and personality. There are definitely some sorts of personality that your social order prefers, so the mixing of personality (personal orders) with relationships is still played out against a social order, even when it gets personal.

To sum this up, personal orders are ways of knowing the world, based on physical experience, childhood impressions, and the unfolding familiarity of everyday life. These are projected in everyday chatter through the display of rhetorical visions, and they are developed with other people within a social order that calls people to account. Personality is a catch-all term for your way of knowing the world and can be presented in different ways (rhetorically). When you find that you both agree about a personal order, then this kind of similarity of personality lays the basis for a relationship. If, on the other hand, you disagree about personal orders—then you assume that dissimilar personalities would create poor relational dynamics and so you avoid potential relationships. If the dissimilarities are not viewed as something you can overcome and yet are integral to the relationship, then you reject the other person as a possible relational partner.

The Answer

All that, then, to answer the chapter's question, is what personality has got to do with relationships.

PEDAGOGICAL EXERCISES

EXERCISE

Write down a list of your friends and acquaintances. List the qualities of these friends and acquaintances in terms of their personality characteristics. Beside the name of each of these people, indicate whether they are fat or thin. Does your list appear to reflect the same kinds of approach to somatotypes as is discussed in this chapter?

ETHICS QUESTIONS

Is it okay to laugh at fat people? If not, then why are such movies as *The Nutty Professor, The Klumps, Just Friends,* and other "fat suit" movies popular?

MEDIA ISSUES

How do the media portray people who are either very fat or noticeably thin? Do they attribute particular characteristics to individuals of different sizes and shapes, do they encourage us to prefer one to the other, and are they right?

References

Allport, G. W. (1955). *Becoming: Classic considerations for a psychology of personality.* New Haven, CT: Yale University Press.

Bartholomew, K. (1990). Avoidance of intimacy: An attachment perspective. *Journal of Social and Personal Relationships, 7,* 147–178.

Blieszner, R. (2006). A lifetime of caring: Dimensions and dynamics in late-life close relationships. *Personal Relationships, 13*(1), 1–18.

Bowlby, J. (1951). *Maternal care and mental health.* Geneva: WHO.

Bowlby, J. (1982). *Attachment and loss, Vol. I. Attachment* (2nd ed.). New York: Basic Books. (Original work published 1969)

Bradshaw, S. (2006). Shyness and difficult relationships: Formation is just the beginning. In C. D. Kirkpatrick, S. W. Duck, & M. K. Foley (Eds.), *Relating difficulty: The processes of constructing and managing difficult interaction* (pp. 15–41). Mahwah, NJ: Lawrence Erlbaum.

Hazan, C., & Shaver, P. (1987). Romantic love conceptualized as an attachment process. *Journal of Personality and Social Psychology, 52,* 511–524.

Heider, F. (1958). *The psychology of interpersonal relations.* New York: Wiley.

Hendrick, C., & Brown, S. R. (1971). Introversion, extraversion and interpersonal attraction. *Journal of Personality and Social Psychology, 20,* 31–36.

Hendrick, S. S., & Hendrick, C. (2006). Measuring respect in close relationships. *Journal of Social and Personal Relationships, 23*(6), 881–899.

Kretschmer, E. (1931). *Physique and character.* London: Routledge.

Levinger, G. (1964). Note on need complementarity in marriage. *Psychological Bulletin, 51,* 153–157.

Lombroso, C. (1918). *Criminal anthropology (L'Uomo criminale).* Roma: Publicazione.

Norwood, K. M. (2007). *Gendered conflict? The "cattiness" of women on Flavor of Love.* Paper presented at the Organization for the Study of Communication, Language, and Gender, Omaha, NE.

Reisman, J. (1981). Adult friendships. In S. W. Duck & R. Gilmour (Eds.), *Personal relationships 2: Developing personal relationships.* London: Academic Press.

Ross, L. (1977). The intuitive psychologist and his shortcomings: Distortions in the attribution process. In L. Berkowitz (Ed.), *Advances in experimental social psychology* (Vol. 10, pp. 173–220). New York: Academic Press.

Ryle, G. (1949). *The concept of mind.* Chicago: University of Chicago Press.

Sheldon, W. (1940). *The varieties of human physique: An introduction to constitutional psychology.* New York: Harper.

Weiss, R. S. (1974). The provisions of social relationships. In Z. Rubin (Ed.), *Doing unto others* (pp. 17–26). Englewood Cliffs, NJ: Prentice-Hall.

4

The Bodily Materiality of Relating

The sketch in Chapter 3 now presents us with two directions in which to proceed.

First, we should carry out a fuller exploration of the ways in which material physical issues affect your personal experiences and rhetorical visions of the world. It is not enough merely to connect it to personality. There is much more to say about the way in which physical appearance and material experiences in the world in general (e.g., poverty, ill health) affect the way in which a social order understands the nature of relationships.

Second, we need a fuller exposition of the way in which talk influences the intersection of personalities in a way that helps people to share meaning within their social order.

In fact, the above two directions are the ones that I will follow, but the premise for all of these explanations must be stated first. It appears to be a simple follow-on from the previous chapter, but it gets much more sophisticated the further we look into it.

The basic premise is this: At some key moments in life, we recognize through a succession of teaching, observation, and dawning epiphanies that we share understanding of the symbols that others use. At the same time, we become aware that *we ourselves* (that is, our bodies and behaviors) are perceptual objects for them to observe. Our bodies and behaviors can be seen, judged, assessed, and evaluated by other folks relative to the social order of symbols in a particular society. We can be evaluated as positive or negative examples of those symbols on any of the criteria that may be used. Strongly tending to be influenced by the social norms of our social order, that dramatic recognition of our symbolic relevance to others influences significantly what we do or how we perform.

Once the premise is clarified and filled out so that the full impact of the recognition of our being perceptual objects for other people can be understood, then on that premise, much can be built. In essence, the point of the next three chapters in the book is that we are physical beings who are *socially* affected by the structure of our body and its symbolic meaning to others, that the material circumstances of our life, our material possessions, and our physical behaviors—whether performed through choice of clothing or by nonverbal behavior or simply embodied in our physical structures—may be symbolic to other people. Our physical and material features therefore have relevance in the construction and conduct of relationships. We are aware of the fact that our bodies, our movements, our physique, our gender, our nonverbal expressions, and even our possessions may be read and judged by others who observe us and interpret us as "suitable," "desirable," or "too weird" for relationships. (You may want to take another look at the exercise "Listen in on Your Own Life" in Chapter 1.)

The next three chapters therefore focus on different elements of these material and physical influences on relating and the effects of our awareness of others' judgments in the social order. The present chapter deals with our awareness of ourselves as perceptual objects for other people. Chapter 5 deals specifically with the influence of our gender and sexuality as embodying socially evaluated criteria, performative expectations, and judgments about our suitability for certain types of relationships. Chapter 6 deals with the role of our possessions and material circumstances in the conduct of relationships and in particular takes a close look at the way in which the giving and sharing of possessions can be used to affect relationships. Yes, birthday presents can build or even end relationships!

The key point from here is to understand the variety of ways in which material and physical influences steer people's thinking, knowing, speaking, and relating.

Symbolically Connecting the Material World to the Social World

Communication researcher Jill Tyler (2007) points out that anyone who grows up in a small farming community may never know or understand city life in the ways familiar to someone who has lived in a city all of his or her life. Likewise, a city dweller may never fully understand a farmer's attachment to the earth and the seasonal rotations of experience. For the farmer, subways, skyscrapers, gangs, or city buses are entirely alien forms of experience, just as the grain elevator, the cow, and the fertilizer packet are to the city dweller. Although both people may have knowledge of these concepts in an abstract sense, the actual experience of living with cows or riding on a crowded subway every day limits what one knows in a real sense.

In the same way, people with the most resources still have quite different experiences from people who have fewer material and cultural resources. Being poor is not just a material circumstance (lack of money), but it affects your choices, your opportunities, a lot of other elements of life, and also what you know.

Some simple examples from the Western culture are that poor people may have no access to physical assets and relational resources that many people take for granted: cell phones; the Internet; TV; a good meal; a roof; a bed; safety; the likelihood that tomorrow will not be your last day on earth; and the certainty that you will not die from starvation, leaving your family

> Poverty affects time. People on the subsistence level spend most of their time trying to find food so they can stay alive long enough to look for the next day's meal (or perhaps the one that they will find next week). People in wealthy countries do not have this concern, so they can spend their time relaxing, reading, thinking about the design of their new apartment, watching TV, or spending time with friends just chatting. Extreme poverty and relative wealth therefore affect the opportunities that a person has to spend time "doing friendship."

and dependents to struggle for themselves. At the same time, they are deprived of the ability to see different places or collect a range of knowledge, or ever have the experience of inviting friends around for an exotic meal cooked by the pool on a fancy barbecue. Even worse, poor people find it difficult simply to stay alive, and they may be led by reduced circumstances into crimes that produce access to the basic necessities of life. The material experience of hunger can certainly affect the way you look at life in any case, even if you are not poor, but I want to take this more broadly and suggest that physical experience makes you look at social life and friendship differently. Access to the resources of material wealth constrains and influences one's experience and view of the world, including relationships and forms of sociality. Thus, the material experience of the world is also epistemic. I will cover all of these kinds of material influences on relationships in much more depth in Chapter 6.

THE REFLECTIVE ORDER IN THE SOCIAL ORDER

What you need to think about, then, is the symbolic connection between the material world and the social world. To make this move, I have to introduce the work of a sociologist, George Herbert Mead (1934), who believed that your social experience comes from material experiences and the shared interpretations of them in a given society.

According to George Herbert Mead, mind and self emerge in individuals from society out of interaction rather than vice versa. In other words, you become members of society by coming to accept the interpretation of your experience of the material world in terms that a society first gives to you during the time that you call "childhood." In childhood, you gradually learn what society means by certain symbols, and you become a truly social being who shares a meaning system proposed at first by your parents or caretakers.

Instead of lots of individuals coming together to make a society, Mead said, it is from your inevitable membership in a society during childhood that you get your sense of what symbols mean in the first place. He believed that one must begin with *material experience* as the basis for developing any system for understanding human life. For example, touching a hot stove teaches you about pain. The fact that someone else says "Ouch!" or "Mind the hot stove, it hurts" gives you a basis for interpreting and adding symbolic and linguistic meaning to your sense of material and physical pain. All knowledge arises from material experiences that are then interpreted for you in some pre-existing common framework of meaning, probably by your parents or caretakers at first. There is no self and no mind apart from this type of (social) *action* that interprets experience by use of symbols. This involves both your own material experiences and other people's interpretations of your behavior in symbols (including language) that you understand.

MAKING THE WORLD ORDERLY

Mead does not see objects as existing in the world in ways that are independent of mind (that is, independently from an interpreter). Until someone perceives (and hence categorizes) it, "the world" is just a bunch of stuff. You learn to make sense of it by seeing—and not seeing—it in various categories that suit the social order around you. Mead suggests that you recognize that your social order separates out those objects that are meaningful to it from other objects that are not relevant (the ways of seeing and not seeing; terministic screens).

Making Orderly Sense of a Disorderly World

As you saw in Chapter 1, when thinking about Eskimos and snow, different social orders perceive different sorts of distinction in the world—different categories of objects and events that they see as actually being "out there in the world." So Mead is pointing to the fact that you perceive what is useful to your social order by splitting that world into "things" only relative to perceiving minds (you, me, and the people you know). "Things" all turn into meaningfully distinguishable items and objects only when a perceiver looks upon them and is able to classify and distinguish them somehow with reference to that social order.

In other words, the physical nature of the world is objective and real (the "stuff" is really there), but it is also relative—in that language allows different cultures (and individuals) to construct and classify objects in different ways. Therefore, the world is not inherently ordered but is given an order by perceivers who want to talk to one another—and so turn the world and its objects into meaningful items, categories, and actions. Your own personal order is derived from the larger social order into which you are incorporated through the learning of its language and symbols. This connection between the objective world and language occurs through interaction, first between the perceiver and the material world and second between different perceivers who come into social relations with one another and *talk* about their perceptions and persuade you about them.

Reflection on Experience as a Way of Making Sense

Mead argued that reflective intelligence involved the manipulation of physical objects by the hands and then subsequent description of those objects and experiences in terms of symbols meaningful in a social order. Mead's doctrine of *objective relativism* suggests that objects exist only relative to some perceiver, and each perceiver is relative to an object in a strange sense. The object is distinguishable from the world of "stuff" only when a perceiver makes a distinction: The perceiver gives the object its existence by the act of perceiving and distinguishing the object from other "stuff," but the perceiver gains existence also from this act of perception and differentiation. Because objects cannot be distinguished from "stuff" until a categorization is made by a perceiver, the object has no name until it is perceived, but the perceiver is not doing anything until distinctions are made between the objects and "stuff." Hence, perceiver and objects are interdependent. This odd and somewhat difficult fact would not matter if you lived alone, but becomes important because you do not. Through membership of a social order, you perceive objects in ways that are shared or created by others in your social group, who share and use the same symbols and terms that you do. For example, you do not know what "a relationship" or "a banana" is until you connect with other people who talk about the world in ways that give sense to it in a social order so you can interpret it in the same way that they do. You make sense of it in ways that you and they can talk about in the same symbolic terms.

To put it another way familiar from the earlier chapters, your *motions* (immediate physical material experiences) are turned into *actions* (motion with meaning) by reference to the social order that helps you explain and interpret them in a particular way. Following the earlier example, when a child touches a hot surface and screams, an adult is likely to interpret this material experience for the child in linguistic terms understood in a social order: "That's hot, and I bet it hurts." From this, the child learns to call objects "hot" but also begins to learn that other people understand what it feels like to touch hot objects and feel pain. The child recognizes that other people understand what the child just felt. The child's material experience is therefore translated into the symbolic framework of language that allows him or her to talk to other people about experience, knowing that they also understand what the *experience* was like.

MIND AND MATERIALITY

There is no knowledge without action, but more surprisingly, there is no having a self without action. Individuals have a self only through their actions (motions connected to meanings), and Mead suggested that everything that you know comes from what you do by turning motion into action (by giving it meaning), whether you yourself give the motion a meaning or whether other people do. You weren't born with much particular knowledge wired into you or just given knowledge that then immediately made sense to you. You have to learn to use it, and you do that by reframing your personal and material experiences in terms of the social order that labels them with its own language and terminology. You acquire access to this code progressively, especially through infancy and childhood but actually all through life. You explain your experiences in a particular way that fits and accepts the social order. In other words, what just happens to you (motion) isn't as important as what you—and, importantly, what other people—*think* about when these things are happening and how you and they organize them into meaning (action) through language, labels, interpretations, and symbols.

The Derivation of Consciousness From Material Experience

Hence, for Mead, *consciousness* develops when motion turns into action (through understanding, language, and symbols); when you connect your motion to the social order; or when other people attribute meanings to your actions using their complex social order of symbols and understanding. For Mead, the insight is that the material and social worlds cannot be separated, for one depends on the other. Knowledge and understanding of both the physical *and* the social world emerge through interaction with the material world and with other members of that socially ordered world. We all confront the world in two ways—first physically (as motion), and then we represent that experience in symbolic ways that are comprehensible to one another (as action) in language or other nonverbal means.

Mead's explanation of the nature of experience thus combines the physical, the social, and the emergence of self. For Mead, the physical materiality of the world is particularly important in acquiring knowledge about the world and in the development of self. You come to experience the world first through touch and the manipulation of physical objects. All infants learn through their hands or mouths, and they are taught to explain these experiences through the symbols of language by reference to the social order with which they are becoming acquainted ("hot," "hurts"). Hence, infants, children, and even adults turn experiences into something that becomes meaningful action or at least begins to describe their experiences in terms that make it possible for other people to understand what everyone else in the same social order is talking about. The physical nature of the world and your experience of the world tell you only about the material nature of the world—heat, cold, flatness, roundness, pain—but your sociality translates that physical experience of the world (motion) into something that means something to other people and to yourself (action) because you become able to symbolize it and hence to think about it in the abstract (think of pain and something negative will come to mind).

Different Ways of Thinking About Experience

One way of thinking about an experience as motion is in terms of how long you've been doing something. You are an experienced student when you have been one long enough to know what it feels like to be a student. You have attended classes, written papers, perhaps taken tests, read books, and spoken with classmates and instructors. You know how the system works, what to expect, and what matters. However, these are the *motions* of being a student. Just because you are going through the motions of being a student, it does not follow that you are *good* at being a student. If you have thought carefully about all of these activities and understand them all, then they are now at least actions.

There is a better way to think of experience. Distinguish between an *experience as an event* and *experience as what you make of something or how you understand it* (experience as action) (Duck, 1994). To put this another way, there is a difference between time served in the job versus knowledge gained. One of the worst teachers I ever knew was always telling me how experienced he was because he had been doing it longer than anyone else. It's true that he had been doing it a long time, but he still had not learned to do it very well. There is a difference, then, between just going through the motions, and understanding well what you are doing and learning to adjust to feedback.

The Material World and Sociability

The above discussion applies also to your thinking about reality and therefore also to relationships, as an aspect of the world about which people have concepts. All of your relationships, even those that are casual, loose ties—relationships with people you do not know all that deeply in a personal way (Granovetter, 1973)—influence your thinking because they are part of your experiences and you cannot always escape that. When you focus on only the freedom of choice that you may have thought you had at the opening of Chapter 1, you *de*-focus from the context and the backgrounds against which it is made, the contrasts from which it is distinguished. Choice is not only about free will but also about fighting against constraints. It is also action in Burke's (1961) sense; it is shaped by the ways in which you construct the situation, the things you see as opposed to, or contrasted with, those you do not see, the experiences that occur to you (motion) and those to which you attribute meaning and sense (action).

MATERIAL INFLUENCES ON CONSCIOUSNESS AND RELATIONSHIPS

In Mead's terms, "the material" influences "the consciousness," and in its turn, consciousness influences relationships (just as the object influences the procedure and vice versa). At the purely physiological level, forgetting for the moment that physical aspects of life influence relationship worlds, consider how your knowledge and feeling are affected by your microbiology. Alcohol causes changes in perspective; aging (a physical and material constraint that affects your ability to lift, bend, last, stay awake, and tolerate fools) changes the way people view their experience; and sickness affects the way in which you experience the world. As another example of the effects of the physiological on the mental, women have menstrual cycles and men don't, and at times, these cycles affect willingness to engage in relational activity or to be sociable. This point of view therefore illustrates the embodied ways in which women and men experience relationships periodically. The hormonal changes that occur in adolescents have a very significant influence on the way in which individuals perceive one another as sexual objects. Furthermore, Mead would say that if you are very fat and others react to you by constantly looking away, then that is reflecting their responses to you as a self but also as a relational object. Their response informs and influences the way you feel about yourself and your relationships. Confidence or lack of confidence that results from these experiences is a style of action based on the framing of circumstances that result from it.

The same distinction applies to relationships themselves: What happens to you in a relationship can be different from what you make of what happens. As you saw in Chapter 3, secure and avoidant people might react differently to a relationship break up, so in the two cases, they are making something different (i.e., making a different action, a different personal experience) out of the break up (motion). Also, a social order projects onto its participants a sense of what is acceptable, good, or bad about relationships (and relational types) and also about the characteristics that are relevant to desires about relationships or even relational membership.

Applying
Meaning to Events

The formulating of events into meaning, or the turning of motions into meaningful actions, yields the sort of experience that is systematically and symbolically organized, then, rather than simply an occurrence (motion). For example, a man with depression may not be inclined to respond positively to his wife, and that disinclination may be given a meaning (rejection) by the spouse when that was not the man's intention (which was just a motion, a physically induced withdrawal from interaction). The wife's response nevertheless makes it into an action that is treated as threatening the relationship (Segrin, 1993). As such, it fits the ideas that Mead has been offering here where interaction with the material world becomes meaningful as a result of reflection and thought. Other people in your social order may interpret your behavior in a particular way (i.e., their reaction gives a motion a particular interpretation that sees it as an action of a particular sort): "That was hot, and I bet it hurt" or "You are withdrawing and rejecting me."

What this means is that when someone else interprets your behavior (even motion) as meaningful, then it becomes (for them) an action, as something having (relational) implications. The behavior (motion) becomes loaded with social meaning (action), and the person must recognize that these

Listen in on Your Own Life

Listen for ways in which you, your acquaintances, your friends, the media, and other sources try to make sense of some unfolding event. Listen for changes in the motives and interpretations that are offered and the way in which these transform the *meaning* of the event. Consider over time the ways in which particular events are reinterpreted and reinvented—the Oklahoma bombings were first attributed to Muslim extremist groups before it became apparent that it was the work of a white supremacist. At the time of writing this book, Tiger Woods has just gotten himself into trouble, and it has been interesting to notice the way in which the media first reported the incident as a simple driving mistake, and then went on to look for deeper reasons why the back window of the car may have been smashed by a golf club, and eventually a confession was offered for transgressions committed against the marriage. By the time you read this, there may well be more to the story than I know at the time of writing, but the general point is that the interpretation of events is essentially unfinished business that occurs in an existing social order that needs to find meaning and to continue to understand things that happen. Consider a recent event that has become the topic of conversation with you and your friends and determine the ways in which your interpretations change as a result of discussion with people you trust.

actions are treated as meaning something by others and so must be treated as meaningful behaviors by the self as well. For example, the depressed man may apologize to his spouse for being withdrawn and may need to make explicit the fact that his emotional withdrawal was not an intentional rejection of the partner, but merely a retraction of the availability of self.

MATERIAL RELATIONSHIPS

The same is true for different sorts of relationships: Meaningful distinctions are made in any given social order between the different types of relationships that occur there and how they may be symbolized materially or physically. Wedding rings, kisses, holding hands, having sex, getting presents, or sleepovers at someone's house are all material ways of indicating relationship, but they are not ways of doing so in all social orders and cultures.

The Social Construction of Events

So neither material objects nor relationships have any type of inherent meaning in them. They are *socially constructed,* that is, other people talk to you about them in terms that are created by the social order and that you will understand. This connects to the ways you come to understand one another's personality in the social context of meaning that I discussed in Chapter 3. You do it by separating off relevant behaviors, gestures, postures, or clothing choices and then classifying them as "extrovert," "lonely," or "team player" behaviors.

To put this another way, your physical material appearance (e.g., physical attractiveness [PA] or your physical behaviors such as nonverbal communication) comes to mean something in your social (and eventually personal) orders because people interpret your behavior, your physical shape, your PA, and your gestures and facial expressions as meaning something specific in your culture. Bodies, PA, or old age do not mean anything by themselves until a society/social order interprets what they mean. Likewise, the separating out of behaviors that are symbolic of relationships relies on social order. Relationships exist in a social order that creates meanings about the form, nature, and quality of relationship that it expects its members to have.

A social order has many symbolic ways of looking at relationships, and this is a story you need to look at before I go on to the deeper lessons of what this chapter tells us. Shape (i.e., physical embodiment of self) influences personality, as we learned in the preceding chapter. But how else does embodiment and performance—the physical behaviors of our bodies—play into the social world? What other sorts of physically material evidence can we see about the nature of relationships? You see wedding rings, team-supporter shirts, flags flying over embassies, and lovers walking hand in hand. All of these serve as examples of physical, but also deeply symbolic, statements of the relationship between one body and another or between one body and a larger organizational unit, such as a marriage, support group, or country.

Material Manifestations of Relationships

Sociologist Erving Goffman (1959) wrote about the *tie signs* that are used to demonstrate and perform relationships, and these can be merely physical and yet also carry symbolic overtones. For example, a wedding ring is a material but symbolic tie sign; a T-shirt that identifies you as a supporter of a particular sports team or as a student of a particular university community is a physical material tie sign; holding hands with a romantic partner is also a tie sign but a physical, performative, and behavioral one. These are signs that other people would be able to interpret if they are members of your culture (social order) and the signals that are used to indicate relationship.

Tie signs can be abstract and linguistic as well as material. An example is the nicknames that people have for one another in close romantic relationships (look at any Valentine's Day supplement

> Research shows that you will tend to sit closer to friends than you do with strangers (Rubin, 1973), and this is a symbolic indication of the relationship that you have with them.

in a newspaper). It is understood also that, for example, merely saying "We are going on vacation next week" signals a relationship between the persons described; "we" does the tie sign work. Tie signs, then, are particular ways of representing relationships in language or material ways that are symbols.

MIND, SELF, AND SOCIETY

Your brain is probably bleeding out of your ears as you begin to think about this, but the point is actually quite a simple one. It is society, or the social order in which you participate, that gives particular meaning to physical appearance or to the physical acts that count as "relating." The materiality of your body (e.g., the shape that is valued as attractive) is something that you learn through interaction with other people and the symbols used in your society to give particular meaning to those shapes and forms. You are not born thinking that a female hourglass figure is attractive in this society, but you learn through interaction with other people in your society, from the media, and the discourse that you have with other people that you should treat it as if it matters and is "better" than some other shape in this society. You also learn by the same means whether your own particular embodiment of physical appearance is attractive or not.

Such interaction with other people also teaches you how to do and perform relationships, what matters in relationships, what counts as a relationship, and how to do and perform them. That interaction also helps to shape your preferences (personal order) about physical appearance, whether or not it matters, and if so, how.

It is important also to point out that the meanings attached to objects and behaviors by a social order are multilayered. At a most basic level, members of a society share the same symbols and give the same meanings to those symbols. For example, when you use the words "shoe" or "friend" or "marriage" or "hookup," you are, on each occasion, referring to the same object that the other person has in mind. Members of a society subscribe to a social order that attributes meaning in ways that allow fellow members to interact with one another because they all use the same symbol system and they all attribute meaning to physical appearance and physical activity in the same socially approved ways.

However, important differences arise in the connotative meanings (overtones) associated with symbols. Different people with different personal orders will feel differently about or draw different associations from the same object; for example, a shoe means one thing to a wearer, has different connotations for a cobbler, and means something entirely different to a foot fetishist. It is these meanings that allow one person to see books and education as important tools for achievement of success and another person to see them as confinements and restrictions that enforce conformity of evaluation. It is the latter level of meaning that is particularly important in separating individuals and their personal orders from the social order that shapes behavior. It is this personal meaning that gets constructed through interaction and acts to shape knowledge of the world. Thus, the social order and the personal order are both likewise constructed from familiarity with symbols and their use with others—especially the language terms that fill out a linguistic symbol system. Our vocabulary exists as a social creation relative to a symbol and classification system used by other folks.

EXPERIENCING THE MINDS (AND JUDGMENTS) OF OTHERS

The same logic applies to *minds*. Minds and objects exist relative to each other, as we saw before. The important deduction is that your own perceptions of the world start to be most meaningful to you only when you can also see that those categories are understood by and useful to other people as well. Something is meaningful only when you can place it in a social order that is shared with other people.

Color and sound can exist only relative to a perceiver, but how do you know that other people see the same colors that you do; hear the same sounds;

or perceive the same item, like a chair or a friendship? You can get some idea because you observe people making appropriate responses to the chair (sitting in it, for example), so you know that they describe and perceive it using the same terms that you do (as a "chair"). Hence, from the appropriateness of their responses to "things," you get some glimmer of the fact that they understand the world in the same way you do. By seeing that other people treat objects or relationships in ways similar to you, you are able to compare their responses to the ways you would treat the object or relationship. This requires that you know that other people understand what a particular symbol means if it evokes the same response from them as from you. Therefore, you know it has some symbolic meaning and serves some symbolic function in conveying information. If a symbol evokes a response in you, then it probably evokes a similar response in other people, and therefore, you know it has some symbolic meaning in the social order.

DISCUSSION QUESTION

If a tree falls in the forest and nobody hears it, does it make a sound, according to Mead?

You can then make the intellectual leap to say that they must know the object or relationship in the same way you know it, because they treat it in the same way that you do. That makes a social and epistemic connection between others and self because your physical and material experiences are given a meaning by the social order and you come to understand that you share meanings with other people. You understand ideas, objects, concepts, or relationships in the same symbolic terms. By use of symbolic terms, you also permit talk and the ability to move out of the present through meaning and imagination: in short, through the development of a *mind*.

In the present chapter, therefore, we have moved from looking at how physical materiality influences how you come to know the world to exploring how far your knowledge of even the physical world hangs on the fact that you are a social being who talks to other people (and, by talking, therefore uses the same symbolic systems). Talking with other people helps you to see that you and they share common ways of understanding the same objects and categories for classifying the world. Your knowledge of the world about you gets shaped by the social fact that you (need to) communicate with other people and so learn to use their words to describe your experiences. From that basis, you go on to relate to other folks.

MOVING BEYOND THE PRESENT

Minds arise through this talk using shared symbols, including the symbols of language. However, symbols have another key advantage: They are *timeless* and can refer to things past (memory) or things future or counterfactual (imagination). Key to the process of the mind, then, is when in the experience of an organism, it breaks out of a present. For example, you go beyond the present experience and say, "Ah, this happened to me before" or "I'll try to have this experience again tomorrow" or "I'll never get into decent relationships, because I am so short and bald."

Mind requires that you don't just feel something, but that you can go beyond it and step into a future or a past or an imagination, into a language that can describe the experience without it actually being there right now. For example, you could tell a friend that you had an experience, and the act of telling about it takes you beyond the experience. Although it's over, it can be re-created in your imagination and relayed to your friend in talk through symbols.

One of the facts about human beings that you know for sure is that we all think about the future and the past, and don't just live in the present. You have plans and an agenda for tomorrow evening on your schedule. You may have travel plans, might have a date coming up, you can remember where you were yesterday, you have made hotel reservations and planned vacations. You can think about people who are not there. You can conjure up pictures of relatives or your romantic partners or teachers in other classes or people in some place where you are not present. Just reflect on how much of your relational life occurs when other people are not physically present. You can daydream, and the relationship grows; you can reflect on a past interaction and get angry with your partner's rudeness; you can plan your wedding alone; and you can imagine that someone loves you or what it would be like if he or she did.

All of this means that you are breaking out of the present; you can go to memory or imagination or anxiety or daydreams or hopes or fears or relational possibilities. You can plan the perfect date. You can describe your feelings and desires to someone else, because you are able to imagine that he or she will be able to understand you and at least grasp your point of view, even if he or she does not share it or evaluate it positively. In short, you are describing something knowing that the other person will understand what you are saying and where you are coming from. He or she will be able to temporarily adopt, even if not thoroughly accept, the representation of it.

TAKING THE ROLE OF THE OTHER

Mead's statement about taking the role of the other is a bit obscure, so I will present it and then reinterpret it to help you see what he is saying. "The effect of taking the role of anyone is to eliminate the peculiarity [subjectivity] of the environment of any one individual and to substitute for any concrete individual an abstraction—a generalized individual—the thinker" (Mead in Miller, 1980, p. 178). What this means is that as soon as you learn to understand that other people can see objects like you do and see them in the same sort of way (whether this be chairs, hot stoves, or hot relationships), then the items become something you can reflect about (as meaning something within a social order). You "get" that you are not alone, but that other people inhabit your same world of thought and meaning.

In Mead's (again obscure) terms, which I will again present and then reinterpret for you, taking the role of the other allows and instantiates generality and abstraction, undermines solipsism (the sense that you are alone in the world), and creates an abstraction. In less obscure terms, this means that you come to recognize that there are broad abstract categories such as "chairs," or "relationships," that you can think about (and thus talk about). You, like other people, can *imagine* those things and can talk about them when they are not actually there to be seen or touched, and you also recognize that other people have the same imaginative abilities. You realize that the world of abstractions may exist in terms of memories, imagination, hypothesis, plans, regrets, and alternative conceptualizations of events. You come to appreciate that the *meaning* of these terms is something you can use in interacting with other people in your social order precisely because they can make the same imaginative leaps that you can make. Although your experience starts out as a material and personal experience, it can be translated into imagination, thought, and symbols through mind and language—and therefore shared with other people. It can also be a basis for or a supplement of relationships.

This is also done when the organism becomes an object to itself, such as when the person achieves not only consciousness but also *self*-consciousness and is aware that it, too, could be an object for perception by other perceivers who might form an opinion about how he or she behaved. This self-consciousness is based on role-taking, or the ability to understand the role from which someone else could know what you mean and are talking about. It would also be role-taking if you decided that another person would not get it, so there would be no point in telling him or her. To take the other's role, you have to imagine what capacity someone else has to understand what you will say, based on your personality as he or she knows you.

The way you work out that someone sees objects and ideas the same way you do is because he or she *acts* the same way you do toward those objects and ideas. If people stop their cars on a red light just as you do, then you realize that they understand something similarly, the way you do. Mead's point is that other people's behavior toward the world indicates that they have a reaction similar to the one you have, so you know that they share your social order, or that their personal order overlaps with yours. You draw your inferences about the way people are thinking by observing the behavior that they carry out. When you understand that someone else has understood the same stimulus in the same way that you have, then this creates a social connection with that person, and that forms the basis for a relationship because you can understand that they know what you are talking about.

Perception is itself ultimately based on a kind of *reflective consciousness.* You have to recognize that you have seen this sort of object before and know what it means, and you categorize it using past reference. I once saw a terrific example of this in one of my local schools. The kids were just playing, like kids, until a bell rang and they instantly ran toward the same part of the playground and lined up and went into school. So these kids have developed a single meaning system that depended on them knowing what a bell meant they had to do next. They all responded immediately, and all responded the same way when the bell rang, although they weren't salivating like Pavlov's dogs. Having observed this, I conclude that there is a symbol system in their world, and that the bell symbolizes the end of recess. The lining up works only because of the symbol system that intervenes in their mind between the bell and the action. On the other hand, the observer can recognize the existence of a symbol system from their actions and might be able to work out what it is. By observing their behavior, you can deduce that there is a symbol system in their world.

So this is an important step forward. Not only can minds make distinctions about what they observe in the universe, but they can recognize that other minds do the same, because ultimately those other minds tell them how to do so using a shared system of language. Communication and relationships are natural derivatives of this observation. You recognize that people are living in the same symbolic universe of meaning and that you can talk to them about it.

THE GENERALIZED OTHER

Mead also introduced the notion of the *generalized other*—a sort of "social eye in the sky" that you assume might see and have opinions about what you do and that you take into account in preparing and enacting your behavior. If you go downtown and you decide to do something illegal, your judgment about what might happen to you doesn't hang on knowing which specific people will be around that time, because it doesn't matter. There will be "generalized others" who generally represent this society and who might respond to you doing something illegal, whoever they are. You might be restrained by anyone who is there. You just have to know that generalized members of the society might step in and prevent you doing something illegal or else you hope that they will do nothing. So your behavior is sometimes guided not by your knowledge of specifics but by your expectations about what people in general might think.

The generalized other functions as a sort of conscience or as an awareness of the likely reactions that other people might have to your behavior. Good examples of this are the frequent thought "What will the neighbors think?" or "I couldn't have done that! My professor could have walked in at any moment," or "I know everyone will think I am crazy, but it felt right to me at the time."

The generalized other is really an organization of perspectives, an awareness of how the behavior of individual role performers will connect with your own, especially in judging it. Your behavior is moderated and controlled by your expectations that others could see and evaluate it and that life is not simply about the behavior that you produce freely and independently in a social vacuum or a darkened closet. All your behavior (including anything that you might happen to do in a darkened closet) is something you think of as possibly visible to others ("Oh dear, what I am doing here in this cupboard is really evil and if anyone ever found out . . .").

Even these imaginary social interactions are epistemic because they affect what you know and how you feel. In the closet, for example, you might feel guilty and that you are a bad person even if no one, in fact, finds out. It is merely enough that you know that if other people did find out, then they would be critical. This is particularly relevant to relational behavior and fears about "being seen as a slut" or "looking like a relational jerk," which are often the sorts of impact that a generalized other has on someone's relational behavior (Senchea, 1998).

DISCUSSION QUESTION

The generalized other is a complicated abstract idea, but can you think of concrete examples that make the point? Think of occasions when you have been concerned about what other people may think or when you have been embarrassed. Why did these matter, and why were you embarrassed?

This process of comparison of self with others is a key part of your ability to evaluate and adjust behaviors to comply with social order, and it is an important point that your knowledge of and responses to the social order are derived as much from your awareness of the social order in its generalized, distant form of relationships (neighbors, professors, crowds, public opinion) as well as from your intimate ones. All the same, you are probably more influenced by the likely reactions of your intimates.

All this analysis matters all the more for changing your views about relationships once you return to the idea that relationships are open-ended, unfinished business. Far from being permanent and fixed, this view stresses very strongly that knowledge is never static. Continual perception of and engagement with the material and social world frames your frequent updating and interaction with life. Hence, the open-endedness of relationships is very real, based on experience of not only the relationships and the world, but also your comprehension and your expectations of the reaction and evaluations of other folks. Accordingly, a personal order is never static, either, but is continually tested and modified through experience, access to new information, reinterpretation of the past, and discourse with other people.

SELF OR SELVES?

As far as Mead is concerned, all experience is continuous and open-ended. That is, it is not made up of little events that happen on the spot, but goes on all the time and is continually modified within interpretive and symbolic frames. You also have a *sense* of self that is continuous and open-ended, to use the term I employed earlier. That is, you imagine a self that is continuously having experiences: The person is feeling the hardness of the seat and the grip of the pencil, seeing the room, thinking about the end of the lesson, or imagining a weekend trip. Your self is continuously experiencing a stream of events and is open-ended in its development, but all the while you feel a sense of constancy, of consistency, based on the epistemic thoughts that you have in your personal order.

An interesting implication of this continuous experience is that you have different selves in relation to different people, or, to put it differently, different aspects of your range of performance are drawn out by different people at different times in different circumstances. Many people are aware that they act differently with parents than with roommates, for example, and you may note the pleasure that you get from being with someone who makes you feel like your true self as compared with the way that other people make you feel. This is the sort of difference in experience of self that Mead is talking about that connects different symbolic experiences to relationships. Different symbolic experiences with different people bring out different selves from your repertoire of selves.

Most people have had the experience of talking to a friend who makes you feel good, and then you talk to someone else who makes you feel bad. Some of us have felt awkward, shy, or intimidated in the presence of a particular person and we start acting ineptly. We may have been lucky enough to find a partner

---

Questions to Ask Your Friends

Ask your friends if they have ever felt as if they act differently when in the company of one another as a group than they do talking with any one person in the group separately. Do they see themselves as having one self or many selves? How do they explain the variety of experiences that they may report in different interactions with different persons? How would *you* explain it?

who relaxes us so much that we feel like "the *real me*" in his or her company. Has any of this happened to you, and have you ever wondered what it might mean?

You are the same person, in the physical sense, and so it must be the other person who makes you feel different—that is, to know and experience the world in a different way. How does that happen? Mead suggests that the other person is the source of the change. Parents can make you feel like you are 6 years old again. Your partner lets out the secret you. The principal calls forth your inner rabbit. To repeat, your experiences are continuous, but they can change as a result of the people with whom you interact. The people who are in material interactions with you can change the parts of your experience that are most central to you or that are occupying center stage at a particular moment.

Experiencing a Material Self

Apart from carrying around your brain, your body serves a purpose that is also *social* in nature. Your social order tells you what bodies mean, and so others treat bodily and physical symbols the same way that you do. Through symbols—or more accurately, through your understanding of what symbols mean—you are able to "get" what someone else is up to when he or she is lean and hungry, wears a wedding ring, uses a tie sign, or waves a patriotic flag. You are able to understand his or her motions as meaningful *actions* and as actions that connect to the social order. That shared system of meaning is one that you understand because you belong to the group of people who understand it in the same way as the person who does the action. The body and its physical appearance are both symbolically meaningful in the social order.

So what are you to make of this? You may not have previously thought about some of the above factors as influences on your relational experience, especially not as material ones. Even if you have, then you need to put the thought in the context of the processes I am talking about here concerning symbols, the social order, and the epistemic. There's a close connection between the physical, the social order, the symbolic, and the way in which you experience life as a person who has relationships.

GETTING PHYSICAL

So now let's get physical. Start with the way that physical experience influences your perceptions of the world. Examined in the way proposed in this book, perception of the material world involves you in taking into account some present object (say, your physical shape) by way of the senses and connecting it to what you suppose people will think about it. In other words, if you think about or reflect on the way other people will respond to your physical materiality (for example, your body or your PA or your age), then this involves you in the *attitude of reflection* that I first mentioned in Chapter 2. In Mead's terms, it involves you reflecting on the likely responses of a generalized other.

This involves you thinking about how other people will think about you, your body, or your attractiveness level—how you appear to them in their mirror as it were. This reflective consciousness takes into account some absent possible object (for example, the generalized other people whom you imagine might think about you) or an imagined or remembered situation. All of this reflection requires a recognition of symbols. These acts of reflection are an important way to recognize that your body might serve a symbolic function for other people and might therefore have meaning over and above its simple, physical appearance, for example. You reflect on how you may look to others (that is what mirrors are for, after all).

In short, the way you look symbolizes something to observers, and you know that the most obvious (but by no means simplest) example is whether you look like a man or a woman. "Man" and "woman" evoke different symbolic responses in other people. Other examples from the previous chapter would be whether you look fat (jolly?) or lean and hungry (dangerous?). However, the importance of the way in which gender represents an embodied experience or a performative activity—literally your body carries your sex with you—is a key issue (Butler, 1990, 2004). Before we get to that point, it is necessary to think about the way in which other material experiences more generally are connected to perception.

YOU ARE AN EMBODIED SELF

Your self is an *embodied self*—a physical experience inside the body, inside something that responds to pain, inside something that has a shape, inside something that will spasm if you put electricity through it, inside something that needs to be fed. Your self is inside a body that may feel sick with influenza, and your sense of self is influenced by your physical state or may be affected permanently by the materiality and social expectations that go with your gender (Butler, 2004; also see Chapter 5). There is a connection between the embodied bits of your experience and the mind that goes along with them, or, putting that into my earlier terms, the physical experience goes along with the epistemic. In a pithy phrase, the eye sees, the brain perceives. That is, the eye receives the light (motion), but the brain organizes what it means (action). The brain adds meaning to the data that the eye merely collects.

As an embodied material organism, your physical experiences are continuous. All over your body, little impulses are continually telling your brain how hot, wet, or uncomfortable you feel and whether you are hungry, afraid, or tired. These signals are even telling the brain whether you are walking, what you are seeing, how broadly you may be smiling, and so on. It is your choice, then, how to cut this continuous ticker tape of experience into specific sections that can be labeled as being notable or remarkable or in need of some sort of explanation.

On the other hand, your body is also an object from the point of view of other people, and they will treat your body as well as your personality in various ways that affect your self-concept. Of course, other people's way of treating you depends on some of the facts that are true about your body, conveying as it does so much information about you that your social order recognizes as meaningful. PA, height, sex, and race, for example, all lead to (ways of experiencing) reactions from other people and hence affect your (epistemic) way of knowing the world in terms of what to expect from it.

PHYSICALITY AND KNOWLEDGE

The important implications of the physical entity that you are, and the influences of your body on your relational capacities and on your thinking, extends to effects on knowledge. Remember that in Chapter 2, I said I would talk about "embodiment"? Well, this is what I meant. This embodiment serves to give physical form to symbolic action (for example, a physical handshake symbolizing greeting or friendship). Also, the physical has symbolic force too: Think of what it means in your social order to be old or the way in which a symbolic claim to reserve a chair can be made by the physical act of putting your coat over the back of it.

Experience of relationships is affected by such features as physical build, but it also affects the way you know the world and the world knows you (what and how you know about the world) and how that changes as your body ages or fails, for example. People spend time looking in the mirror to see if their physical state is as close as possible to the way that they want it to look. People connect their embodied self to some experience of the world, to some effect that they expect their body to have on their life in that world, and to other people's responses to them. You might be able to think of many examples of the way your physical nature influences your experiences of life. Your sex is the obvious one; men and women experience the world somewhat differently, as you already knew.

YOUR BODY IS A SYMBOL TO OTHER PEOPLE

You are born into the world as a physical being with physiology that affects how you feel, and you grow up having a body that produces sensations and allows you to speak, laugh, and move around. The body also "speaks" your sex, your nationality, and perhaps even your sexual orientation. But you may have limits (only some people are good athletes, tall enough to reach high shelves, and strong enough to open sticking bottle tops). You are either male or female, might be good-looking or average, thin or fat, right-handed or left-handed, and you may have a physical disability or a very large nose or strikingly attractive eyes or a large wart in the middle of your forehead.

Physical Bodies and Relationships

You have a body that facilitates or restricts your physical movement and your sense of being in the world. Your body also is something perceived as a social, relational, and even sexual object with value or interest to other people and so has a bearing on your sense of worth. Therefore, if choice is the basis for sexual pairings, then you can bet that PA will have a strong role. Hence, those who are physically attractive might experience relationships differently from those who are not, whose relational choices are thereby restricted.

All of the above physical characteristics therefore do not just happen to be descriptors of people's bodies but could have an important effect on the person's impact in social situations and may perhaps enhance or constrain abilities to relate to other people. I am going to explore the ways in which physical factors influence your *thinking*, especially your thinking about relationships. For example, when I was younger, I worried about being short because our social order places such emphasis on height as a determinant of male attractiveness and authority. After about 20 years, I gave up worrying about it. Now, I worry about being bald and looking old.

If you have ever wanted to change your physical shape in any kind of way, then this is something to do with the fact that you feel you would be treated differently or might have different experiences or different concepts of self if your physical embodiment changed. You might feel that you would look different to others and be treated differently by them as a result. In short, you feel that they will know you differently if you appear to them in a different physical form. You will go on to see that you, too, understand the world in a different way if you have a different physical state, the most immediate examples being when you are drunk or sedated or suffering a disabling illness, but it all goes deeper than that.

Any emotional life occurs in the context of many different sorts of physical materiality, only one of which concerns various physical circumstances of your life such as your body (PA and your sex and whether or not you are drunk or sexually aroused). Your experience of the world is affected by your physical possessions, your living accommodation, the physical structure of your social world, and the material gifts that you give to others. These, too, are material aspects of relationships (discussed at length in Chapter 5, on sexual behavior, and Chapter 6, on physical environment). There are physical and physiological changes that take place during sexual arousal (Floyd, 2004) and that connect physical results to psychological desires. You also indicate love and respect by giving physical gifts on birthdays or other occasions (see Chapter 6).

The Physical and Performative Self

Judith Butler (1990) has pointed out the importance of the notion of *performativity* in our physical world. The notion of performativity is based on linguistic philosophy that points out that some forms of talk perform certain actions or bring about certain results, simply by their being stated. "I now pronounce you husband and wife" makes it so when spoken by the appropriate official. "This meeting is now adjourned" ends the meeting when spoken by the chair. These utterances are therefore performative in that they bring about a state that they declare to be the case.

In a somewhat strangulated expression on this concept in relation to gender, Butler (1990, 2004) essentially argues that people become their gender by doing it at a particular time. More than this, performance varies according to circumstances, making gender less an essence of a person than a dramatic effect (rather than a cause) of our performances of selves as "men" or "women" or "feminine" or "masculine."

In effect, this separates the group previously seen as "men" into lots of separate performances of the social order view of what manhood entails and likewise for females. There is more to be said about this position, for it is a provocative view that is somewhat consistent with the one offered in this chapter and to which we will return in more detail in Chapters 5 and 8. Essentially, the point is that language reinforces gender that is performed in a social order that sanctions behavior by means beyond language. The idea that identity is free-floating and not connected to the essence of the individual and must instead use a performance is one of the essential ideas that is represented in the growth of queer theory in which these identities are a dramatic consequence of our performances in social life. Clearly, this is consistent with some of what I have said so far and helps us to see the ways in which categorization of individuals is "a way of seeing that is also a way of not seeing."

It must therefore be borne in mind that although these categorizations are given meaning in talk and discourse, the *symbolic* meaning of the body is far more important than its physical state in most circumstances that are of interest to relationship researchers. Clearly, for a physician, the physical materiality of the body trumps its symbolism, but for us, our body is a social object that is categorized and carries symbolic force in social worlds that we inhabit.

The Physical Embodiment of Relationships

The physical embodiment of relationships is also conveyed by such symbols as wedding rings or by holding hands, too. These are arbitrary symbols of relationships accepted by your social order. Why should the particular physical symbol of a ring on a third finger mean "I'm married," for example? Why not a blue tattoo on the nose, or a head shaved across the middle from one side to the other? Several centuries ago, a haircut could indicate whether a man was a monk if he had a tonsure, that is, if the middle of his head was shaved but the rest was not. In order to understand how physical materiality connects to the symbolic world in this kind of way, you need to revisit your old favorite: epistemics.

Physical materials have symbolic force, and the shared symbolism about physical objects is part of the social order. The recognition of similar meanings attached to physical objects is an important key to the recognition of similar personal orders. It is based on a key observation of Kenneth Burke (1961). He noted that there is an obvious difference in the human approach to people and their approach to things. People are entities capable of symbolic action; to various degrees, they can be addressed, reasoned with, petitioned, persuaded (Burke, 1961, p. 40).

PHYSICAL APPEARANCE AND RELATIONSHIPS

Within such broad groupings as race and sex are many physical variations that could affect relationships and their associated ways of knowing and being (their epistemics). Physical stature in terms of height and shape attract many stereotypes that nevertheless affect the ranges of people with whom you are expected or even allowed to associate. For example, men are expected to be taller than their female dates, and so short men are not expected to date tall women. Older women are not expected to marry younger men. If an attractive young woman marries an old man, then everyone assumes he must be rich. Crude stereotypes exist about "butch" women and "effeminate" men. Also, homosexual relationships operate within a set of epistemics about what physical features are attractive to members of the same sex (Huston & Schwartz, 1995).

Physical Attractiveness

Studies of the impact of materiality on interaction in social life have shown some interesting effects of PA on the ways in which such men and women interact with the world. Harry Reis and his colleagues (Reis, Nezlek, & Wheeler, 1980) showed that the level of PA was *not* predictive of the rate of social participation for women, that is, women were as likely to lead active social lives, whether they were physically attractive or not. Actually, PA level, as independently rated by a panel of judges, affected men's levels of participation (positively) more than for females, meaning that physically attractive men engaged in more social encounters than the physically less attractive ones. For women, the number of reported daily encounters was unaffected by the women's PA level.

Instead of looking at the numbers of interactions that people have, what about the ways in which physically attractive people actually interact?

> ### Listen in on Your Own Life
>
> Note the number of times that your own or other people's physical appearance is the subject matter of talk and the ways in which that is related to the symbolism of such items. How is nonverbal communication interpreted? How are clothes, physique, and material objects rendered "accountable"—that is, how are such items evaluated in relation to the social order?

In a study to understand if attractive people disclose more, Bill Stiles and his colleagues (Stiles, Walz, Schroeder, Williams, & Ickes, 1996) covertly taped 6-minute conversations between strangers. The participants were rated by 11 researchers on a scale of 1 to 10 (1 = *extremely unattractive*, 10 = *extremely attractive*), and then associations were analyzed to see if there was a correlation between being attractive and the amount of intimate self-disclosure that occurred. Indeed there was: People who are physically attractive are much more likely to offer a high level of self-disclosure, possibly because they confidently assume interest from the other person.

Whereas you might see this as showing some simple and direct effects of PA, what is actually having the effect is not PA but a way of knowing—the way that physically attractive young people have experienced treatment from others, the sorts of social order norms they hear about the ways they may relate, and the sorts of experiences that they get as "trophy partners." Interesting that there are such norms, or ways of knowing and structuring the world!

There are clear and strong social markers about who is attractive and who is not. However, my point is not that such stereotypes exist (who knew?) but that they are governors of people's ways of knowing. Physical materiality (embodiment) broadly influences people's experience of the relational world. Hence, you can assume that PA specifically will affect everyday relational experiences. PA is a material influence on relationships, and several studies have shown that people tend to like PA people more—unless they are really extraordinarily attractive (in which case they are envied) (Norwood, 2006) or unless they appear to be using their attractiveness for personal gain (such as con artists often do), in which case they are treated punitively, especially by juries (Aronson & Linder, 1965).

Physically attractive people, especially physically attractive women (Norwood, 2006), risk the animosity of others to such an extent that people circulate such Internet links as "Women you'd love to see fat," which portrays modified photographs of famous film stars. In the United Kingdom, retailers Marks and Spencer ran an ad campaign celebrating women who are not physically attractive (the infamous "I'm normal" campaign), based on the desire of people not to have to live up to model perfection. In the United States, the parallel is the "Dove Women" campaign.

You are probably aware of the role of clothing and physical appearance on the success of relationships and have often heard about the importance of appearance as an effect on first impressions. "Dress for success" we are told, and a host of ads reminds you to primp your hair, pluck your eyebrows, join Hair Club for Men, and use the right deodorant if you want to have any hopes of romance or business success or even happy family life. You dress up for interviews and first dates, and you also carry around in your head some sense of your own PA. Of course, you register the PA of other people whenever you meet them and may even comment on how well someone looks or how different or attractive they appear after a haircut or a tanning session.

Stereotypes About Relationships

You also know that the relationships of young people who can move about fast and freely are different from those of really old people who cannot sustain rapid mobility or, in some cases, any mobility at all (Lyons, Langille, & Duck, 2006). You also know that men and women are viewed differently in key ways in most societies. All of these material elements of relationships are easily overlooked, but they can significantly affect not only your sense of well-being but also your ability to communicate with other people and to have relationships with them.

Consider one piece of evidence from communication researcher Paul Mongeau and his colleagues (Mongeau, Hale, Johnson, & Hillis, 1995). Men who ask women out on dates are seen as acting in an expected way ("normatively"), and their behavior raises no particular eyebrows. It's what men do in this social order—especially tall, dark, handsome, muscular, he-men "players"—(although it is stressful and occasionally downright anxiety-provoking to get up the courage to ask out someone whom you really, *really* like). On the other hand, women who ask men out on a date are seen as acting against that trend ("counter-normatively"), and their behavior is evaluated as forward or demanding or even as a sexual invitation when it really isn't and is just a request for company. According to studies of gay relationships, men who ask other men out on dates in clubs are seen as sexual adventurers, whereas those who make the offer elsewhere are seen more positively (Huston & Schwartz, 1995).

You can probably think of life experiences you've had that relate to this, but you'll find that it does seem that sex differences in material biology are related to different sorts of social and personal expectations about relating. These have unwittingly affected the ways in which you know the world (your epistemic personal order), are reacted to by the world, and go on to perceive it in the future—including in relationships.

Similar issues arise with respect to other aspects of materiality, such as race. Stereotypically, African American men prefer "thick women," those who have more ample figures and larger girth than is the prototypical preference in White America, and in Brazil, "bunda" is highly regarded (Google it!). In some cultures, there is a pronounced preference for large body size, and in some cases, such as a food-poor country, high weight is a sign of status (because if you are fat, it indicates that you are so wealthy that you can afford to overeat). A Chinese colleague of mine once thought he was complimenting me when I returned from a long trip and he remarked with admiration, "Ah, Steve, you have put on a lot of weight." Had I not understood something of his cultural epistemic, I would have punched him. In particular cultures, then, different physical features may be regarded as indicators of PA, some valuing the slim figure and some the larger. Also, if you look at pictures of "beauty" across different ages and different cultures, it is soon self-evident that this is the case (compare pictures of film stars from the 1920s, 1940s, 1960s, 1980s, and today who were regarded as the essence of femininity or masculinity).

Physical Experiences That Influence Relationships

Here, we will look more broadly at the ways in which physical restraints or facilities in your life affect the ways in which you relate to others, and hence affect the aspects of self that are drawn out, and also the way in which you experience the situation and the relationship.

If your physical shape and bodily activity affect not only the ways in which you experience the world but also the ways in which people react to you, as well as the sorts of relationships that you can attain, then what happens if you experience significant physical changes whether gradual (as in aging) or sudden and unexpected, as occurs in spinal injury (Grewe, 2006) or car crashes (Secklin, 2001)? How is the ability to conduct relationships affected by chronological aging, and its physical effects, for good or ill? What about acquired deformity, chronic illness, or disability (Acitelli & Badr, 2005; Lyons et al., 2006)? How do these material restraints affect a person's styles of communication, sense of self, and ability to be a member of a community or a relationship? The deeper and more important questions are: How (and why) do these material differences affect your senses of self; relationship; your satisfaction with life; and your communication patterns, personal order, and epistemics relating to personal relationships?

PHYSICAL AGE AND CHANGES IN SOCIAL BEHAVIOR

Let's start with age and development. Aging turns you from mewling, puking infants to grown adults, and during that process, much alters in your social experience. You grow from childhood to adulthood by acquisition of sexual characteristics that affect the ways in which other people respond to you and the ways in which you expect to respond to other people. As time rolls along, so you turn from fit young adults to aging and aged crones with restricted mobility and limited physical capacity. These changes in your physical and material experience change and influence the ways in which you experience yourself, other people, and life in general—and, tragically, the way in which they experience *you*. Of course, at different ages, the effects are different. Adolescence brings new physical experiences, whereas old age often takes away familiar and accustomed ones. The relationships you have at a younger age are not the same as those you have at an older age. For one thing, when people are sexually mature, this changes their way of thinking about life, and the relationships that they have—and the types that they seek—change in character.

Patterns of relationships are not constant across the life cycle and are responsive to physical material change, some of which is due to chemical changes in the capacities of the brain and consequent changes in interpretation and use of context. In particular, in childhood, the brain grows, and there are many consequent changes in mental (cognitive) functioning that affect relationships and the capacity to understand other people, particularly concerning the understanding of others' motives and personality.

DISCUSSION QUESTION

Giving examples from people you actually know, what differences have you observed in people who are well as compared to those who are sick or have aged? How do your grandparents seem now as compared to when you were 10 years younger?

Children's relationships are also different in the course of development rather dramatically as a result of the way that they think and how they can understand other people as social objects. Children's reasons for having friendships are based on material considerations, such as the fact that another child has a nice climbing frame or good swing set. Later, they attend to personality, such as loyalty, trust, or insight. Across the different stages of childhood, friendship changes as the child matures (Bigelow, Tesson, & Lewko, 1996). At first, friendship is localized and inconstant, with children focusing on the attractiveness of other children who have large resources (lots of toys, a big house). At later stages of childhood, the emphasis falls on cooperation, companionship, and loyalty, and eventually, by the time people move through early adolescence, their choices of friendships are based on increasingly sophisticated analysis of the attractiveness of the *personality* of the other person (Selman, 1980).

To rephrase this point, the developing child's capacities to form friendship and romance are somewhat affected by the physical development of the person's brain, consequent cognitive maturity, and different needs—changes in their epistemic. The latter are essentially physical material and embodied influences on the ways the person can understand the world. Likewise, they affect the way a person encounters various relational forces, and so *how they know* affects *how they relate*. Later, adolescence arrives, although it is not all about cognitive change but is also quite a bit concerned with physical alteration: The change in materiality is more directly influential in experiences of relationship epistemics.

ATTRACTIVENESS IN ADOLESCENCE

In adolescence, people not only change in observable physical ways but are also subject to rampant hormones that redirect their attention from the childhood elements of life to S*E*X (see Chapter 5). Their microbiology connects with their physical re-formation to make them aware of, and look for, different sorts of relational connection to other people. Alas, at the same time, they learn more directly about social orders concerning PA. They learn more about the real effects of prejudices and biases of the social order about physical appearance. They learn how the material circumstances of one's self can affect one's social worth or appeal to others, especially because adolescents are increasingly aware of their physical embodiment. Consider the (slightly modified and rearranged) song by Janis Ian: *I learned the truth at seventeen: that love was meant for beauty queens and high school girls with clear skinned smiles who married young and then retired . . . and those of us with ravaged faces, lacking in the social graces . . . we cheat ourselves at solitaire, desperately remained at home, inventing lovers on the phone. . . . To those of us who knew the pain of valentines that never came and those whose names were never called when choosing sides for basketball . . . dreams were all they gave for free to ugly duckling girls like me.*[1]

What Janis Ian is pointing out is that not everybody gets treated the same way. When you get to be an adolescent, you learn that certain kinds of experiences and expectations are acceptable for some people but not for others, and that the attractive ones get the romance. Physical characteristics (embodiment) again make a difference to how you get to experience relationships. Adolescents start to learn something about their social value to other people on the basis of physical appearance. That material circumstance therefore causes different kinds of self reflection and assessments of whether you are an appropriate person for relationships with other people.

PHYSICAL HEALTH AND RELATIONSHIPS

We can extend the previous focus on physical embodiment in terms of PA and how this affects your daily experience in two ways. First, in this chapter, I will look at physical changes that occur over the life cycle and affect relational epistemics, and in the next chapter, I will look at sex. In Chapter 6, I will look more broadly at material circumstances outside the body (e.g., in places, environments, situations) that affect relational epistemics, experiences, and performances. Material influences affect relationships in terms of the expectations of others and how you learn what they believe about you, based on material factors and how you understand them in return. I will also look here at the physical effects of chronic disease on relational expectations and knowledge about relating.

At the end of life, the physical circumstances of your health will affect what sorts of relationships you have, how many people you can sustain in your network of friends and acquaintances, and whether you are physically capable of going out to meet them and sustain conversation with them. For example, the development of deafness constrains many friendships and restricts contacts by phone and other means, which is why some older people actually like e-mail (what a TFG among the younger folks!). However, many older people, especially men, have to learn to type in order to use e-mail. In their day, men did not do typing; women did, and by no means all women. Old age can restrict physical capacity in these ways and so also restricts the ability to conduct types of friendship.

In addition, at the end of life, one of the hardest events is the death of friends and the sense of isolation and dangling on the end of a string of disappeared shared knowledge and memories. The loss of a close friend is the loss of history and shared experience. Such loss brings changes in access to knowledge and to *shared knowledge* that affect the way a person sees self. In short, it changes older people's epistemic. Part of being an older person is this epistemic shift about self. There are fewer and fewer people to share or validate your experiences and to do the emotional integration that goes with those experiences (such as knowing what it was like living through the Great Depression or fighting in World War II).

There are a couple of other effects of lifetime physical aging on perception of people and on the broader concept of the appropriateness of relationships that are worth noting. First, when you are as young as 4, you can have sleepovers with both sexes, but when adolescence brings sexual change, so segregation of the sexes occurs. Even patterns of relationships are not the same across age. For example, 4-year-olds change friends often, whereas long-term loyalty is expected in adults. As another example, parenthood influences your selection of friends because it is well-known that parents tend to form friendships with the parents of their children's friends (Bigelow et al., 1996).

Second, note that age affects social judgments of appropriateness of friendship and romances between people of certain ages, with some seen as OK and others not. Partners within about 15 years of each other are OK, but what about larger age gaps, and why does a social order care whether the female is older than the male? Part of it is probably to do with the belief that marriage is about the production of children and so the social order looks with suspicion at a partnership where the woman is beyond the age of fertility. Such relationships elicit mild or severe sanctions, although these differ somewhat as a result of the direction of the difference (old rich man and young wife strange but OK, extremely old [112-year-old] Somali man and 17-year old bride [front-page news as of November 2009], old rich man and a child [pedophilia] definitely not allowed), and a 75-year-old woman marrying a 20-year-old man would soon find out that relationships are not all about free personal choices. The media, reflecting their social order, take an interest in relationships, too, especially when those relationships diverge from the age patterns typical in the social order.

IN SICKNESS AND IN HEALTH

Some other physical material circumstances affect relationships and how you see yourself: chronic illness. How does chronic disability affect relationships, and how does it affect various kinds of knowledge that people have about their rights and relationships? Something noted by people who become chronically ill is the fact that their social and relational lives become restricted and they cannot be as socially energetic or relationally giving as they used to be (Lyons et al., 2006). To reconnect to Weiss in Chapter 1, their ability to help and support others is infringed, and so they feel bad because they are unable to provide one of the necessary provisions of relationships (namely, physical support). They then feel dependent in unwelcome ways.

Various kinds of chronic psychological illness likewise materially affect people's behavior in certain kinds of ways, such as chronic depression. This disease is thought to have a physical/chemical basis in reduced production of serotonin, but its social manifestation is a view of self as worthless or powerless and so less valuable to, or respected by, others with whom one could relate. Depression tends to create a physical manifestation in terms of slouched posture, reduced physical liveliness, lower eye contact, and tendency to slump when walking (Guerrero & Floyd, 2006; Segrin, 1993). Thus, depressives show their way of knowing the world in the physical ways that they behave. However, their social behavior is altered, too, and they tend to withdraw from, and feel discomfort or uneasiness in, social relations, even with spouses and children—and depressives can drive their families crazy (Duck, 2007).

Relational experience is likewise reduced in many cases of serious chronic illness or disability (Lyons et al., 2006; Lyons, Sullivan, & Ritvo, 1996). Obviously, if your legs are immobilized, then you become reliant on wheelchairs in order to get around, and you cannot get into social experiences as easily as before. You are more reliant on other people to get you around to any social events.

Another thing that people with wheelchairs point out is that you're always *physically* lower than other people and so people *literally* look down on the disabled, although there are now new wheelchairs that put users at eye level with other people (Grewe, 2006). Mobility is also affected, and material circumstances therefore affect what you can do in this particular respect as well. It even affects where you can go and sit in a cinema. This depends on where the management has made provision for the disabled to be placed, whether or not this happens to be your preferred location for viewing a movie, and it may isolate you from the rest of your family, who is watching the movie from somewhere else in the theater. People do tend to sit with their friends and relatives when they go, even though they normally do not converse with them after the movie starts.

Chronic illness spills over into people's social lives and has negative effects on their ability to take part in social activities. It is not merely a physical restriction. Can you think of examples from your personal experience or elsewhere? If you have no personal examples, then consider the way in which a person in a wheelchair would be restricted from involvement in any kind of dancing.

Nondisabled people report feeling dissatisfied when they are not able to sit next to their friends because there are not the right number of seats available in a particular row, and likewise, the relocation of disabled people to particular parts of a theater can feel awkward and dissociating.

Obviously, also, illness and disability increase dependence on other people and reduce opportunities for spontaneity. Many diseases ultimately call upon people to plan much more consciously, because they have to take medical equipment with them, such as respirators, injection devices, various supplies of medication, or machines that mean they have to plan ahead and cannot simply be spontaneous. It is no longer possible to be so often or openly or freely available if a friend just calls up and says, "Hey, do you want to go downtown and do something together?"

Social Consequences of Illness

Sick people often are able to remain active only for shorter periods and also may need longer to recuperate afterward. This inevitable certainty can make them fear being party poopers because they become exhausted before everyone else, not to mention that they are often treated as victims and are asked patronizing questions (Secklin, 2001). So the nature of their relationships is also changed as a result of the changes in physical circumstances.

Sexual dysfunction (or at least lack of function at the customary level) also can attend these illnesses and affect people with certain kinds of losses (for example, loss of limbs, appearance, or vigor). Often, those with depression, too, see themselves as sexually unattractive. So they go through a self-concept change and don't see themselves as having the same characteristics they used to have as sexual beings (Lyons et al., 2006). This, of course, changes their relationships and their sense of self. Epistemics kick in here, too.

Basically, these illnesses and changes in physical or physical/psychological circumstances mean that people become less available for others and so less able to take part in the spontaneous activities that people do when they have friendships or close intimate relationships (i.e., these material changes in embodiment affect performance of relationships). So chronically ill or disabled people see themselves as less desirable, and this is a consequence of both the nature of their illness and the psychological results of adapting to the social experiences consequent on it, such as loss of independence and helplessness (Lyons et al., 1996).

Sick people may also feel a sense of guilt because they can't give back in a relationship, and they constantly have to ask others to do things for them but can't supply others' needs in return (again, revisit the Weiss provisions covered in Chapter 1). So they don't see themselves as the kind of persons who can provide the relationship experiences that other people are expecting. In particular, they are physically unable to provide physical support because of their illness. Instead, they keep needing it from other people, and patients can become obsessed with giving thank-you gifts for very small tasks in order to release them from the guilt of their dependence (Secklin, 2001). Adults who have reached old age noticeably increase their number of references to this increasing imbalance in the relationship checking account.

They often express the desire to disengage from social activities for fear of being a burden on their more able-bodied relations and friends. Evidently, these days, in this culture, the value placed on elders' wisdom has lost its significance.

Social Results of Physical Illness

Some illnesses are invisible, and you might think that the person is just being difficult or unsociable, because you can't see any reason for the person not being as lively and enjoyable as he or she used to be. You may even treat the person as if he or she is making it up, whether something like depression or lupus (Routsong, 2007). It is hard to understand what problems a person has to deal with in making the relationship work at all when people have a disability (or are an embarrassed adolescent or a 70-year-old).

The physical form in which you embrace life is one that ultimately affects and contributes to your understanding of the world and the ways in which you may relate to other people in it. Look for examples; they are everywhere. PA is epistemic, not just the characteristic of a person in a purely physical sense, but also in a *symbolic* sense.

Why does that matter, apart from the fact that it causes people personal pain? For one thing, reduced opportunities for relationships also change and reduce opportunities for knowledge. For another, they are symbolic in the social order. Being old means something symbolic in a culture. Some cultures equate age with useless redundancy, and some equate it with dignity and respect, where elders are more knowledgeable and wiser folks whose views carry greater importance because they have learned so much through experience.

Conclusion

The physical material body through which you experience the world actually shapes and forms the experiences of the world, not only in and of itself, but because you can assume an attitude of reflection that tells you how other people will respond to you and to your physical materiality. Hence, the body becomes a matter affecting what you know as well as how you know it. Although the chapter started from the relatively complex idea about the way in which minds arise from the interaction and from physical experience, from this we have been able to work out some direct and much simpler connections to the conduct of relationships. Observation of the effects of PA on relationships and your knowledge of them, then, has ended the chapter by claiming that all physical features of your world affect your knowledge of relationships and everything else.

PEDAGOGICAL ISSUES

EXERCISES

Spend 15 minutes in a well-known local store and find a magazine that has an ugly person on its cover.

Watch the original (Charles Laughton) version of *The Hunchback of Notre Dame*. (It may help you to know that Charles Laughton loathed his own appearance and felt that this role particularly suited him.)

Rent a wheelchair for a day and use it as if you were disabled. How does your worldview change? What differences are there in how you see doors, curbs, counters in supermarkets, public telephones, and . . . (fill in the blanks)?

ETHICAL QUESTIONS

There are equal-opportunity rules that govern the hiring of men and women, minority groups, and persons with disabilities. Should there also be a rule about the hiring of physically attractive versus ugly people?

MEDIA ISSUES

How do the media (TV, magazines, YouTube . . . even university recruitment documents) influence the way in which we think people ought to look?

When you have completed the exercise above, how many magazines did you find that were devoted to issues of dress and appearance?

Watch *Slumdog Millionaire*.

Note

1. Janis Ian (1975), "At Seventeen" from the album *Between the Lines*. Columbia Records.

References

Acitelli, L. K., & Badr, H. (2005). My illness or our illness? Attending to the relationship when one partner is ill. In T. A. Revenson, K. Kayser, & G. Bodenmann (Eds.), *Emerging perspectives on couples' coping with stress*. Washington, DC: American Psychological Association.

Aronson, E., & Linder, D. (1965). Gain and loss of esteem as determinants of interpersonal attractiveness. *Journal of Experimental Social Psychology, 1,* 156–171.

Bigelow, B., Tesson, G., & Lewko, J. (1996). *Children's rules of friendship.* New York: Guilford.

Burke, K. (1961). *The rhetoric of religion.* Berkeley: University of California Press.

Butler, J. (1990). *Gender trouble: Feminism and the subversion of identity.* New York: Routledge.

Butler, J. (2004). *Undoing gender.* New York: Routledge.

Duck, S. W. (2007). *Human relationships* (4th ed.). London: Sage.

Floyd, K. (2004). Introduction to the uses and potential uses of physiological measurement in the study of family communication. *Journal of Family Communication,* 4(3,4), 295–317.

Goffman, E. (1959). *Behaviour in public places.* Harmondsworth, UK: Penguin.

Granovetter, M. S. (1973). The strength of weak ties. *American Journal of Sociology, 78,* 1360–1380.

Grewe, B. (2006, April). *Relationships on the rocks: How a relationship changes after a person acquires physical disability.* Paper presented at the annual meeting of the Central States Communication Association, Indianapolis, IN.

Guerrero, L. K., & Floyd, K. (2006). *Nonverbal communication in relationships.* Mahwah, NJ: Lawrence Erlbaum.

Huston, M., & Schwartz, P. (1995). Lesbian and gay male relationships. In J. T. Wood & S. W. Duck (Eds.), *Under-studied relationships: Off the beaten track* (pp. 89–121). Thousand Oaks, CA: Sage.

Lyons, R. F., Langille, L., & Duck, S. W. (2006). Difficult relationships and relationship difficulties: Relationship adaptation and chronic health problems. In C. D. Kirkpatrick, S. W. Duck, & M. K. Foley (Eds.), *Relating difficulty: Processes of constructing and managing difficult interaction* (pp. 203–224). Mahwah, NJ: Lawrence Erlbaum.

Lyons, R. F., Sullivan, M. J. L., & Ritvo, P. G. (1996). *Relationships in chronic illness and disability.* Thousand Oaks, CA: Sage.

Mead, G. H. (1934). *Mind, self, and society.* Chicago: University of Chicago Press.

Miller, D. L. (Ed.). (1980). *The individual and the social self: Unpublished work of G. H. Mead.* Chicago: University of Chicago Press.

Mongeau, P. A., Hale, J. L., Johnson, M., & Hillis, J. D. (1995). Who's wooing whom? An investigation of female initiated dating. In P. Kalbfleisch (Ed.), *Interpersonal communication: Evolving interpersonal relationships* (pp. 51–67). Hillsdale, NJ: Lawrence Erlbaum.

Norwood, K. M. (2006). *Women in conflict: An exploratory study of conflict between women in initial interaction.* Unpublished master's thesis, University of Arkansas, Fayetteville.

Reis, H. T., Nezlek, J., & Wheeler, L. (1980). Physical attractiveness and social interaction. *Journal of Personality and Social Psychology, 38,* 604–617.

Routsong, T. (2007). *"We call those my lupie days": Communication in families with lupus.* Unpublished doctoral dissertation, University of Iowa, Iowa City.

Rubin, Z. (1973). *Liking and loving.* New York: Holt, Rinehart & Winston.

Secklin, P. L. (2001). Multiple fractures in time: Reflections on a car crash. *Journal of Loss and Trauma, 6*(4), 323–333.

Segrin, C. (1993). Interpersonal reactions to dysphoria: The role of relationships with partner perceptions of rejection. *Journal of Social and Personal Relationships, 10,* 83–97.

Selman, R. L. (1980). *The growth of interpersonal understanding.* New York: Academic Press.

Senchea, J. A. (1998). *Gendered constructions of sexuality in adolescent girls' talk.* Unpublished doctoral dissertation, University of Iowa, Iowa City.

Stiles, W. B., Walz, N. C., Schroeder, M. A. B., Williams, L. L., & Ickes, W. (1996). Attractiveness and disclosure in initial encounters of mixed-sex dyads. *Journal of Social and Personal Relationships, 13,* 303–312.

Tyler, J. I. (2007). *Media clubs: The interpretation of media texts in social networks.* Unpublished doctoral dissertation, University of Iowa, Iowa City.

5

Sense and Sensuality

The Relationship Between
Sexual Activity and Knowledge of the World

The preceding chapter dealt with basic bodily materiality and its role as a symbolic force in relationships, and I looked at different sorts of meaning that are embodied in the physical forms and structures that you take into relationships. You have already seen in earlier chapters that personal orders for relationships are affected by general social orders about the ways in which relationships should be conducted, and this chapter looks closely at the ways in which the most personal enactment of relationships (sexual activity) is constructed by your social order. Another term for personal enactment that I have used is *performance,* a key issue these days when discussing materiality, physical embodiment, and the nature of gender. However, in this chapter, I am writing about sexual activity itself, not gender.

PHYSICAL PERFORMANCE OF EMOTIONS AND FEELINGS

We will still be looking here at the physical form of relationships as an expression or performance of symbolism, looking at the way in which the physical relationship between two people says something not only about self and social order, but also about *knowledge* and a social order's interest in overseeing what its citizens know. A recent news story indicated that while Natalie Portman was making a film in Jerusalem, she passionately kissed her costar at the Wailing Wall and was immediately faced with outrage by Orthodox Jews, who found it extremely offensive that she would do that activity in that particular place. Why does religion or society care about the places where people express passion? Why does popular music tell us not only how love is felt and expressed, but how it should be controlled (sometimes) or openly performed?

The immediate question is about the connection of passion to some more refined sense of love, but also indicated is that bodily *performance* (embodiment) of feelings that are otherwise rated positively by society (love, devotion, commitment) can be evaluated separately from the feelings themselves. The feelings themselves are honored in the abstract or are allowed limited expression (in private); they are less clearly accepted if they are expressed and performed in public or in special holy places. Why?

Performance and the Audience

Evidently, the public performance of (even mildly sexual) physical behaviors and religion don't mix. Even on TV and in the movies, sexual behaviors are expected to be observed, if at all, by certain people and not others—it is assumed that children are in bed by the 9:00 TV watershed. More adult situations can be performed after that hour. It is also taken for granted in our social order that children should be refused entry to view movies that are R-rated. Parents should be cautioned (PG) or strongly cautioned (PG-13) if the movie contains even indirect references to sexuality. Why is that? Perhaps some social orders place a demand of highest loyalty and affection toward a Higher Being. However, most religions specifically note that sex between *married* partners is one of the Higher Being's better ideas. In that case, why would such religions still say that it is wrong to express affection in particular places associated with holiness (e.g., even for married people to have sex in churches, graveyards, altars, synagogues, mosques, Shinto shrines . . .)?

Unfortunately, this chapter will be hindered by the fact that researchers on relationships and researchers on sex and sexuality tend to work in distinct groups and do not hold long conversations with one another (see McKinney & Sprecher, 1991, for an exception, but note that it is almost 20 years old!). The influence of sex and gender on many aspects of life has also been researched by groups of scholars that have no particular direct interest in relationships themselves, and although the thinking about gender is particularly well advanced (Butler, 2004; Dow & Wood, 2006), the application of gender theory to personal relationships specifically is quite limited (for counterexamples, see Wood, 2001, 2004).

DISCUSSION QUESTION

Type "Vaigar" into your word processor and see what happens. Are you offered the option of correcting the error to "Viagra"? Then try typing "warfrian" and "Vaigsl" to see if you get offered "warfarin" or "Vagisil" as a choice for correction. I didn't. What do you think that says about the social order and its acceptance of products dealing with specifically male sexual dysfunctions, as distinct from general heart ailments [or rat poison] or women's infections?

Sex and Society

When society tells you that love is generally a good thing, why does it limit the places where love can be expressed? Such a question asks about the *symbolism* inherent in doing something in a particular place. Why would a society make a distinction between doing something in one place and doing the same thing in another place? On the other hand, for sex, it is generally understood that privacy

Did you know that *profane* means "in front of/outside of the holy temple" and hence refers to behaviors or events not suitable for holiness? *Obscene* means "offstage" and not suitable for public view. The words for unacceptable actions, then, refer even in their etymological roots to material *places* where certain acts should not be done or seen by others.

enhances intimacy. Why is that? The answer is because sex is not motion but action, and so it is loaded with social significance and symbolism.

The Symbolism of Sexual Performance

The present chapter keeps the focus on material, physical bodies and symbolism but looks at it all in reverse—the most materially physical form of relationship—sex—as the expression of symbolism, not only about self and relationship but also, perhaps surprisingly, about the social order. The social order chooses to encourage sexual activity between legally joined partners as the highest instance of the embodiment of love. Curiously, at the same time, it also seeks to regulate both the public performance of sexual behaviors and their performance by other people who are not legally joined (that is, joined in the sight of the social order). The reasoning often offered for this is that it is inherently indecent to show love in that way in the presence of other people, and also that it would break down the structure of society by inducing corruption (usually of minors) if such regulation were not carried out. (We never get told where all the already corrupted people have ended up.) Note also the idea of "conspicuous affection": It is rather like the idea of conspicuous consumption, like parading your Lexus. You got it, and someone else did not. So the display enhances envy, but also conformity, by limiting the forms of expression.

Thus, the social order imposes on private individuals some constraints about how they should enact their relationships, even though you started out believing that relationships are truly private and that emotions of any great depth are regarded as the pinnacle of privacy and intimacy. But if they are private, then why do governments and religions regulate them and seek so strenuously to confine them to certain material places and circumstances? This chapter will explore the relationship between private behaviors and public structure, examining the ways in which sexual behavior is represented as a way

Write down or make a mental list of the ways in which society restricts sexual activity (define that however you like), and give any reasons for these specific restrictions. You could end up being very surprised at what you take for granted.

of knowing the world and therefore as something in which society at large has a legitimate interest.

Most people don't give any thought at all to the ways in which society and its active practices influence how you *perform* relationships. You are now beginning to be aware of these influences. In particular, consider the way in which certain kinds of relationships are disapproved of or even banned by society (e.g., adultery and pedophilia) (Duck & VanderVoort, 2002). The different way of looking at how relationships operate, by focusing on this and taking the focus off emotions, helps to explain the connection of personal and social orders about relationships.

Sexual Intercourse as a Material Way of Knowing

I wrote earlier that sex represents a way of knowing (that is, that sex is an epistemic). Society's various attempts to regulate it derive in part from the suspicion of how people will know the world if they are not guided and regulated to do it in the *approved* ways.

This claim may have struck you as rather odd as there are a couple of unusual ideas there that need unpacking. The first, and one that follows from previous considerations, is that bodily materiality—how you use, view, or experience your body—is connected to knowledge. We've already addressed this in some detail in the preceding chapter, drawing on Mead's (1934) ideas that physical materiality generally is the basis for creating mind (which you could represent as the sum of all the ways of knowing that a person has). For Mead, minds spring from the physical manipulation of the world. These embodied, material activities produce a kind of experience that leads to mental imagery, to symbolism, and basically to mind itself. Hold that thought, and move on to look at the materiality of sexual behavior and how it connects to specific parts of mind. Also, as you saw in the preceding chapter, your physical form and your experiences of your own body can make you feel attractive, valuable, isolated, or stigmatized as a social being. The way you look can affect the way you feel as a social object. Well, you already are partly there: The way sex works is also connected to these material and embodied issues through that direct connection to the epistemic and to the social order.

You could see sex as purely physical activity, as the relentless primordial grinding of animal impulses based on hormones and biochemistry. Indeed, at some level, all physical activity (motion) is of this kind. It is indeed true that there is a physical basis to sexual behavior. Young people need to acquire certain bodily development not only at the physical organic level (maturation of sex organs), but also at the physiological level (production of the necessary hormones). Until the adolescents' organs and biochemistry are appropriately developed, sexual intercourse is not really possible and reproductive aspects of sex are simply not going to happen. Even for adults, physical aspects of sexuality affect interest in and performance of sexual behaviors. Men with prostate problems or erectile dysfunction often cannot have sex or cannot have sex often. Women have a menstrual cycle that injects hormonal rhythms into their sexual interest and performance levels; men have refractory periods (a sort of "recovery time") that limit the frequency with which they can ejaculate successively in a given space of time. Women, too, though in less restricted ways, have refractory periods between orgasms.

Despite medical evidence to the contrary, particularly about chocolate (Darn!) (http://www.webmd.com/sex-relationships/modern-love-8/chocolate-answers?page=2), popular beliefs indicate that certain foods can enhance sexual performance and interest. Such claims have been made for oysters, rhinoceros horn, and some vegetables, as well as chocolate, since Aztec times. Other chemicals (especially alcohol) can depress performance if taken in excessive quantities—and yet in small amounts can raise interest in sex while also lowering inhibitions.

SEX AS MOTION VERSUS SEX AS ACTION

You probably knew that already, and hence you already knew several ways in which the material embodied aspects of life affect performance, motivation, interest, and desire for sex. That part of the move to discuss sex as materially influenced is therefore not a hard one to make. In these cases, however, bodily life—the material knowing part—and sex are represented merely as motion, the unthinking physical reaction to stimuli and internal chemistry. But it is more interesting to look at sex as action, not motion. Given that you now know about the distinction between action and motion, you can see that the *meanings* that surround particular motions (and that make them into actions instead of just motions) are an important way of understanding their significance in broader terms.

Embodiment and Performance

Just as family dinner talk is more than food consumption, and daily routines can embody knowledge and perform personal and social orders, so, too, can sex be just "doing it" (an animal reflex activity) or meaningful. From this point of view, sex acts become more than motion whenever there is some sort of reflection taking place or some sort of enactment of a relational meaning that gives them significance. They then achieve the sort of importance that actions do more generally. Thus, when the enactment of sexual behavior becomes meaningful—as a symbolic expression of love, as some indication of the growing strength of a relationship, or as something that must never happen between the two people now beginning to do it (e.g., incest)—the motions become actions that are more than just fluids, muscles, and biochemistry.

If you see the motions of sex as motivated and placed in a social epistemic order that gives them meaning, then they become actions that are symbols built on to bodily movements. If sexual activity becomes an act of love, or a sexual conquest, or a sign of being grown up, or even a symbol of power and control, then it has that meaning as a result of some symbolic baggage and not just as a result of the behaviors (motions) themselves. The symbolic baggage is a representation of some way of knowing the world through those symbols.

Symbols and Performance

Symbols, whether about sex or anything else, are ways of connecting events in the world into meaningful groups or presentations of some form of understanding. This symbolic (way of knowing) aspect is one reason why sex can also be put into a moral context. For example, people can talk about "good sex" (see any magazine this week) and so can presumably treat the description of acts of sexual behavior through a terministic screen differentiating it from . . . bad sex? Yet, like pizza, even when it is bad, it is still pretty good relative to a bowl of plain rice.

Such a differentiation must refer to something other than the physical acts alone, because the physical activity is the same whether good or bad. The distinction between good and bad here depends actually on symbols and on treating sexual behavior as action not as motion alone, so it fits right in with what I've been writing so far. It requires only that you think about ways of knowing, epistemics, and the connection between relationships and knowledge of the world. Motion is less than action, and because social orders work with action, there are symbols and lots of epistemics built in even to sex. You can't defend yourself against a rape charge by saying, "It was just sex." You have actually violated the rights of another person and hence have violated the person's symbolic status as an individual in society.

If you can grasp that point about the connection of symbols, meaning, and action, then the activities of sex by themselves are not what makes them significant or interesting to the society as a whole. Rather, they assume importance precisely because they signify something symbolic and so take their importance from the ways in which they symbolize . . . something. When that symbolism intrudes against the social order, then private action intrudes against the public social order. When you realize that it does not help to explain society's interest in sexual regulation if you focus on the activity itself (motion), then you must turn to the thought or framing that goes into making the mere bodily activity (motion) into an action.

You could also consider that sex may be treated as a symbol of love, where either consenting to sex or actually engaging in it can carry messages about feelings for another person. It therefore signals something symbolic over and above the act itself and brings private action into the realm that is of interest to the social order. Sex could also symbolize other things (power, possession, immorality, subordination, disdain, respect), but the point is the same: It is the *symbolism* of sex that is important between/for the two people in the relationship, but one that also carries meaning to the public social order. Hence, the importance of sex in society is not the activity itself (motion), but how society gives it meaning (action).

DISCUSSION QUESTION

Although sex is often the subject of legislation dictating how and where it may happen, much of the legislation commercializes sex and recognizes that lap dancing parlors, sex shops, and the like should be allowed, but only in certain parts of the city, for example. Thus, society both regulates and, in contradictory ways, permits sexual behavior outside of the usual types that occur. Why is this?

SEX, MEANING, AND THE EPISTEMIC

So here you are again, looking at the idea that performances of behavior are actually a reflection of the epistemic. That is, the ways in which you choose to carry out behaviors are themselves representations of something symbolically connected to the ways in which you know (and your social order knows) the world. You carry out sexual activity with a particular person as a means of satisfying not only biological needs but also symbolic social requirements to demonstrate love and caring, partnership and acceptance, relationship and significance, power and control, possession, maturity—the list goes on endlessly, depending on the person, situation, and circumstances. The *meaning* of the activity can, of course, be different from time to time as the circumstances change between the same two people. That is because the symbolic meaning of the activity can be different from time to time also; for example, the act of sexual performance may be done for love one time and for mere duty the next. Hence, sexual behavior becomes an action that has overtones about the ways in which you see yourself and your partner and the meanings that you attach to the relationship and its form on particular occasions.

Sex and the Social Order: Language

Now it might be more obvious why society has an interest in regulating sexual behavior. Forms of sexual activity, construed as actions, represent meaning and hence cast sex as epistemic, a way of knowing the world. In that case, sex could represent a form of knowledge (personal order) that the society does not endorse in its social order and even does not like. Following the brilliant analysis of sociologist Murray Davis (1983), I will now look at this notion a lot more deeply.

Consider first the uses of language itself for sexual behavior. There are two codes of language in use at any one time in society in general: a high code and a low code. High code is characterized by formality, complexity, and structure. An example of high code is found on public notices or official proclamations, such as airline crew announcements of the form "Please discontinue the use of all electronic equipment." The other type of code is a low code characterized by informality, looseness of structure, and relatively simple format. An example of low code would be a flight attendant saying, "You guys shut down your laptops and toys" (I've heard both).

At least in the case of bodily terms, there is also a sort of middle ground that allows people to be familiar without being regarded as downright crude, a sort of euphemistic slang form that is not regarded as either too formal to be used among friends and not too informal to be used in front of family. Good examples of the use of these terms are provided in the language used to speak to very young children, where it is OK to say in public, "Do you want to go potty?" but not "Are you currently motivated by a predominant, urgent need to defecate?" or the rather less likely "Do you want a shit?"

In the realm of sexual behavior, these codes are quite marked and quite markedly different, taking the forms of a professional code and a common or vulgar code. The same sexual referents, acts, body parts, and processes can be described in Latin (high code, professional, and detached words, such as "penis" and "copulation"); middle-form, relatively inoffensive slang ("willy," "doing it"); or the Anglo-Saxon (low code, vulgar, crude words, such as "cock" and "fucking"). Yet the *referents* are the same; whichever form of language is chosen, the same objects and activities are being talked about.

Perhaps, Davis (1983) argues, the language worlds represent different experiential worlds (or in my terms, epistemics); one of them—low code—is immediate and present, and the other—high code—is distant and abstract. When you are involved and attentive to sexual activity, then you are more likely to use the crude forms and "talk dirty." When distant and uninvolved, as when you talk to your physician, it is deemed appropriate to use the professional terms. Doctors talking to you in a detached, clinical way about sex will use the high code forms of terminology in order to symbolize their professional position of clinical detachment when talking professionally ("Does this patient have a genitourinary tract infection?") and the middle form in order to indicate connection with the patient's real life ("How are the waterworks?" or "Do you have any trouble peeing?" for example).

Such differences in code indicate something about the relationship of the two people, and they do so through the symbolic nature of the codes themselves. When a physician wants to be welcoming to the patient, then use of codes familiar to the patient (middle or low code) will be more successful at achieving such a welcome than will high, distant, formal, expert, professional codes that are entirely appropriate for use by one physician talking with another. The *relationship* between the speaker and audience is coded in the language form that is used to talk about the topic.

Sex and the Social Order: Moving Between Symbolic Levels

Now think about the activity of sex itself. Which code usage would make you feel most involved in intimate behavior and which the least? Do you think that your physician uses high code to talk to a partner when having sex? When in the arms of a passionate lover, it is much more likely that the physician will experience a role shift from professional to lover and so switch from professional high code to lower codes and thereby become a more involved and engaged participant. Getting in tune with the situation, then, can be done by a linguistic choice, although this is not the only way. It is an important one here, however, because language is the most immediate form of symbolic action that concerns us and most clearly connects the argument about relationships, language, knowledge, and epistemics.

Moving between one level of experience and another is quite important as an epistemic shift. Imagine that you're having a physical exam with a doctor of the opposite sex and the physician suddenly switches to a low style. This might be seen as crossing a boundary from the professional to the indecent or unacceptable.

In the actual activities of initiating sexual activity, one of the things that people do is to try and move out of the present material world and into an abstract fantasy world. They leave the external characteristics so that they can go into an interior world where they're feeling connected only with one another and leave the rest of the world outside of this. For example, people may make a shift in atmosphere by altering lighting or sounds or fragrances to make themselves feel comfortable and create a little world separate from the rest of the world. Indeed, the lights are turned low partly so that you cannot see—to be distracted by—the real material world. It is just you and your partner in a bounded physical and epistemic space, making an epistemic shift from engagement with the outside world to engagement with the partner specifically and alone. The shifting from one style to another can be important in creating atmosphere for sex, as anyone knows who has ever purposely adjusted the lighting in the bedroom or rearranged pillows, furniture, and ambient sound.

THE MATERIAL AND SYMBOLIC WORLDS OF SEX

What is all this about, and how does it connect to the ideas in the book so far?

If you want to move into a symbolic world that makes sex a meaningful action (rather than just a physical motion) that expresses relationships and love, then you need to move out of the world that focuses only on physical movements and localized sounds with its emphasis on surrounding local activity. You need to be focused centrally on what only the partner and self are doing and feeling. You need to move your mind-frames (epistemics) into symbolic expression of deep and significant emotions; you need to move from the immediate real world into an erotic symbolic world. In other, familiar terms, you need to move from the obscene reality into an erotic fantasy, from a literal, material, physical epistemic of motion (where grinding groins are just the movement of bits of human meat) into a symbolic epistemic where physical activity is an action that has deeper relational meanings and is a richly symbolic representation of love, involvement, caring, power, or even duty. The key point is that there are two forms of knowing (real and fantastic), and one is not "sexy" whereas the other one is. Both are forms of perception and knowing. Fantasy may be a preferred or desired perceptual state, but reality is one to which one may become resigned or may just accept as a perceptual state. There is a lot that gets "settled for" in everyday life.

Davis (1983) says you need ways to keep you in the unreal fantastic world epistemically, because sexual activity is a form of epistemic in which you are experiencing the world in a different, fantastical way. If I see things in this broadly fantastical kind of way, then it follows that I'm *not* seeing them in a real and everyday routine kind of sense—and that second way of seeing must be kept out if I am to continue to see the activities in the fantastical way. Terministic screens mean that when I see the world in an erotic way, I'm *not* seeing it in the regular way; to stay in the erotic fantasy epistemic, I have to work to keep it that way.

An important element of shifting from detachment to fantastic involvement or getting in tune with the erotic situation is to defocus from the external, intensive world of other people and external stimuli and be in an isolated psychological space containing just you and the partner. This creates a place where there will not be frequent interruptions by people or activities like telephone calls or office mates or talkative servers who will frustrate the couple's intent to focus on each other over a candlelit dinner.

A focus on each other is, of course, a specific way of knowing, a way that limits what is in the mind and makes it central to one's experience. For example, taking a phone call in the middle of sexual activity is

---

Question to Ask Your Friends

Think about "cougars" and whether they threaten, challenge, or actually conform to the social order. Are they asserting feminist values or playing into the image of women as sexual objects?

setting aside one's focus from the relationship, as the Laura Linney character in *Love Actually* discovers when she interrupts a promising sexual encounter to answer a phone call from her mentally ill brother. The right moment is lost forever.

SEX AND THE SHIFT OF EPISTEMICS

Davis (1983) goes on to suggest that this is one instance of a general truth about sex and relationships. The activities of sex are intended to take you from one realm of experience to another and so, in my terms, from one epistemic to another—from a simple material epistemic to a complex symbolic epistemic. This is what is happening when you create atmosphere in setting up sexual activity. The lowering of the lights, arranging of the smells and experiences in the environment, setting up of the situation in enticing and relaxing ways, and the other preparations that you and your partner do are done in order to focus you both away from the normal material ways of knowing the world and on to a special and erotic way of knowing the material in symbolic ways.

Consider how the intrusion of reality breaks the focus on the partner or the event. Intrusions tend to disrupt successful engagement in sexual activity, as when the alarm clock goes off, a loud ambulance passes by, one of the cats jumps on the bed, or somebody's stomach grumbles (or worse). All of those intrusions from the outer world, those reminders of the different realm of epistemic experience than the one in which you are attempting to participate, tend to disrupt flow, concentration, and enjoyment. They bring you back, with a start, to the real world rather than leaving you in the world of fantastic erotic mystery. They remind you of the solid, sordid world of objective reality that you are trying to escape for the delights of an erotic fantasy world.

Shifting From the Real to the Fantastic

Davis (1983) argues that much of the thinking behind sexual moves is basically to redirect the partners away from the objective and real epistemic—where bodies are objects—to a fantastic and erotic epistemic—where bodies are symbolic or idealized or become fantasized. The move is from an objectified outer world to an experiential inner world where feelings are paramount. The objective material expression of reality can be kept at a distance while the two partners move into another epistemic world where they will have more pleasurable involvement in the activities. They will sense themselves as entities moved from the insistent present to a time-free unreality that heightens their pleasures in one another. Some activities keep you in the unreal world of sexual experience—such as "dirty talk" or intensely pleasurable physical sensations that keep one focused on the erotic sensuality—and some bring you back to earth and hence out of that realm of difference and altered experience. Such events intrude on your fantasy world or make you aware of the world outside the erotic, such as those listed before or a prosthetic device falling off or a CD "sticking" in the background or a piece of clothing that stubbornly refuses to come off smoothly.

For Davis, then, the actions of sexuality are performances that make the relationship shift from one realm of experience to another and move the participants from the real world to a fantasy world. Of course, in my terms, a real world and a fantasy world are different ways of knowing, different epistemics, and they are separate and importantly different. Hence, difficulty arises if there are sounds, events, or mistakes that distract the people from moving into or staying connected to the fantasy world. The main issue here, then, is that in Davis's analysis, which is consistent with mine, sexual activity becomes a form of epistemic. You know and experience the world in a different way because of various attempts to move one's self and one's immediate material focus away from the present and real into the abstract and distant world of passion.

I am hoping that all of this has sounded to you very much part of an epistemic analysis but also has made you think once again about terministic screens! Isn't this analysis suggesting that when you see things one way (erotic fantasy), you do not see them another way (objective reality)? In addition, isn't the same idea suggesting that both forms of experience are ways of knowing the world materially and responding to it symbolically? With respect to something as intimate and immediate as sexual activity, they are acutely dichotomous epistemics.

Why "the Fantastic" Might Threaten a Social Order

If this argument so far has brought you along with it, then the next step follows quite easily. This step suggests that a fantastic epistemic can represent a dangerous concept for the social order, namely, an alternative way of seeing reality that may not conform to society's preferred way of knowing.

Clearly, if you can have two ways of seeing things, then these can be in conflict with one another. The way that one creates an epistemic during sexual behavior can differentiate one way of seeing from another way of seeing, and the social order might not like this alternative. If sex (as an action rather than a motion) is a way of knowing the world, then it can be consistent or inconsistent with other ways of knowing the world. Just as forms of relationship are forms of knowing, that sensual way of knowing the world can be one that the social order at large finds acceptable or one that it does not. At one level, the removal from the present realm of awareness into erotic fantasy is a difference in experience for the partners alone. At another level of analysis, it also presents, in symbolic form, a way in which the world can be understood and addressed. So it might be one that can contest or oppose some other ways of seeing the world that exist in the social order.

SEX AS AN OFFENSE AGAINST THE SOCIAL ORDER

Davis (1983) proposes that this is why there is such effort in legislation and by religious groups to control (or to completely de-control) sexual expression. The battle, Davis argues, is not so much about sex itself (at least not about sex as motion or as a set of bodily functions) as it is about the ideology that is represented by the different ways of knowing the world as represented by erotic fantasy (itself an *action*), on one hand, and objective reality, on the other.

Davis asks why society is so dedicated to the stopping of displays of sexual activity. Look at the lists of repressions of sexual activity that you noted down at the start of this chapter and consider what they achieve. Why *can't* you do it in the road? What did you say when you wrote your list at the start of the chapter?

Remember from earlier in the chapter that there are a number of different issues here, some of which connect to the commission of the acts themselves and some of which relate to witnessing them instead. Society has always assumed that it is "dangerous" or "corrupting" for children, as I noted, to see certain kinds of sexual activities. Hence, society has regulated the circumstances in which children may see, for example, sexual activity in the cinema or on TV, which it does by means of rating certificates and warning notices to its delegated societal police—parents.

It also used to be thought improper for certain topics to be discussed when ladies were present, and the Victorians invented a complex, euphemistic language to avoid describing anything sexually related, such as pregnancy ("she's in a delicate condition" or "she's in the family way"). However, society is also concerned that innocent citizens should not unwittingly come across other people doing anything that is legal only when it is done privately. Indeed, some fears about the Internet could be traced to the concern that witnessing sex is contagious and disrupts a social order.

The Social Order and the Regulation of Sexual Behavior

Society thus seeks to regulate not only the occurrence of certain sexual behaviors, but more significantly, their being witnessed inadvertently by people who might be harmed or offended by them. For these reasons, the British Parliament (January 29, 2003) advised that it was considering legislation that proposed to regulate and punish the occurrence of sexual activity in public in case other people should inadvertently witness it. For example, having sex in a garden that can be seen from the public street would be a crime,

Listen in on Your Own Life

What do you make of "virgin promise rings" and virgin balls where girls and young women dance with their fathers and pledge their virginity? What about celebrities who pledge their virginity or, conversely, change partners quite frequently and publicly? In your circle of friends, has anyone adopted either of these styles?

whereas performing the same acts in a bedroom with the drapes open would not be because the participants are in their own private space. The legislation was also concerned with whether doors in public toilets are open or closed, for example, when sex acts occur between homosexual partners (closed is OK, open is bad).

For relationship scholars, there are some interesting points there: (a) Private activity is normally assumed to be no one else's business, and (b) the reasons offered for the legislation are all about bystanders unwittingly seeing other people "at it." If you follow this argument through to its conclusion, then it should be the case that society would be perfectly happy to allow any sorts of private acts to occur as long as other people did not see them happening. In fact, there are closer regulations about some acts, and they are banned whether or not anyone sees them. For example, incest, rape, and pedophilia are illegal whether or not anyone witnesses them, and consensual anal sex between consenting adults is illegal in some states in the United States whether or not anyone else observes it happening.

Sexual Behavior and the Disruption of the Social Order

Davis (1983) argues that those who fear sex or fear observing sex must believe that it will change them (and, in my terms, change their epistemics) fundamentally whether they see or take part in it, and that it will change them for the worse by corrupting them. In other words, those who fear sex must see its very occurrence as morally degrading and too ready a reminder of the animal origins of the human species. They must fear or at least acknowledge the animal instincts and the animal urges represented there. It would be easy to analyze such concerns in terms of ways of knowing: The ways in which animals know are far too reminiscent of inhumanity as compared to those ways in which humans know the world.

Psychologically, there is a balance between inclusion and exclusion, on one hand, and guilt, on the other hand, if the audience is observing. Hence, to adopt an essentially animal way of knowing is to degrade humanity or to induce guilt or corruption in witnesses. Indeed, comparisons with a person and animal life are often used to degrade or vilify people, especially enemies. For example, when Saddam Hussein was finally captured, it seemed to be important to both politicians and the media to report that he had been caught "like a rat in a hole" or that he came out "like a dog with a tail between its legs." Note also that repeated sexual predators (a value statement in itself) are often characterized by the media as "sex beasts," a term emphasizing their connection to the animal (not human) world.

The importance of distinguishing sex as animal motion from sex as human action leads to a further point, namely, that because *both descriptions are simultaneously possible*, something must be done to move people from one realm (animal motion) to another realm (human action). Such ideas play to another layer of analysis of this whole topic, because for Mead and others, psychological changes come from physical experiences or physical changes, as you saw in Chapter 4. In line with Mead's ideas, many writers refer to sex as a *transformative activity*, and in many of his stories, D. H. Lawrence wrote about sex as an experience of dissolving or melting together, a metaphor of transformation.

In this way of thinking, sex has effects on our epistemic and personal order, it can serve as personal change or as personal affirmation, or it can bring about a sense of renewal of self. All of these are, of course, changes in a personal order. However, the transformation can be good or bad, depending on how self is affirmed and identity acquired. An activity that turns someone into an "animal" or that emphasizes the animal aspects of their sexual activity might degrade them in ways that an emphasis on their spiritual being might not. Hence, people are more likely to describe their best sexual experiences as enlivening spiritually, making them feel satisfied not as animals but as people, fulfilled as lovers rather than emphasizing, for example, an animal level of physical exhaustion except insofar as that shows the fullness of their satisfaction.

Three Theories of Sexual Epistemics

Given this background analysis, Davis (1983) goes on to distinguish three theories or ideologies about sex that can be contrasted and understood as different epistemics (in my terms).

JEHOVANISM

Davis uses the term *Jehovanism* to describe those approaches to sex that are based on religion and formal appeals to the social good or to morality in the social order. This approach sees sex as a dangerous threat to the separation of mind/soul and body; sex is bodily and animalistic, whereas the human quest is a divine one for spirituality. Sex is dirty and disorganizing and connects you too easily to your biological and animalistic roots. Authority for these kinds of views is usually sought in Biblical, Koranic, or similar sources, and the emphasis falls strongly on the distinction between animal and higher order instincts and goals. In this approach, sex is a source of vague regret that humans need to reproduce in order to maintain the species. It is regarded as a necessary evil or as a simple duty that must occur—but only between those who have entered a religious contract to fulfill God's will to do their bit to help restock the Earth and especially to restock it with believers.

In this view, the flesh is inherently animalistic and evil. It is to be punished so that the soul—the essentially human aspect of people that differentiates them from the animals, not only birds and bees, but more especially beasts and swine—can survive. The flesh generally must be punished and restricted so that the soul can escape its imprisonment. Hence, sex is not to be treated as a pleasurable relaxation but as a source of corruption, sin, and evil if used incorrectly.

Sex reminds Jehovanists too strongly of the closeness of evil to the soul and that the physical embodiment of temptation can deny the soul and its higher purposes. Jehovanists see only one pure and acceptable form of sex. This occurs within marriage, for purposes of procreation, as a fulfillment of a divine rule to repopulate the earth.

Other impure and unacceptable forms, especially adultery, masturbation, and homosexuality, are all represented as being done willfully and in pure gratification of animal lusts. In essence, then, the distinction here lies in the purposes for which the person entering into secular and potentially corrupting activity does it. If it is done in fulfillment of a divine injunction for married people to repopulate the Earth, then it is OK, but if it is in satisfaction of some lower order animal desire, then it is bad.

Of course, when it is stated that way, you were thinking, "Two different ways of knowing: secular/animalistic versus divine/humanist." If you didn't think that, then think it now! These two forms of motivation are differentiable (according to Jehovanists): One represents a holy and acceptable way of knowing, and the other one does not.

For Jehovanists, nature is unholy because of the original sin in the Garden of Eden. Therefore, sex must be regulated for the good of humanity, and in order to help everyone save his or her soul, all sex, and not just public sex, has to be regulated so that it occurs only in its good, sanctioned, soul-saving forms. Sex is to be regarded as connected to the Divine when it is performed by the approved sorts of people (husband and wife) in the proper places (in the home) and circumstances (as a result of love), and when it is done in fulfillment of a sacred duty (to reproduce and so to repopulate the world). The sacred duty between husband and wife, as duly approved in religious ceremony by a properly appointed priestly representative of the Divine who blesses the official marriage of the two participants using accepted sacred rites, exists in the use of their bodies for the fulfillment of the holy requirement to restock the world with believers. On this epistemic, marriage is explicitly regarded, in the ceremonies of most religious forms, as God's way of channeling the otherwise unbridled animal carnality of the human species into a civilized expression that, Jehovanists believe, lifts it out of the gutter, cattle trough, or animal farm.

Pornography, prostitution, masturbation, and sexual deviancy/difference are rejected by Jehovanists as bestializing the divine aspects of sexuality and reducing the sexual act to only its mechanics (motions) rather than to its human relationships or blessed and divine purposes (actions). Such critiques focus on the ways in which pornography, prostitution, and particularly homo-sexuality objectify their subjects, both men and women. At the same time, they pay no attention to the warm and acceptable sentiments of true love and devo-tion that "proper relationships" would not only entail but also celebrate. Forms of sexual behavior other than those aimed at reproduction are vilified by Jehovanists as simply animalistic lust and as reducing their perpetrators to the level of cattle and swine bent only on their own pleasure and without any con-cern for higher order issues that represent a spiritually driven epistemic.

I will not dwell on that inherent epistemic here nor focus on the ways in which this represents a particular ideology for sexual relations. By now, you ought to be able to see where I would place emphasis: on the fact that physical performance of certain behaviors is connected first to the underlying motives, and hence to the forms of action that are implied. Second, sex is connected to the epistemic that those forms of action represent and hence the forms of society and structures of social order that they either challenge or sustain.

GNOSTICISM

The second form of approach to sex is labeled by Davis (1983) as *Gnosticism*. This approach (or epistemic) sees sex as dirty and also disorganizing, just as the Jehovanists do, but crucially, the Gnostics also see it as socially subversive, and they especially see it as *politically* disruptive. Gnostics glorify sex as a tool for expressing defiance of repression and the social order. Recognizing that sex-ual activity represents "dirtiness" as seen by the rest of society, Gnostics also recognize that what is "dirty" must be offensive, and what is offensive to society must also be threatening to it.

They also see sex as a uniform activity in that it equates all people who do it, not respecting separations of rank or degree or wealth or education: Everyone who has sex is, at that moment, equal to anyone else having sex. They are not honorable or superior or powerful or respectable or admirable; they are just having sex. Hence, Gnostics regard sexual activity as an open attack on the prevailing structures of society and see sex as both creating individual freedom and also making for social equality. Hence, for them, sex serves to remove hierarchical orders.

Gnostics *like* this social disruption. "Make love, not war" people cried in the 1960s, and when John Lennon and Yoko Ono had a "love in" in a bed/bag in their hotel room, the press showed up in hordes in order to take pictures of the bag, presumably with them inside it busily disrupting society.

DISCUSSION QUESTION

What is the effect on social order of a person walking into a sex store? How does it reflect on that person's personal order and the kind of relationship that he or she tends to enact?

As a general idea, sex and sexual expressiveness are both construed by Gnostics as attacks on social order because they are seen as doing three things simultaneously. First, sex liberates the individual by allowing the person to escape the social constraints of the Jehovanists and simply be a socially untrammeled human being doing what comes naturally. Second, sex equalizes individuals because all people who have sex voluntarily are experiencing the same bodily sensations, enacting the same motions, and getting more or less the same results. Even if you have a royal title or a presidency, you still have sex in the ways broadly available to everyone else, too. Third, for Gnostics, sex reconnects people with their true nature in a "back to basics" sort of way that resists and removes the trappings of a society that has tried to restrict and undermine the truly natural life for which humans were really intended. The back-to-nature point is made very well for Gnostics by the fact that in order to have sex, people usually divest themselves of their clothes and hence of any marks of rank or status. This is a symbolic way of divesting themselves of inhibitions, social norms, and the restraints of modern society.

The Marquis De Sade, a particularly well-known Gnostic, was attempting to disrupt society when he advocated sexual libertinism. He wrote, "Virtue is an illusion whereas vice is real" (quoted in de Beauvoir, 1961, p. 52). In this phrasing, he is identifying the thought that sexuality expresses the true nature of human beings and that the sexual act itself is freely open, bare of pretense, and nakedly real. Virtue, restraint, modesty, and morality, for him, are false, illusory, fake, and absurd impositions of a social order. For this reason and from this perspective, sexual freedom serves to liberate and equate everyone by stressing the fact that everyone is truly animalistic under the skin and that human beings are, at root, no more than animals in their true nature. Gnostics like the Marquis de Sade claim that sex can destroy the socially ordered and hierarchically structured universe. Their more general point is that it *should* do so, and that its power is a force for the creation of equality in the world (an interesting idea from a noble marquis, even one who spent a lot of his time in an asylum pretending to be Geoffrey Rush in the movie *Quills*).

More recent examples of the same basic idea include rock stars such as Alice Cooper and Marilyn Manson, whose bisexuality is sometimes articulated as an attempt to overthrow social order or at least as an attempt to question sexual classifications and hence to invite open discussion of the social orders based on sexual differentiation. Such sexual social orders—the obvious one that presently privileges men and heterosexuality, for example—are often key targets of such Gnostics who want to increase tolerance for other expressions of sexuality. However, this epistemic way of knowing the world—a way that stresses the moral equivalence of all forms of sexual expression—is only one part of the Gnostic agenda. Although Gnostics typically seek equal treatment of different sexual styles, thoroughgoing Gnostics believe that this is only a first step and that other forms of social equality can be initiated through sexual liberalism also.

For Gnostics, pornography is purposely intended to be antisocial (not just antiwoman) because Gnostics use it to degrade and equalize everyone. Its purpose, for Gnostics, is not solely sexual stimulation but stimulation to social revolution. It is also intended and perceived by Gnostics as an implied attack on society and any form of social order that structures people hierarchically, and so (as Gnostics see it) deprives them of their natural state of animalistic equivalence. Note that in the sexual revolution of the late 1960s, "free love" was one of the slogans, and the suggestion was a conscious attempt to attack social order by proclaiming the value of random and unattached sexual activity as a means of overthrowing the state. People evidently had a lot of fun—but the state is still here.

You may however like to consider whether the recent rise in campus hookups is an attempt to overthrow some sort of repressive social order (Paul, 2006). What do you think? Can you see it in those terms at all? You might like to discuss this in class, even perhaps as an example of a sense of politicalization that ultimately represents a desire for political change.

NATURALISM

The third epistemic for sexual behavior is labeled by Davis (1983) as *Naturalism*. This view sees sex as pure unalloyed joy that is grounded in biology, seeing sex as natural rather than dirty and something that can also be enlivening and uplifting because of its natural release of pent-up biological energy. Sex is interpreted in terms of nature, and the sexual directive is seen as a part of human nature without any overlay of moral evaluation. Sex is something that people naturally do because of genetic and biological programming that is not really under their control. It is not seen in terms of the sacred (as in Jehovanism) nor is it seen as political (as it is by the Gnostics). Sex is seen by Naturalists as no big deal, or else is understood as a positive force for the individual and benign in effect on people generally. It is, for Naturalists, simply a biological function, and that's *all* it is. Sex has no metaphysics and no cosmic meaning for Naturalists. In essence, the Naturalist position treats sex as little more than motion rather than action; hence, Naturalists just get on with it and don't make it into a big deal of any sort at all, something having connection neither to society at large nor to religion—it's all about pelvises and that's it.

Various famous social scientific reports about sex tend to be Naturalist in tone, but also blow away the fantasy/hypocrisy for many people as well. The Kinsey reports in the 1940s and 1950s (Kinsey, Pomeroy, & Martin, 1948; Kinsey, Pomeroy, Martin, & Gebhard, 1953) and the Hite Report in the 1970s (Hite, 1976) served to naturalize and hence to normalize sexual activity by means of the presentation of statistics. The Internet has also had a similar effect more recently by broadcasting the activities that other people are up to. Once people begin to read about the frequency of use of different sexual practices; variety of sexual positions; frequency of intercourse in people of the same sorts of social groups as themselves (age groups, economic groups, religious groups, for example, the sorts of groups created by demographers to analyze their results), then people begin to say, "Hey! What I am doing is normal" or else complain that "I'm not getting as much as everyone else."

Such statistics and Internet images raise people's awareness and create both contagion and envy. The statistical presentation of information tends to set people both standards and targets by implicitly suggesting that what is most likely (or most common in the population) is also most acceptable and correct. It also stimulates them to a different understanding (epistemic) of what is moral or acceptable.

Statistical evidence presented by the above reports and by Internet images tends to naturalize masturbation or adultery by reporting on the frequency and generality with which it occurs, using such reports as implicit justifications for the activity ("If everyone else is doing it, then why shouldn't I?"). If the activities that were previously suspected and outlawed (by Jehovanists) can be demonstrated statistically to be quite prevalent (and masturbation was found by Kinsey and others to be almost universal), then the very fact that everyone is doing it tends to render it pragmatically, if not morally, acceptable.

Naturalists see inhibition of sexual activity as an infringement of natural human life but do not give it a greater deal of significance as a part of life than any other features of humanity, such as diet, exercise, liberty of conscience, or education. Rather, they naturalize it as part of the human right to the pursuit of happiness. Sex is just a part of the whole but not an unduly significant nor weighty part.

DISCUSSION QUESTION

When should any kind of sexual activity happen within a relationship? If you went on a third date and there was no sexual activity, have you really missed the boat? Have you ended up in the "friendship zone" where it will never be possible to make a move?

Epistemics and Various Social Orders

In all of the above three epistemics—and for different reasons and with different purposes—repression of sexual activity is a repression of knowledge, but for the Jehovanists, it is a necessary, religiously inspired strictness; for the Gnostics, it is a sinister political repression; and for the Naturalists, it is just a silly, pointless, and overdone repression.

In the discussion, I have treated the subject matter as something about which there are three epistemics. I have not addressed the issue of whether there is a men's epistemic and a women's epistemic, or a gay epistemic and a lesbian epistemic, yet all of these exist and are similar but different. I'm going to leave some of this for your own reflective contemplation but will address the double standard for men and women in sexual behavior below. Note that in heterosexual relationships, the female is normally the gatekeeper of sexual activity both in fact and in law (rape is defined in terms of the withholding of the woman's consent, not just in terms of the violence inflicted). You should also think about the effects of being made responsible in this way. In addition, in gay and lesbian relationships, the issue of gate keeping is one surrounded with dilemmas as an issue of role management, where one or both persons also assumes, accepts, or refuses the responsibility (Huston & Schwartz, 1995).

The above discussion has focused on sex in relation to epistemics and has only implicitly connected it to the prevailing social order. I have noted that most social orders approve of marriage and disapprove of sex outside marriage, but this takes more than one form. The form that attracts less social disapproval, on the whole, tends to be sex *before* (outside) marriage. Although many religions stress that sex should not occur until marriage has approved it, Western societies are more tolerant of youthful experimentation than of other forms of sex after (but outside) marriage, namely, adultery.

It is rather interesting to explore the work that has been done on affairs (Duncombe, Harrison, Allan, & Marsden, 2004), adultery (Kipnis, 1998), and inappropriate relationships (Goodwin & Cramer, 2002), because it is clear that the conduct of an affair connects quite directly to the epistemic, surprisingly. People feel that they know the world differently and are different people—their true self—when they engage in affairs and report that affairs liberate them and give their true self an expression that is not felt within the constraints of marriage (VanderVoort & Duck, 2004).

ILLEGAL, MORALLY REJECTED, AND DISAPPROVED FORMS OF SEX

All of the above discussion has put the activities of sex into a framework based on what it *means* and how those forms of meaning affect social orders. In commenting in this way, I have so far skirted one important form of sexual relationship, the form that is regarded by all major epistemics as inappropriate within the prevailing social order (such as adultery and incest) (e.g., Goodwin & Cramer, 2002; Duck & VanderVoort, 2002). By definition, these represent a form of sex that is outlawed or at least regarded as morally corrupt (VanderVoort & Duck, 2004). You can see from the previous discussion that any abnormal form of sexual activity can be seen as involving an epistemic shift or at least taking an epistemic position that takes the participants away from the normal way of knowing and toward an alternative universe of understanding, both different and, from the point of view of the social order, deviant, and to be morally condemned.

Quite recently—in fact, surprisingly late into the scheme of things—relationship researchers have turned to the question of inappropriate relationships and the nature of affairs (Duncombe et al., 2004; Goodwin & Cramer, 2002). You may now be able to see several reasons why these sorts of relationships are of some interest when they are seen not as random motion—merely irresponsible biological fluid exchange (so romantic!)—but an action that can contest a social order. I will go into some issues here in detail in a minute, but can you say why you might feel uneasy if your father admitted to you that he is having an affair? How would you feel if your sister told you that she is a lesbian? What if your brother announced to you that he is a pedophile? How about if your mother told you that she had sex with about five dozen different men before she got married? What about *after* she was married to your father? And how about you? Do you ever look at pornography or imagine your friends or bosses naked? How would you feel if your CEO or class instructor called you into the office and proposed having sex right there? And would it make a difference if there were windows in the office that allowed others to see in?

These questions are intended to get you thinking about the boundaries around your sexual comfort zone, as it were. What aspects of sexuality do you find disturbing, if any? Are some forms of relationship more shocking to you than others? This is a big question. Where one person is disempowered, the other is empowered, and the power balance is essential for there to be an equivalence between relationship and the sexual act. How do you and how does society organize its map of what is acceptable, what is doubtful, and what is abominable? As you will already be thinking on the basis of the previous discussion, why does society even care about this? Perhaps there can be a fear of chaos, threats to the social order, conformity, law and order, and sanctions without any need to be a Jehovanist or a Gnostic.

> At the time of writing, Tiger Woods, previously a symbol of purity, had just been discovered to be having multiple affairs, and this has engendered much discussion in the public sphere. By the time you read this, you will know a lot more about the outcome than I can possibly guess, but I am certain it will continue to get a lot of press coverage and attract expressions of moral outrage.

Society—the social order—does not like people to have affairs: You may have sex with your spouse, but you may not have sex with someone else's spouse. Society has a definite opinion about the appropriateness of partnerships, and the generalized other (see Chapter 4), often in the form of media such as TV or popular magazines, takes a curious interest in such partnerships. It is not just abstract media that do this—you watch and buy these media products, so you are complicit in the effects of media on society. Why is this? It needs a closer look, and you now have the tools to understand it in terms of epistemics and the relationship of epistemics to social orders.

Let's start with a topic mentioned in the Ten Commandments: adultery. Most societies condemn it, and in some religions, the punishment is particularly brutal, especially for the woman—stoning or beheading, for example. Why is adultery so important that it is one of only 10 subjects discussed directly between God and people? After all, at some level, adultery is just two people doing what married people do, but in this case, they are not married to one another but to other people. How does this activity apparently threaten society in its own eyes and offend its gods? And what do you make of the fact that according to some surveys, 70% of Americans say that they have committed it (Kipnis, 1998)?

Adultery involves a transgression against the social institution of marriage and its explicit prescription that the two partners who marry each other henceforth will have sex only with one another. We've already seen, earlier in the chapter, how such vows are positioned within an epistemic based on Jehovanist religions. It might follow, then, that people committing adultery

> Queer Theory is proposing new approaches to a social order of heteronormativity that essentially destabilize assumptions about relationships and how they may be embodied or performed. Several social scientists have used Queer Theory to explore the ways in which heterosexual norms are often subconsciously queer, counternormative, disruptive, and challenging to the social order.

know that they are breaking rules and so see one another and themselves as contrasted with the epistemic that the religion encourages them to adopt. In short, they may see themselves as contrasted with their social order. To put this another way, the adulterers must see themselves as different people from those who follow the conventions of their social order. They are above it or transcend it as far as they see it. They have enough arrogance to balance or overwhelm the guilt.

AFFAIRS AS WAYS OF KNOWING AND BEING

Do you, then, know the world differently when you are in affairs as opposed to regular intimacies? According to Kipnis (1998), an affair transports its actors, if only temporarily, from ordinary life, while assuring them that ordinary life will be there waiting when they return, as long as they succeed in hiding the transgression. If you ask people who have affairs, have extra dyadic relationships, or cheat (Dunscombe et al., 2004), then you rapidly find that they say that the affair makes them feel like the real person that they are. In other words, they report (as Mead's work discussed in Chapter 4 might predict) that having an affair makes them feel about the world and themselves differently, and it makes them feel real. They report that it makes them feel more fulfilled, more themselves. Note, however, that "real" is equivalent to "free" in this context. They are unencumbered by roles and responsibilities and rules within role definitions. They haven't had to do the vacuuming and pay the bills or mow the lawn on that particular day.

In contrast to the negative images of marriage as a routine, and eventually somewhat boring, arrangement, affairs are reported as liberating and fantastic epistemics. Cheaters and adulterers can easily present themselves as risk-takers who feel, if only briefly, able to re-create their real, true selves and take a more positive view of their lives. Kipnis (1998) reports that adulterers rejoice that discontent is not an inescapable human condition; rather, affairs snatch moments of passion and sublime joy from months and years of vague unhappiness (Kipnis, 1998). This contrast with the routine predictability of mundane marriage gives affairs a special feel, or a new way of knowing. In Tolstoy's *Anna Karenina*, Anna believes that she and her lover will be punished for being so happy. There is not only the obvious risk of social disapproval if they are found out, but also the punishing pain of her own inability to leave her husband, translated into excuses about not wanting to hurt him or the children and feeling obliged to honor her marriage vows. This unwillingness to engage with and challenge chronic unhappiness at its source is what Kipnis (1998) sees as the heart of the matter and one that entirely fits my analysis in terms of not only personal but also social orders:

> My point is that what is so ordinary and accepted as to go quite unnoticed in all of this is simply that toxic levels of everyday unhappiness or grinding boredom are the functional norm in many lives and marriages; that adultery, in

some fumbling way, seeks to palliate this, under conditions of enforced secrecy that dictate behavior ranging from bad to stupid to risky to deeply unconscious; and that shame, humiliation, and even ruin accompany the public exposure of this most ordinary of circumstances. (Kipnis, 1998, p. 319)

Affairs are special ways of knowing because they disconnect adulterers from the ordinariness of daily life. Typically, they are carried out in epistemic settings other than the physical spaces and material regularities of ordinary life—in hotels, resorts, conferences, fast cars, back rooms, snatched moments of illicit joyfulness separated from the tedious monotony of the everyday life that the partners otherwise lead. Whereas the failures and drawbacks of spouses are a familiar complaint in affairs ("My partner does not understand me"), most adulterous partners never have to be experienced in the context of a continuous and ordinary life or the boring household routines, decisions, and everyday talk in which a spouse is necessarily involved.

For adulterous relationships, there is a lack of contact with mundane reality, and the erotic fantasy of the affair is made possible by its lack of contact with the trivial, routine life that is normally the married partners' experience of one another (laundry, cleaning, cooking, doing the dishes). Because adulterers can remain happily ignorant of the routine and trivial aspects of each other's lives, their idealized fantasies about each other remain unchallenged and are easier to accept, and often lead to them experiencing themselves as different beings, as Mead would predict. The removal from one epistemic (the mundane and the trivial) to another (the idealized and fantastic) itself makes it possible to forget what ordinary life is like and hence to experience self in a different way from the customary one.

The other level of analysis (social order) applies here, too, in that the social order condemns affairs because they "threaten the very fabric of society" as is usually pompously stated each time a famous person is caught in the act. Society likes marriage and family and sees them as stabilizing factors, as noted earlier. Therefore, adultery is an implicit threat to that stability in that it threatens the institution of marriage. Adulterers thus must be publicly condemned even though so many Americans admit that they have committed it. Interestingly, it's all about epistemics, one of which, alas, is the place of women as under the control of men. Therefore, in some societies, the punishment of women caught in adultery is largely disproportionate to the punishment meted out to the male partner.

The social order is threatened if there are lots of people going around out there saying to themselves, "I am more 'me' when I am an adulterer than when I am just a married person." Such a sentiment would tend—if it became widely known as something that millions and millions of people were thinking—to create a statistical normalization of adultery and hence to undermine people's confidence in marriage (and the family) as a source of personal satisfaction and as a normal and natural state of humankind. Violent punishment of adultery is thus to do with the preservation of institutions in the social order.

Kipnis (1998) took a slightly different view, which is nevertheless consistent with my analysis, namely, that the institution of marriage is both necessary to social stability and also one inherently dissatisfying for very many people. Because it is necessary to society, Kipnis argues, society must treat dissatisfaction with the institution as an individual fault and failing rather than as a societal one. Hence, punishment of adulterers is calculated to castigate their individual weakness and moral disgrace, partly, Kipnis says, as a way to deflect everyone else from questioning the value of marriage as an institution in itself.

Either way, the analysis of sexual behavior, the reasons for society's interest in it, and the way in which it is regulated all relate to social orders of relationships and to an implicit hierarchy of relating that validates preferred relational forms and at the same time reinforces certain social values. Epistemics, hierarchy, and terministic screens about relating reflect the fact that relationships are ways of knowing as well as ways of expressing or ways of being.

The chapter has continued the connection between relational behavior and epistemics or knowledge, and between personal and social orders. In both normal sex and the activities of both sexes that are not permitted by a society, individuals are performing and embodying selves, personal orders, and epistemics that may conform with or confront those of the social order. However, at its root, sex is about epistemics, knowledge, and the way in which those connect personal orders to social orders. Even in the most apparently private activities, epistemics and social orders still rule. It is quite a shame that personal relationship researchers and researchers in sexuality do not work more closely together, because this would represent a clear development from the old ways of thinking about relationships. Perhaps this chapter will encourage people to think along collaborative lines because sexual activity is rarely dissociated from relational considerations in everyday life.

PEDAGOGICAL ISSUES

EXERCISES

Consider the number of times that your friends and you discuss anything to do with the nature of sex or sexuality. Evaluate the number of times that you discuss another person's sexual behavior in terms of a social order of moral standards.

ETHICAL QUESTIONS

Are hookups ethical? What about friends with benefits? Is it ethical to date your best friend's ex-partner? Give your reasons for your answers to all of these questions and debate them in class.

MEDIA QUESTIONS

There are TV shows about "cougars." What is that fact doing to affect social orders about the sorts of behavior and relationships that are acceptable in society? I just watched a CNN analysis that complained that one of the cougars came across as "too needy." What does that tell you about social beliefs about women, sexuality, and the connection between all the women and power? If the programs are intended to promote a certain view of women, but the commentators about those shows relate it directly to the existing social order, then is the social order likely to change?

References

Butler, J. (2004). *Undoing gender.* New York: Routledge.

Davis, M. S. (1983). *SMUT: Erotic reality/obscene ideology.* Chicago: University of Chicago Press.

de Beauvoir, S. (1961). *The second sex.* New York: Bantam Books.

Dow, B. J., & Wood, J. T. (Eds.). (2006). *Sage handbook of gender and communication.* Thousand Oaks, CA: Sage.

Duck, S. W., & VanderVoort, L. A. (2002). Scarlet letters and whited sepulchres: The social marking of relationships as "inappropriate." In R. Goodwin & D. Cramer (Eds.), *Inappropriate relationships: The unconventional, the disapproved, and the forbidden* (pp. 3–24). Mahwah, NJ: Lawrence Erlbaum.

Duncombe, J., Harrison, K., Allan, G., & Marsden, D. (2004). *The state of affairs.* Mahwah, NJ: Lawrence Erlbaum.

Goodwin, R., & Cramer, L. (Eds.). (2002). *Inappropriate relationships: The unconventional, the disapproved, and the forbidden.* Mahwah, NJ: Lawrence Erlbaum.

Hite, S. (1976). *The Hite report on female sexuality.* London and New York: Macmillan.

Huston, M., & Schwartz, P. (1995). Lesbian and gay male relationships. In J. T. Wood & S. W. Duck (Eds.), *Under-studied relationships: Off the beaten track* (pp. 89–121). Thousand Oaks, CA: Sage.

Kinsey, A. C., Pomeroy, W. B., & Martin, C. E. (1948). *Sexual behavior in the human male.* Philadelphia, PA: W. B. Saunders.

Kinsey, A. C., Pomeroy, W. B., Martin, C. E., & Gebhard, P. H. (1953). *Sexual behavior in the human female.* Philadelphia, PA: W. B. Saunders.

Kipnis, L. (1998). Adultery. *Critical Inquiry, 24,* 289–327.

McKinney, K., & Sprecher, S. (Eds.). (1991). *Sexuality in close relationships.* Mahwah, NJ: Lawrence Erlbaum.

Mead, G. H. (1934). *Mind, self, and society.* Chicago: University of Chicago Press.

Paul, E. L. (2006). Beer goggles, catching feelings and the walk of shame: The myths and realities of the hookup experience. In C. D. Kirkpatrick, S. W. Duck, & M. K. Foley (Eds.), *Relating difficulty: Processes of constructing and managing difficult interaction* (pp. 141–160). Mahwah, NJ: Lawrence Erlbaum.

VanderVoort, L. A., & Duck, S. W. (2004). In appropriate relationships and out of them: The social paradoxes of normative and non-normative relational forms. In J. Duncombe, K. Harrison, G. Allan, & D. Marsden (Eds.), *The state of affairs* (pp. 1–14). Mahwah, NJ: Lawrence Erlbaum.

Wood, J. T. (2001). The normalization of violence in heterosexual romantic relationships: Women's narratives of love and violence. *Journal of Social and Personal Relationships, 18,* 239–262.

Wood, J. T. (2004). Monsters and victims: Male felons' accounts of intimate partner violence. *Journal of Social and Personal Relationships, 21*(5), 555–576.

6

Wealth, Place, Gifts, and Rituals

The Material Structures and Practices of Relational Experience

OK, it's all right to put the lights back on! I have stopped writing about sex, and I'll now look beyond your own physical structure to the material world around you and its effects on relationships. Instead of the physicality that carries you around the world, I will turn it about and look at the physical or material world that encloses your relationships. I will now look at other aspects of the material experience beyond your own personal bodily structure. This exploration will connect your relationships to the material circumstances of your life (poverty? riches? modern times? ancient times? good neighborhood? bad neighborhood?), to the solid goods that you exchange with one another to symbolize friendship (gifts, benefits, objects, bequests). Finally, I will explore the physical, ritualized material performances that you carry out as ways to embody or to symbolize relationships. Yes, a hug or holding hands both are material and symbolic; a marriage ceremony is both an embodiment of a social order and a symbol of relational connectivity. All of these matters will concern you in the present chapter. (Keep asking yourself: Where did choice and simple emotion go?)

These are rather different ways to look at the role of embodiment and materiality in relationships from the ones in the preceding chapters on body and sex, but they demonstrate the same principles. Relationships are not simply about choice and emotion but are influenced by the physical world around you and what you do in it. You now know from the previous chapters some of the implications of the fact that embodiment is directly involved in the materiality of knowing and having relationships. What other material factors in life can be relevant to the nature of relationships and how you know them? Material aspects of the broader social world and of living conditions

Listen in on Your Own Life

Make a quick list of your friends, acquaintances, or romantic partners. When the whole list comes to 10 names, stop and indicate for each one whether they are the same race as you, the same religion as you, the same socioeconomic class as you, the same educational level as you, and whether they live more than ten miles away from where you live now or lived when you first met them. Keep this list for later.

more generally also affect your experience of the world and your relationships in it. The present chapter will explore that impact at some length, looking at the economic resources you have available to you—the location of your house in a city or in the country, for example—and the effects on your relationships. This chapter is probably going to be more shocking than the previous one because it deals with things you would never suspect as influences on relationships at all.

The notion that close relationships are private enclaves away from the sight of others has already been challenged earlier, but the notions that relationships should be intimate and that they are based on privacy are also relatively modern. Until quite recently (about 200 years ago for most families, although even then not for very poor ones), people conducted all of their lives in the direct presence of other folks and had virtually no privacy, in the sense that you understand that notion today. Furthermore, your ancestors often believed that relationships were based on loyalty rather than liking, because their physical world was such that reliance on other people was less from love than from necessity, less for emotional support than for assistance.

Your ancestors relied on the help of other people just to be able to eat and stay alive, and that reliance depended not on love but on help with the harvest and the daily tasks of living. If I needed your help in order to stay alive (e.g., I need your help in harvesting the corn that will be used to make the bread that I need to stay alive), then it is not seriously relevant whether or not I like you or would choose you for a conversational partner in a free world.

Consider also how poverty changes one's access to places for conducting relationships, which necessarily occur in more public and open places because one lacks the resources to seclude oneself in a big mansion or private grounds and invite only the people you *want* to come near you. You probably cut back on social networks so that you are not being frequently put into situations where you need to "pay back" someone's invitation to dinner. You may even, in the worst conditions of poverty, be spending your time just looking for any food at all.

This chapter will consider the restrictions on communication that are imposed by access to "place" and ways in which knowledge of the propriety of relationships has changed as a result of these material modifications. I will also look at the ways in which wealth is "moved about" to show affection symbolically in gift giving between friends and relatives, and I will explore some of the meanings of gifts for relationships—including some ways in which gifts *end* relationships!

The Material Circumstances of Relationships

MATERIAL WORLD AND
HISTORICAL FORCES: LIVING WITH DEATH

This section relates relational beliefs and performance directly to various aspects of material existence, looking at availability of resources, nature of place, structure of social rank, and material social exigencies such as poverty and death as factors in how you conceive of yourself in relation to others. So once again, relationships are not just about choice.

To set this up, think about what it is going to be like when you have kids. Will it be a joyful occasion? Something to plan for? Will it be good having them around? Is it good to have kids?

Materiality and Expectations About Love and Childbirth

Will you make a will before you or your partner goes into labor?

Margaret Duck of Egton in North Yorkshire, England, expected to die in childbirth, and as a matter of fact, she was right and died February 8, 1557. She lived in Tudor England in circumstances of reasonable affluence and relative comfort for the time. Her will (dated January 13, 1557) is involved and extensive. She leaves a variety of bequests and gifts ranging from numbers of sheep; quantities of corn; items of furniture (a spinning wheel, a dresser); bedding (two linen sheets, a mattress, two pillows); two specific items of clothing; gowns; kitchen equipment (a brass pot, a little pan, two saucers, and three kettles); and various pieces of hardware, such as a pair of tongs and an iron fire basket with a pot hook, all tools or implements made to order specifically by a blacksmith and therefore expensive. The people who received these bequests would probably have felt quite lucky, although it would be pretty hard to get excited about the bequest of a pillow or a pair of saucers nowadays!

> Objects—not just those left in a will—can remind people of the relationships they were in—sometimes in quite enduring ways. The meaning of gifts is talked about, as well as other material elements. A romantic gift such as a teddy bear could be held on to by an individual as a reminder of a terminated relationship.

Historical Materiality and Beliefs About Relationships

For all her affluence, though, she lived in material circumstances bounded by the prevalence of disease, poor hygiene, and restricted diet (even the humble potato had not yet arrived in England, so she must have died without ever sampling that staple of modern English cuisine, fish and chips). She could have expected only the most basic medical services, founded on superstition, prayer, folk wisdom, and a large element of trial and error. She was probably also afraid of witches, and she specifically requested that when she went into labor, she be "bound in the chains of St. Peter," a church-provided remedy for the pains of childbirth that involved binding the woman in chains that had been blessed by a priest and were obviously, in her case, only as effective as it sounds as if they would be.

How might these circumstances have affected her relationship with other people in her contemporary world, always bearing in mind that I am inviting you to ask yourself the same question about your relationships? Well, for one thing, my research into my own family tree indicates that she would have seen herself as the "natural" inferior of men of her own rank, and as a devout Catholic, she would have trusted that her priest was a directly privileged line of contact with God, as was the common belief at the time. She probably believed that poorer people were simply of a lower order of humanity and hence were there to do her bidding and could be whipped if they did not. She would never have expected to vote, assumed that the best evidence in court cases came only from open confession however extracted (even by torture), thought it right that heretics should be burned alive, and had probably been to a few public hangings.

She would have accepted as perfectly obvious the right of a father or husband to take away and use a woman's possessions for himself unless she had written and duly executed a legally binding will that established her own rights over matters that women were legally permitted to control at that time (in her case, money, some kitchen property, and animals, but no land or other real estate). She would likely not have expected to be asked whom she should marry and would have seen it as her father's right to make the choice for her, although in fact, the style of her will suggests that she was a strong, independent (and, incidentally, unmarried) woman who might have had her own ideas about that. But she would have shared some other interesting, more personal, relational ideas with her contemporaries.

Material Circumstances and Parental Love

For one thing, life was precarious, and attachments were a reflection of that. Stone (1979) notes that Tudor parents rarely formed strong attachments to their children, mostly because those children were almost guaranteed to be dead before they were 5 years old. Why make the emotional investment?

In any case, contraception was not widely available, and you'd probably have another replacement child by next year anyway. Children were sometimes given nonunique names in the same family because parents assumed that, at best, only one of them would make it to adulthood, so by naming three consecutive sons "John," say, they stacked the odds that one of the Johns would make it to the age where he could take over the family name and the family farm. Often, new children were given the name of the child who had most recently died. Likewise, in the Chosun Dynasty in Korea (1392–1910), parents did not record children's names in the family register until they were 10 years old because of high child mortality rates (Cho, personal communication, April 14, 2009).

One in 10 women died in childbirth during her fertile years, one in 30 births was stillborn—all that trouble and pain for nothing (or was it a relief?), and one in 20 births resulted in the death of either mother or child. *One in 20.* Think how you might view the world differently if that were still true today, where live births are 95% of all births (https://www.cia.gov/library/publications/the-world-factbook/geos/us.html) and the death of the mother in childbirth is as low as 12 per 100,000 in the United States.

Power in Relationships in the Face of Death

In Margaret's world, most people died young, and there would be few old people around. Life expectancy even 100 years later, in 1640, was less than 32 years. One in four kids died before the age of 5, very often—and here's the interesting *relational* point—because of culpable neglect (child endangerment). Particularly in less wealthy families, for most people—especially city dwellers—at that time, kids were economically crippling nuisances who simply interfered both before birth and after birth with the ability of the mother or of both parents to carry out their work, hence endangering the family's economic survival. Infants were invariably swaddled (meaning that they were wrapped up so tight that so they could not move about and be a problem).

On the farm, as opposed to in the city, where material circumstances were somewhat different, children were more likely to be welcomed only because they represented a potential growth to the labor pool, and once they could walk about, they would be put to work.

Large families became problematic later in their lives, however, because the farmer had to bequeath his (yes!) farm to someone, and the rule in Tudor times was that the eldest surviving son got it all, with no provision made for daughters, younger sons, or the farmer's own wife, except in special circumstances. The farmer (or his inheriting eldest son) could choose to be generous to his other children and his wife, but this was by no means expected, and even the wife and other children themselves would not have expected it. They *knew* that the rule was "eldest son gets it all," and so they lived with the idea.

For these reasons, the father and the eldest son had tremendous power over the other children and the wife/mother, who had no legal rights of her own. Thus, in Tudor times, as also later, there was a strong and direct relational connection between wealth, resources, and family dynamics. That makes the point of this chapter over and above the ways in which material circumstances of living influenced people's general views about children and other people.

Relationships With Children in a World of Uncertainty

Children were seen as closest to the natural state of (precivilized) human beings, and hence were still bearers of the original sin that characterized fallen man. From this line of reasoning, it apparently followed that children were in need of perpetual beating to have the sin thrashed out of them. Consequently, the parental relationship was rather closer to being one of ministering angel of death rather than loving, as you understand the term. Kids probably had very good reasons to hate their parents, who no doubt treated them very harshly; abused them both physically and psychologically; and dealt with them arbitrarily with respect to inheritance, career disposition, and marriage arrangements (about which the children were rarely, if ever, consulted).

> Violence between parents and children was not at all uncommon 400 years ago, and the whole idea of a "rule of thumb" has been suggested to reflect the thickness of the stick with which a man was allowed to beat his wife and children!

Thus, you cannot presume that parental love of children and vice versa is natural. Rather, it is *historically and culturally bound* within a particular social order of expectations and beliefs. It is no more than a fashion in the history of humankind that depends on and relates to the persons' knowledge of what is or was acceptable and appropriate behavior between parents and children—their epistemic and their social order.

Epistemic Effects of Materiality

More than this, other relationships were materially and epistemically different also. Of course, marriage itself was arranged by parents or other circumstances (such as the luck of the draw about who in your local village area was of marriageable age when you became marriageable yourself). Stone (1979) has calculated that the average length of marriage at this time was a little more than 10 years. Three out of every four first marriages ended during the first 10 years, often through the death of the wife in childbearing. The modern divorce rate (at 50%) therefore is little more than a substitute for the ending of marriages that was previously brought about by death. Once again, the social order and the relational assumptions current at the time are quite different from the assumptions that you make now.

How many people do you know who have had smallpox, cholera, typhus, diphtheria, or malaria? Cholera and typhus were largely caused by the proximity of disposal of the waste of human life to the water supply, but this dangerous connection was not realized until about 1850. Until that time, poverty and disease were very common, and death from unexplained causes was quite familiar. People must have expected to drop dead inexplicably and saw death all around them fairly frequently. You don't—and this affects the respective ways that you have and they had relationships.

You expect your relationships to last for many years, and most people are not particularly concerned about immediacy of death until they are old. This goes away if we have a near-death experience (Secklin, 2001). So the ways that you have relationships and see relationships may be different as a result of these historical circumstances and the fact that relationships can be expected to last longer. If death is so present in your living experience that you don't know whether people you see here today will be here tomorrow, your belief about their value as friends might be diminished and your willingness to invest emotion in them might be decreased. Nowadays, as those who have had a near-death experience can testify, we are more likely to appreciate the friend's presence and to fully cherish and value the relationships that are dearest (Secklin, 2001).

Also consider other aspects of modern material and relational life. Not only are you restrained and enabled by your abilities to move around freely in cars or to contact distant folks by email or telephone, but your physical environment and physical circumstances affect the ways in which you communicate and relate. In some ways this is obvious: for example, if my sister is at Michigan State and I am in a school in France, then I have to communicate with her via phone and email rather than face to face and that may be OK. In other ways, its consequences are unimagined.

Consider also the role of transport, not only in its effects on ability to get together (or to get away from each other), but also in what it does to concepts of relational possibility. The ability to travel less than 20 miles a day must affect expectations about contacts, who is a stranger, and who can be reached. Patterns in 17th-century marriage suggest great unlikelihood of anyone marrying out of the parish (Stone, 1979).

MATERIAL EFFECTS ON RELATIONSHIPS

Why bring this up? Well, obviously, all these examples serve to make the point that the surrounding material circumstances of your life make a difference to your expectations about relationships with such issues as children, marriage, and love. If your life is hard, cruel, and arbitrary, then your relationships with other people are of a different sort from the ones that you nowadays expect as normative in a society where material circumstances are more favorable. In explaining relationships even today, then, it is always important to keep in mind the material situation and the everyday circumstances in which they are conducted, including the historical situations and circumstances.

You may be horrified at, or enlightened by, knowledge of historical circumstances applying to relationships long ago, but in fact, you are equally constrained and enabled by your own material experiences in ways comparable to those affecting your historically distant ancestors. Like them, you take the circumstances so much for granted that you do not typically articulate them. They weren't all sitting around seeing themselves as some step on the next progression of social evolution and wishing they had mobile phones, any more than we see ourselves that way and sit and dream about the changes that the next 200 years will bring to our descendants' relational life. It is literally unimaginable (or at least not accurately imaginable). Yet in 200 years' time, people will sit around and wonder uncomprehendingly at the way we do things, just as we do about the 1700s and 1800s. We'll probably give them a good laugh! And if any of my descendants are absorbing this on Phinkobame, "Hi from your great-great-great-grandfather! Good luck with your genomic certification and relationship permits from the government."

Remember once again that your ways of presenting and processing information arise from social interaction (Chapter 4), and that social interaction always, even today, occurs in historical, social, and economic circumstances that you usually do not notice because, like the air, they are all around you and hard to see because they are so obvious and taken for granted.

There is a rather fine and well-preserved Roman latrine at Housesteads in England consisting of some 20 seats arranged open-plan in two facing rows, where apparently a considerable amount of social interaction took place. The bodily activities therefore were not truly private in those days but conducted communally, and they were often accompanied by social conversation, a bit like Facebook with toilet paper (although the Romans used their own personal sponge on a stick).

MATERIALITY OF LIVING: LIVING WITHOUT PRIVACY

The broad point about material circumstances has other elements that can reconnect you to the present day more directly. As already noted, it is only quite recently that people have had so much access to privacy and the choice of whether or not to forfeit it. Before the 1600s, people lived in large communal huts or castles and other shared dwellings and performed all of their life functions in those places, eating, sleeping, excreting, and copulating where other people could see.

Hence, the concept of privacy as you understand it had not yet flourished, and until the architecture of buildings was changed, the idea of privacy did not really catch on at all. Even the four-poster bed, with curtains mostly intended to keep out the drafts rather than prying eyes or ears, would most likely have been in the same room as the place where the servants and children all slept, namely, the family/household bedroom. Stone (1979) notes,

> The most striking change in the life-style of the upper classes in the seventeenth and eighteenth centuries was the increasing stress laid upon personal privacy. The great houses of the fifteenth and sixteenth centuries had been constructed of interlocking suites of rooms without corridors, so that the only way of moving about was by passing through other people's chambers. In the late seventeenth and the eighteenth centuries, however, house plans allocated space to corridors, which now allowed access without intruding upon privacy. Inventories of goods show a decline in the practice of putting truckle beds here, there and everywhere. Most bedrooms were transferred upstairs, leaving the ground floor for living-quarters. Although public rooms remained large, there was a proliferation of smaller rooms where daily life was increasingly led. (pp. 169–170)

We could add that as the number of rooms extended, so, too, did the acts performed in those rooms become specialized and appropriate to the space. Instead of eating, sleeping, and socializing in the same communal hall, people started to have bedrooms, living rooms, dining rooms, and even studies and libraries—at least if they were wealthy. Hence, the separation of functions led to the conduct of certain kinds of relating in certain kinds of rooms and not in others. Indeed, the Victorian "drawing room" (nowadays less common than it was, but the second of two living spaces) derives from "withdrawing room," the room to which company withdrew after dinner in order to converse and entertain one another. To underline the point, relationship norms were altered in tandem with changes in the physical arrangement in houses, but only for the wealthy folks with houses of their own.

Material Privacy and Personal Intimacy

You may suppose that we are drifting off the topic of relationship, but we are not. If you reflect for a moment, you will see that your current notion of relationships is based on intimacy, self-disclosure, and personal knowledge of other people. But these concepts have no meaning without a concept of privacy or of a self, a *demarcated* self, and of individuality. There is less to disclose *about* if there is no specifically separated and recognized individual mental activity on which to report. In a communal world where everyone knew all aspects of everyone else's activities, which was, in any case, conducted in public, then any concept of separate identity really meant very little. This element of interchangeability in social life was simply another instance of it, rather like when children were given nonunique names. Indeed, Stone (1979) notes that the broad sense in society at the time was very much based on the notion of the beehive, where one bee is much the same as any other bee and simply helps in doing the communal work without having a special identity. All serve a royal master but otherwise act interchangeably in concert toward the common good.

Although architectural and other material aspects of life thus might seem a little off target for this book, they are nonetheless quite central to the argument that relating and knowing are tightly bound up with embodiment and the physical spaces for relating in the first place. Reorganization of the structure of households is important. A shift from one common dining and sleeping area to places marked off for different purposes and away from other people is a significant shift in *relationship* thinking, because it starts to exclude other people, to draw boundaries around behavior in a way that says, "This is mine. Keep out. Yours is over there, not here."

The relevance of these matters continues today, because changes in household organization tend to bring about relational shifts also. If you look at old pictures of the household in the 1940s, you will see the dining table in the middle of the living area, with an implication of its centrality in social life of the family, and comfortable chairs grouped around a fireplace or perhaps the radio. In the 1950s and 1960s, TV took over, and so furniture and house layouts likewise shifted so that the TV became the center of the layout. The social organization of the living space was focused away from people and onto the TV itself.

The same thing is happening in your time, as people set up computer areas that demarcate them from other members of the family and hence further reduce family interaction, and PlayStation® or videogames do much the same (Mesch, 2006). For this reason, family arguments often occur over the placing of the computer in the household space and whether it should be in a communal area or specifically well away from it, although the development of laptops and wireless networks makes the drawing of boundaries delicately smudged (Duck, 2007). Also consider the implications for romantic and family communication patterns if you have a TV in the bedroom, or only in the living room, or if you do not have one at all (yeah!). Think about the effect of whether you have a backyard, porch, or sundeck.

Materiality, Aesthetics, Household Arrangements, and Relationships

The implications for relating are subtle but significant. If you have no back porch, then you cannot sit outside in the evening with friends and just chat about the day. If you have no backyard, then it means that you cannot have a dog and invite other friends' dogs over to play.

The broad point here, then, is that you should not look only at the aesthetic forms of household arrangement, but also look at what it does materially, what the material arrangements imply for relationships, and what they bring about for relationship conduct. The material layout of the house has relational effects.

You already know (Chapter 5) that people routinely arrange the furniture for "social effect," particularly when bent on seduction. The reason that you do this is because the placing of the goods and the furniture and the lighting affect the material space for relating, and that, in turn, changes what is acceptable, allowable—and expected—relational activity.

Although you have probably had experience of that aspect of the material world, I wonder if you can see how the principle operates more broadly, and are thinking about the way materiality affects the relational epistemic. If you can change the materiality of social space and make a relational consequence, then it follows that differences in materiality of social space affect the relationship epistemic in other ways, too.

To put this a third way, those people in a culture with access to fewer physical and material resources than those available to others in the culture might experience and *know* relationships in a different way.

Therefore, you should not assume that all people in a particular culture share the same view of the nature of relationships in that culture (Duck & McMahan, 2010). Some are able to access certain resources that others cannot; people mix with different sorts of people and so epistemically experience the world and the world of relationships differently from one another. For example, those with greater access to society's material resources (wealth and prosperity) can conduct their relationships in greater seclusion and in expensive private places (large homes) not available to those with fewer resources, who are packed into smaller shacks or crowded living accommodations or much more public places, such as bars (Allan, 2008). The greater your access to space and privacy, the greater your chances of conducting intimate relationships in those private spaces.

Material Social Circumstances and Relationships

A stronger way of making this point is to generalize the idea: Context and material circumstances influence relationships in a number of ways. Sociologist Graham Allan (1998) says that there is no pure form of a relationship. "Its form and content are inevitably influenced by the circumstances—or contexts—under which it is constructed" (Allan, 1998, p. 689). Although I have elaborated this idea in the example from the Tudors, the general notion is that social and material constraints associated with social class shape relationship formation and enactment even today and not just in periods of history other than your own. Because these influences affect the person's epistemic and personal order, it therefore follows that material experience of the world shapes and is reflected through one's material circumstances and that fees affect relationships.

Material and social resources influence the initiation and selection of relationships in some unexpected ways that go alongside those physical, bodily factors that you saw in Chapters 3 and 4.

DISCUSSION QUESTION

List the material circumstances other than embodiment of sex/gender that may affect your relationships. How has the conduct of your relationships been affected by the introduction of Facebook, Twitter, and YouTube? What difference does it make that you have constant access to your friends through your cell phone? Do you ever wish you didn't?

LIVING CONDITIONS AND RELATIONSHIPS

First, the environment in which one lives and works plays an important role in relationship formation. Physical closeness (proximity) has long been recognized as an important factor in formation, maintenance, and dissolution of relationships, and a very early study was devoted to discovering the effects of such closeness on the relationships found in a housing facility. Social psychologist Leon Festinger and his colleagues (Festinger, Schachter, & Back, 1950) showed that

> people who lived close to one another became friendly with each other, while people who lived far apart did not. Mere "accidents" of where a path went or whose doorway a staircase passed were major determinants of who became friends within this community. (p. 10)

However, opportunities to meet other people (such as those created by living near the mailbox where people tended to go quite often) increased chances for interaction, which, in turn, increased opportunities for relationship development.

Festinger and his colleagues made a quite subtle observation here in that *functional* proximity mattered more than actual proximity. The difference here is the difference between opportunities to meet, on one hand, and simple physical distance, on the other hand. *Physical proximity* refers to the actual physical distance between you and someone else; *functional proximity* refers to the ways in which you use that proximity, if, indeed, you use it at all. Also, functional proximity removes human choice or decision and free will, so attraction or at least association is forced by similarity of position. In reality, you are closer, physically, to the person who inhabits the dorm room or apartment directly above yours than you are to the person who is two doors down on your hall-way, but you are more likely to meet the second person reasonably often and not the first one. Hence you are, on balance, much more likely to form a rela-tionship with the person on your hallway (the functionally closer one) rather than the one upstairs (the physically closer one).

Note also that individuals who live in the same sort of place tend to have similar levels of economic resources and so are not only physically closer but also sociologically similar. Because material, economic, and educational resources influence where one lives and works, people in the same location tend to be users of the same material resources. This tends to create more opportunities to meet people of similar rather than different economic cir-cumstances. Consider how unlikely it is that a wealthy bachelor living on a large estate out in the countryside would meet and form a relationship with a single, working-class young woman living in an inner-city apartment. They are socially distant because they are materially different. For these and other related reasons, sociologists have long noted that individuals form relation-ships predominantly with individuals from similar socioeconomic and cultural backgrounds (Kerckhoff, 1974).

OK, so now look back at the list of names and characteristics that you wrote out at the start of the chapter. Let me guess that most of the people are very similar to you in most material and sociodemographic respects. You might like to reflect on this or discuss with friends whether you really have as much real freedom of choice about your friendships and romances as you are often led to believe that you do. Look at how the material circumstances of your life (socioeconomic status, race, living place, and so on) are reflected in your friendships that you "choose." Consider whether you actually exercise complete freedom of choice over relationships that you like to think you can choose, or whether, in fact, it turns out that you "prefer" people whose mater-ial circumstances are very similar to your own. We'll come back to that later, so store it somewhere on a back burner.

Questions to Ask Your Friends

Ask your friends how much freedom of choice they believe they have in their relationships. How many of your friends are introduced to you by somebody else and then became friends later? How many of your romantic partners have a friend in common with you who may have made the introduction between you?

POVERTY, RESOURCES, AND RELATIONSHIPS

Graham Allan (2008) also notes that material circumstances do not simply channel people into relationships with others from similar backgrounds but also influence the way in which individuals in relationships talk and relate to one another and conduct their intimacies. Social and material resources constrain the activities in which individuals are able to participate, shape knowledge and attitudes about how to have relationships with others, and direct the places and ways in which relationships are performed.

As a simple example, activities like yachting, high-stakes poker playing, and eating out at gourmet restaurants with friends all require lots of money. People with poor access to material resources cannot have their friends come to a large and comfortable house for dinner, with a visit to their own personal wine cellar and an evening of listening to sublime Vaughan Williams CDs on expensive stereo equipment. Instead, poorer people are more likely to socialize in common spaces, such as bars or pubs where consumable items are less expensive, and so the entertaining of friends costs less, and being entertained involves one in less demanding levels of reciprocity. If I buy you a beer, then you need only buy me a beer later in order to even things out; you do not have to take me for a four-star meal and give me a bottle of vintage port afterward. In addition, the jukebox provides the musical support for relatively little cost, not all of which I have to pay for myself, if I am lucky. Consider also other material influences on the way your relationships feel and work and are experienced.

You can often experience relationships on the basis of changes in material circumstances. Long-distance romantic relationships can be painful as a result of a change in material situation, and nobody looks forward to the separations implied in a long-distance relationship.

Materiality and Spontaneity

Just as with the relationships of the chronically ill or disabled (Chapter 4), there is a lack of spontaneity—planning has to take the place of spontaneity in a long-distance relationship. People have to arrange to be available at a given time, although the prevalence of mobile phones now makes this easier. Dates have to be arranged thoughtfully and plans laid in ways that are not the case with spontaneous, face-to-face, proximal relationships. The amount of time it takes to get in touch with people these days has created a material change, and the fact that you can get in touch with people more or less whenever you want to is a material difference from relationships a hundred years ago or even 20 years ago, before there were mobile telephones. But again, materiality—in this case, distance or access to technology—affects relational experience for good or ill. Constant availability has its drawbacks.

Relational performance is shaped to a large extent by access to material and social resources. These resources constrain the types of activities in which one can participate and may shape attitudes about different types of activities. These resources also influence relational behavior. Individuals learn how to behave in relationships to a large extent from parents and other social role models, as you saw in Chapter 3. The epistemic defects of material social resources are then reflected in their relational behavior.

Material Gifts and Relationships

SYMBOLS AND RELATING: TIE SIGNS AND GIFTS

As I noted earlier, in her will, Margaret Duck left bequests and gifts to others, and these were signs of her connection with, and liking for, those folks. I'm guessing that she gave the most valuable bequests to the highest status and closest relatives or friends, with the servants getting the less important "thank you" gifts, if they got anything at all. The recipients are supposed to recognize that such gifts will remind them of the person who gave them and also honor the relationship and demonstrate, in material form, the respect with which the donor held the recipient. You take it for granted that people will give bequests when they die, but you might not recognize that there is a system of expectations about who gets what.

Allan and Gerstner (2006) describe the trouble that is caused when family members do not get what they are expecting or feel entitled to receive, and, indeed, the whole will itself may be contested in the courts as a result. The same idea that is bound up with the symbolism inherent in gift giving runs through gifts between the living, however. Material gifts are closely tied up with a relationship symbolism. A gift itself is a token of the nature of the relationship as seen by the donor—a view that may shock the recipient. In this section, I will therefore look at the connection between relationships and materiality in this particular sense.

GIFT GIVING

What happens when you give people material gifts? What does it *mean* when you give someone a gift, and what does it mean epistemically for the relationship? You might take it for granted that a gift is a symbol of some kind, although it is not necessary to assume that it is a symbol because it can simply be a service or actual physical help. I will look here at how resources actually come to be *symbolic* and what that means.

Gifts are given at baby showers, weddings, birthdays, and graduation, as well as other rites of passage and during the reading of wills or testaments.

Every single one of these situations is essentially a rite of passage, but you also celebrate a ritual of relating and so tend to give gifts at holidays or on anniversaries. There is a connection here between the giving of gifts and the changing or recognition of status and status change, as in graduation or marriage. There is a marker here for a particular occasion that changes a person's status.

Weddings and baby showers are cases where there is a practical need for people to set up a new household or develop a reliable bank of goods for use in the support of the new life. People set up a registry for weddings and list the gifts that they wish to receive. Hints may be dropped for birthday gifts, but even in other cases, like weddings and baby showers, the gifts are usually symbolic in some way because these occasions are essentially rites of passage that require recognition of a symbolic change in status. What, then, is the epistemic or symbolic connection between gift giving and relationships?

The giving of gifts as symbols of relationship can be an important way in which you present symbolically your connection to others, but these material representations of relationships are parts of a larger system of symbolic representation of relationships. When I come to write specifically about the ways in which gifts "work" relationally, you will be able to interpret those effects in the larger context of symbolic representation of relationships that range from the bodily (Chapter 4) to the symbolic nature of sex (Chapter 5) to the symbolism in material things (this chapter) to the symbols of connectedness between people that come from the *performance* or *embodiment* of relationships.

Gifts are expected to symbolize changes in relationships as they develop, and the lack of gifts (or giving of underwhelming gifts) is also quite telling—particularly in relational progression. If I begin to date someone and his birthday rolls around 2 weeks into the relationship, the gift is expected to be quite different for that birthday compared to the gift I would be expected to give for his birthday if we were still dating 1 year and 2 weeks later. On many levels, the gift I would probably have to give 2 weeks in would be much trickier to determine, too. If the gift were too extravagant or flashy, it could indicate I was too much into the relationship for only 2 weeks. If it were not nice enough, though, it could indicate I did not know how to select a good gift or that maybe I was not into the relationship at all.

Furthermore, many individuals in relationships (particularly women) are asked why they do not yet have an engagement ring—not why they are not yet engaged, but where the ring is—demonstrating both how the gift is seen as expected at a certain progression in the relationship and allowing the relationship to be discussed in a less personal way (through the ring and not the people in the relationship). This is the way in which the expectations of the social order are allowed to come back to the personal level. As Beyoncé put it in "Single Ladies": "If you liked it, then you shoulda put a ring on it."

DISCUSSION QUESTION

Think of examples where you gave or received gifts that were clearly regarded as inappropriate by you-as-receiver or the other-person-as-receiver. What sorts of feelings did that generate in you, and what kinds of social embarrassment were registered in the situation by either party?

THE MEANING OF GIFTS

There have been several studies of the meaning of gift giving and how the exchange of material resources maps onto the symbolism of relationships. In an important sense, gift giving and resource shifting help to manage relationships symbolically, and I will now consider some of the important implications of the ways in which this works. Although the giving of gifts involves material resources, what you need to consider here is the ways in which those material effects serve symbolic functions as signals of friendship, relationships, and status. There can sometimes be something competitive about gift giving, too.

Gifts are rarely given because of need pure and simple, although in the wedding registry, you have an interesting combination of the explicit needs of a couple setting up a household and the ritualized indication of relational bonds between givers and recipients, with closer relatives bringing more significant gifts. The wedding registry and the whole idea that relatives and friends of the married couple give them implements and utensils to help them to set up their household ties relationships to material resources very closely. Yet also, in some interesting ways, gifts tie the friends and relations to the launching of the married couple itself, thus once again stressing the connection of feelings with material resources.

In the case of birthday gifts, these are not intended to be helpful in the ways that wedding gifts are; they are intended to show that you recognize and value the other person and your relationship with him or her—except perhaps at special birthdays like a 21st or 18th, which parents sometimes mark with material gifts intended to launch the former minor into adulthood. Likewise, with gifts at Christmas, the purpose is not really to enhance other people's material life so much as it is intended to show that you value them as people.

There are rules about reciprocity and there are messages about relationships. When you give someone a gift, you are stating something about a relationship. You are stating clearly that you believe that a relationship exists or could exist in the future. You might expect to get something back reciprocally or set up a sense of obligation or a need to pay off an obligation ("a thank-you gift"). The balance between the two gifts is a sign of the relationship.

What is the most serious mistake you can ever make when giving somebody a gift? Answer: leaving the price tag on it, or leaving the gift receipt in the package. If you show somebody what price was paid for the gift, then you are committing the number one error of giving. Therefore, people take the price tags off of gifts because it is gauche to let the recipient see how much you spent; the value of the gift is its symbolism rather than its price. The symbolism is not only in the giving but in the value of the gift and in the reciprocity. It can be a symbol of love, of affection, of relationship. Obligation is something that also results from a particular stylistic act of gift giving.

THEORIES OF GIFT GIVING

Several theories have been offered to explain the giving of gifts. Veblen's (1899/1992) notion of *conspicuous consumption* is well-known: the idea that people in society establish their status by conspicuously consuming goods in excess of their strict needs. Veblen focused on American society, whereas other anthropologists have looked at other cultures where there existed comparable lavish wastage, notable in the ceremony of the "potlatch," involving extravagant giving away of goods, the highest status essentially going to the person who gave away the most (Seguin, 1986).

Conspicuous Giving

Conspicuous consumption may thus take the form of conspicuous giving, and although it may be an excellent outcome for the recipients, the main point for the giver is that you are *seen* to be a giver or a consumer, even if the effect is ultimately helpful. Some philanthropists remain anonymous until after death, fearing that if they give flamboyantly, then the conspicuous giving appears self-serving despite the fact that it benefits those to whom the gift is given. Buildings are sometimes named after donors, and this is an example of conspicuous giving that results in status attainment. In less generous cases, people drive flashy cars or sport a lot of jewelry or eat at expensive restaurants simply to be seen there. In other words, you don't need to go to expensive restaurants to have food, because you could go to McDonald's. People like to be seen in expensive restaurants because there is status in being seen in expensive places, and you achieve relational status through the amount that you spend publicly on inviting friends to dinner at expensive places. *People* magazine even considers lists of such places: If you want to be in the "in" crowd, then you go to these restaurants rather than other ones. Conspicuous giving is therefore a simple extension of the principle that the more you can throw your money or possessions around, the higher status you acquire symbolically.

Redistribution of Wealth

Another possibility to explain the symbolic connection between gifts and relationships is that gifts are a way of *equalizing wealth*, in which case you would expect that wealthy people would give expensive gifts to other people and would not get such valuable gifts in return. If gift giving is about this redistribution of wealth, then you would predict that older and materially better off people could give significant gifts to less wealthy people and not get very valuable gifts in return. This appears to be what happens. The elderly lose out the most. They don't get expensive gifts, they get pointless gifts that aren't of great monetary value because they are viewed as not *needing* anything. (Yet another box of elegant handmade and personalized soaps for Grandma!) The most expensive ones are between husbands and wives. The husband gives more (and more expensive) gifts than the wife does. Spontaneous gifts have more symbolic weight. The symbolic force of gifts is reinforced at certain times of the year and at certain times in life (i.e., Christmas and birthdays). This means that gift giving has a pattern to it.

Patterns of Gift Giving

Sociologist David Cheal (1986) studied holiday gift giving in detail and identified three classes of factors that situate gift behavior. They are to do with interaction processes within personal relationships, the levels of economic resources possessed by people, and social status of the relevant parties.

Cheal suggests that the relational significance of gifts is particularly evident where one gift is matched by a return gift in a process of gift *exchange* or reciprocity of giving. Cheal demonstrated that reciprocal giving is a notable aspect of valuable holiday gift transactions. All the same, personal income, household income, and the general proportion of household income spent on regular living expenses all appear to affect the level of gift expenditure. One interesting result was that gift-giving did not seem to be strictly functional; that is, extended family did not use the occasion of holiday gift transactions to gradually but systematically redistribute wealth from the older generations to the younger.

Cheal also noted that there was little evidence in Christmas gift activity that supported Veblen's views of gift behavior as conspicuous consumption. Instead, social structures, in the form of kinship and gender position, affect the direction in which gifts flow, with most of the valuable Christmas gifts given to primary kin, especially husbands giving wives the most important and expensive gifts. Gifts between the sexes are generally rather asymmetric, with men giving more and women receiving more. All of this reflects materially the relationships between the parties, then, and acts symbolically to reinforce the relational epistemics that apply.

Gift Giving Within a Social Order

Another symbolic/epistemic function of relationship gifts, though, is an indication of *conventional morality* in the social order. The decision to give makes a statement about one's relationships with the social order in which the person lives and contributes to a sense of moral order. For example, the tendency to give gifts that mark significant lengths of relationships (such as a 25th wedding anniversary) tends to reinforce the social norm of the value of long-term endurance in marriage, and so indicates that a *long* marriage is assumed to be marked as a *successful* one.

DISCUSSION QUESTION

A friend of mine was once given a birthday present during her first year as a wife: a vacuum cleaner from her husband. What message do you think that sent about the nature of the relationship, her role in the relationship, and his perception of it?

However, spouses tend to give one another symbolic gifts that indicate the status of the relationship, sometimes in unsubtle form (see the above discussion question), but usually in a way that reflects emotional connection. Normally, anniversary gifts embody love and affection on such occasions, rather than practical value—although it is quite a noticeable exception that hardware stores tend to emphasize the importance of *practical* gifts to fathers during Father's Day celebrations. This reinforces the role of practical skill and service that a father is traditionally supposed to play in a family in this heteronormative social order.

When people get married, the guests present gifts with a specific purpose that helps the couple set up a household. At other times, gift giving is usually done as a way of expressing symbolic affection. There is a middle-class bias here, of course. But people can give someone a practical gift at a particular marked event, when it might be regarded as offensive to give somebody that gift at a nonmarked event—for example, it is okay to give a father a power drill for Father's Day, but not for a baby shower, because the gifts there are supposed to be focused on either the baby or the nature of becoming a parent.

There are different kinds of giving, and people often need an occasion to give a gift; hence, the nature of the occasion helps to define the context for, and appropriateness of, the gift. Therefore, a boss giving an expensive gift to an employee is treated as acting appropriately, whereas an employee giving an expensive gift to a boss is probably regarded as a Brown Nose. However, there can be unwelcome overtones, too. For example, if a man picks up the tab on a date, is that a gift or an implicit intention to create an obligation for relational or even sexual benefits later on? Apparently, both men and women believe that this is a risk.

GIFTS AND RELATIONAL CHANGE

Julie Ruth and her colleagues (Ruth, Otnes, & Brunel, 1999) explored the effects, rather than the purposes, of gift giving and found six basic relational outcomes of gift exchange that I shall explore below: strengthening, affirming positive relationship, negligible effect, affirming negative relationship, weakening, and severing. Before you proceed, you might like to see if you can guess what some of these are and how they work.

Strengthening Relationships

First, Ruth et al. (1999) note that only one outcome of gift exchange is a simple *strengthening* of the relationship that creates bonding. However, there is a second version of the strengthening role of gift giving that is caused when the gift is a big (but welcome) surprise and so acts as an epiphany and demonstrates that the relationship is more important to the giver than the recipient realized. It then creates a sense of greater commitment, in the case where it is welcome. (In the case where such a gift is not welcome, then it would, of course, create problems, as in the case of Mr. Darcy expressing his affection to Miss Elizabeth Bennet on the first occasion, in Jane Austen's *Pride and Prejudice*.)

A positive example is from a blog:

> Jason surprised me with a trip to New York City this year for my 25th Birthday. Our plan was to spend a couple of nights there and then drive to the family lakehouse. We spent our first day in New York (July 30th) seeing all we could: riding the Staten Island Ferry to get a view of the Statue of Liberty and Ellis Island, standing in front of the World Trade Center Sphere, sitting in the pews at Trinity Church, and walking the Brooklyn Bridge (to name a few highlights). We had reservations at The Boathouse restaurant at the lake in Central Park that night, so we headed back to our hotel room at On The Avenue Hotel in the upper west side. We were about to get ready to go to dinner and were sitting on the bed talking and I thanked him again for taking me there. Then he told me he had something else for me—I was upset that he had gotten me ANOTHER birthday present (or so I thought). He pulled out of his pocket a brown leather pouch. I was confused. It looked like an old, handmade coin purse. I think I might have thanked him for it, but I don't really remember. He told me to open it and inside there was a tiny white jewelry bag. That's when I got really confused!! I opened the bag and there was the ring he had picked out for me. I was in complete shock. He asked me to marry him and I think I said "WHAT?!" probably 50 times in between sobbing and

hugging him. He caught me completely off guard. The entire thing blew me away—the fact that he wanted to marry me, the trip, the ring—everything. When I finally calmed down he asked what my answer was. I hadn't realized that I forgot to say yes or no. Yes, of course.

Gifts That Make No Change to a Relationship

Another way in which Ruth and colleagues talk about gift giving is *affirming positive relationship*. The relationship stays the same but is reinforced and is stopped from slipping back. For example, deathbed gifts can affirm the nature of a relationship without changing it or increasing it; they simply show and confirm commitment, love, and appreciation or gratitude and represent maintenance of that relationship. Thus, most deathbed gifts show recognition and affirmation of the relationship, but can occasionally also send unwanted messages and create family feuds over bequests or even the whole will (Allan & Gerstner, 2006).

A third possibility explored by Ruth et al. (1999) is that there will be a *negligible effect* of gift giving. For example, it might have no effect on how you feel about the person at all, or might be seen as charity, or someone may feel that whatever the giver does can never change the nature of the relationship. Someone may give a gift for a birthday present that is a perfect gift, but even that cannot save a failing relationship nor restore one that has already been ended, because the relationship is unwanted and so is the gift. Gifts do not always work to strengthen or affirm a relationship and sometimes can have a negligible effect.

Affirming a Negative Relationship or Showing Guilt

Somewhat surprisingly, Ruth et al. (1999) found that the symbolism of gifts can be negative and so can also end relationships or have negative effects on them.

Gifts can *affirm a negative relationship*. You can give someone a generic, all-purpose gift that does not indicate any special concern or affection or thought. It's a generic gift and serves to reaffirm the distance already present in the relationship, or it may be a forceful statement of rejection. For example, in 1795, William Duck bequeathed considerable wealth to his other children, but with the gift of only one shilling to his son Matthew Duck, he affirmed his negative relationship with Matthew. (As it turns out, Matthew had been a naughty boy and had an illegitimate son, something that had displeased his father William. Matthew was obviously a bit of a ne'er-do-well and subsequently died in the poor house in 1832.)

Another side effect of gifts on relationships is that they can (attempt to) *exert control or relieve guilt*. Somebody can give you something that he or she has always wanted you to have, and the giving of the gift removes your excuse for not doing or having it. So this is a form of control and does not make the receiving of the gift a pleasant experience. For example, someone may give you a piece of clothing that he or she has always wanted you to wear, but you had chosen not to do so, and so this gift essentially eliminates your freedom and asserts the other person's control over you and your choices. Of course, this can make you feel bad rather than good. The reason, of course, has to do with the epistemic and how you feel treated by receipt of such an insulting gift.

Gifts That Undo Relationships

Gifts can *weaken a relationship,* and do so deliberately or by accident, where the relationship suffers as a result of the gift. Leaving someone a 10-cent tip is a deliberate insult, but gifts can have strings attached, too. "I'm giving you this because I want something from you," and so the gift itself can weaken the relationship because it implies very strongly that it is given only in order to establish an obligation.

Gifts can *sever a relationship altogether.* For example, you can give a type of gift that is known to be associated with endings. The gift of a clock upon a person's retirement from the workplace is a recognized gift that is specifically associated with the ending of the relationship for time served. Apparently, there are equally strong coded messages in certain types of flowers, and some flowers are associated with endings of relationships (for example, the yellow carnation symbolizes rejection, and the marigold is specifically associated with grief at a loss). So you have to know the flower code! Excessive giving or persistent excessive giving is a way to end relationships too, because it becomes inappropriate and seems over the top. Such excessive or overattentive giving is very much associated with stalking (Cupach, Spitzberg, & Carson, 2000). Constant attention or persistent and effusive giving is a way to make a person afraid, or at least suspicious, of this relationship.

Gifts Whose Relational Overtones Are Not Accepted

Returning of gifts is also a recognized way to sever the relationship or to decline to accept the definition of the relationship implied in a particular form. For example, when Iowa City was struck by a tornado in 2006, my wife gave a significantly over-large tip in a restaurant where she personally knew the owner, who had suffered serious loss. The owner later sent her a note thanking her for her sweetly generous thought, but returned the tip, thus recognizing her wish to be kind but declining to accept the patronage implied.

Refusal to accept a gift altogether without explanation is a refusal to accept the symbolism of starting or continuing the relationship, and it is a way of indicating change in relationship status, or an unwillingness to accept a certain kind of relationship (for example, a refusal to accept a bribe).

The Relational Symbolism of Gifts

In identifying these functions of the symbolism of the giving of gifts and the connection of gifts to various relational epistemics, Ruth et al. (1999) argue that "relational appropriateness" is fundamentally important and often supersedes other characteristics of the apparently perfect gift. *Perception* of events rather than actual events (i.e., their symbolism in the epistemic of personal and social orders) now exerts the most power relationally.

The exchange of material signals of friendship and romance are significant ways in which people demonstrate and symbolize the nature of their relationships with one another in an epistemic in relation to social order. Your assessment of the appropriateness of gifts takes part of its force and meaning from the way in which you view and understand the relationship between yourself and the gift giver/recipient. For instance, it is one thing for a mother to buy her daughter's wedding dress as a gift for the wedding. It is quite another—and much more deeply connected and symbolically loaded—if the mother gives the daughter the wedding dress that she wore for her own wedding. In this way, *material* gifts are important to the way in which you understand your relationships with other people *epistemically* and *symbolically*. Hence, the materiality of giving continues the analysis of the relationship between material circumstances and relationships between people, once one takes account of the epistemic, the personal order, and the social order.

> ### Listen in on Your Own Life
>
> Are there any people who are important in your life but to whom you do not give gifts? What sort of relationship do you have with them? Are there any people who are relatively unimportant in your life but to whom you give gifts anyway? In what way are you defining "important" and "unimportant"?

Material gift giving has to be understood in a context of appropriateness and symbolism within a social order. You have a general kind of understanding about how gift giving should occur, and you understand that somebody breaking the rules of doing it is probably sending a symbolic relational message, if, indeed, he or she understands the code. They may not, of course, have realized what their gift really means, much as in Daphne du Maurier's famous novel *Rebecca*. Rebecca's intent to surprise her husband by wearing a particular ball gown turns out to have been a big mistake as it makes her look like his dead first wife. However, the key point is a simple one, that this is another instance of the material influences upon the epistemic and hence a further example of the ways in which Mead's analysis of materiality (in Chapter 4) has direct effects on the way in which you understand your world and, in this case, the ways in which your relationships are understood and conducted.

Conclusion

What this chapter has taught you, then, is that relationships are conducted in a social context of others' opinions and symbols that are performative and contain behavioral restrictions, affirmations, and epistemics. Material circumstances and gifts emphasize various aspects of relationships and place key elements of their performance into the frameworks provided by social orders. All of this affects the ways in which relationships are done, and even your everyday casual chat might seem as if it is doing nothing very much, but it is also subtly reinforcing and challenging certain ways of acting; reframing what is happening by reference to cultural norms, symbols, metaphors, and rituals; and telling you that your relationships must conform.

The ending point of this chapter, then, is that the social order and the partners' personal orders both shape and conform relationships, both through material and behavioral expectations. The next chapter will extend this to commentary about other people's behaviors to the performance of relationships in talk.

PEDAGOGICAL ISSUES

EXERCISES

Try living for 2 days with your cell phone switched off, and keep a notebook of your feelings, your sense of security, and other elements of your well-being. What kinds of messages are left on your phone or your e-mail by friends who cannot get a response from you?

ETHICAL ISSUES

Is it right to give formal gifts to subordinate employees (secretaries, receptionists, office administrators) on holidays, or does it merely emphasize the ritualized nature of the gratitude that you express for their efforts?

MEDIA ISSUES

How frequently do you hear "White Christmas," "Let It Snow, Let It Snow, Let It Snow" or "Jingle Bells" from the end of November, and what purpose do you suppose it is intended to serve?

References

Allan, G. A. (1998). Friendship, sociology and social structure. *Journal of Social and Personal Relationships, 15,* 685–702.

Allan, G. A. (2008). Flexibility, friendship and the de-centering of family. *Personal Relationships, 15*(1), 1–16.

Cheal, D. J. (1986). The social dimensions of gift behaviour. *Journal of Social and Personal Relationships, 3,* 423–439.

Cupach, W. R., Spitzberg, B. H., & Carson, C. L. (2000). Toward a theory of obsessive relational intrusion and stalking. In K. Dindia & S. W. Duck (Eds.), *Communication and personal relationships* (pp. 131–146). Chichester, UK: Wiley.

Duck, S. W. (2007). *Human relationships* (4th ed.). London: Sage.

Duck, S. W., & McMahan, D. T. (2010). *Communication in everyday life.* Thousand Oaks, CA: Sage.

Festinger, L., Schachter, S., & Back, K. (1950). *Social pressure in informal groups: A study of human factors in housing.* New York: Harper.

Kerckhoff, A. C. (1974). The social context of interpersonal attraction. In T. L. Huston (Ed.), *Foundations of interpersonal attraction* (pp. 61–77). New York: Academic Press.

Mesch, G. S. (2006). Family relations and the Internet: Exploring a family boundaries approach. *Journal of Family Communication, 6*(2), 119–138.

Ruth, J. A., Otnes, C. C., & Brunel, F. F. (1999). Gift receipt and the reformulation of interpersonal relationships. *Journal of Consumer Research, 25*(4), 385–402.

Secklin, P. L. (2001). Multiple fractures in time: Reflections on a car crash. *Journal of Loss and Trauma, 6*(4), 323–333.

Seguin, M. (1986). Understanding Tsimshian "potlatch." In R. B. Morrison & C. R. Wilson (Eds.), *Native peoples: The Canadian experience* (pp. 473–500). Toronto: McClelland and Stewart.

Stone, L. (1979). *The family, sex, and marriage in England 1500–1800.* New York: HarperColophon.

Veblen, T. B. (1992). *The theory of the leisure class.* New Brunswick, NJ: Transaction Books. (Original work published 1899)

7

The Language of Relationships in a Social Order

I wrote at the start of the book that much is taken for granted in the ways in which our relationships get done, performed, and articulated within the broad social order, once you get away from the simplistic idea that relationships are all about emotion and choice. This issue, as is seen in all the previous chapters, comes down to the question of how emotion and choice get *performed*.

Performance assumes that

- we are aware of others' oversight of our privacy;
- society holds certain truths about relationships to be self-evident;
- the outward show of private relationships is done within particular constraints of the social order;
- historical and material resources affect the way in which people conduct their relationships.

In Chapter 2, I also asked what lies beneath the process of knowing someone else's thoughts, and ended up connecting the process of social orders, materiality, and epistemics of relationships to the key formative social activity of language use. The present chapter concerns the way in which language steers us into social orders and offers inherent structures that the social order acknowledges as guiding relational activity. The final chapter looks at the explicit performance of language in speaking and discusses the consequences of the new view of relationships for research, relationships, and society at large.

Language in a Social Order

The performance that we call "speaking" uses language and does so much more than reveal inner personal truths. To understand how language presents relationships, we must first take account of forms of language available in a social order and from which the person makes choices in describing experience or presenting rhetorical visions. In short, before inspecting the specific nature and content of speaking by individuals to one another, we must look at the social order represented in a language itself.

One key matter is the social order in which the language is embedded— the hidden connections of language to materiality and the structure of narrative (stories) that is acceptable to the social order within which it is related. For example, a *story* about grief must be structured to employ specific symbols and must also be placed in a relevant context of expectation (it is okay to get upset when your mother dies, but not okay to get so upset when the friend of your next-door neighbor finds a dead fly on the porch—unless you are Jean-Paul Sartre). The *telling*—the performance of the story rather than its structure— must be accompanied by appropriate symbols of emotion (tears, sober looks, somber demeanor).

The social order accepts some contexts as making appropriate certain sorts of narrative. Members of that social order share expectations about "the way things should be done," just as Weiss (1974) identified in his provisions of relationships (emotional integration). Accordingly, I will look at some ways in which language in relationships is based on such shared meaning of how it should buy into the social order. I will explore the subtle ways in which language's hidden structures work with the social order before they work with the personal orders of the speakers. These structures and forms of language reinforce, yet are guided by, epistemics about relationships within that social order.

THE STRUCTURE OF ACCOUNTS

Part of our sharing of the social order depends on the use of the same language, its terministic screens, and the sorts of narrative structure or story forms that hit the right notes for the social order to recognize what is being told. As part of the placing of your personal reports in a social context, you also take account not only of what is known, but of what is presumed to be *right* and *good* and *appropriate* according to the culture in which you live. After that recognition, your personal order

Whereas previously there was some importance attached to official announcements of engagements, now one of the most important decisions that a couple makes can be the question of whether to "go Facebook."

rubs up against the social order, through your personal and relational connections with specific other people.

Think about the forms in which you tell stories about your relationships. You take a lot for granted about what other people understand and judge to be "right." For example, you would rarely tell a story about a relationship that presented you as an unfeeling and selfish egomaniac. Instead, you would report your actions and performances in a way that made them look . . . a little better. Recall from Chapter 5 why people don't openly declare to everyone that they've been committing adultery or having affairs or cheating behind someone's back and why they are often ashamed when other people find out. If relationships are just and only about personal preferences or choices and not about social context, then why does the form in which you talk about them to anyone else matter at all?

In many different parts of everyday life, people swamp one another with self-justifying stories (accounts) of their experiences. In reports about the ending of relationships, people usually have a story about how their own behavior was largely unblemished and the partner's was not. And so the world turns. Whether your report is about the way in which a shop assistant treated you or how your lover has been behaving lately or why you got out of a relationship, you are *accounting* for yourself. This involves presenting your ways of understanding/knowing what happened in a form that will make sense to other people so that your behavior is pardoned, excused, or seen as justified.

At the same time that you describe anything, you are also presenting a spin on the description and endorsing a particular social order for knowing the world of other people. Other people can accept your reports to the extent that they conform with or deviate from the social order expectations. (Against this social order background, any personal accounts present your specific ways of comprehending relationships and their unfolding as much as they depict your personal orders about the world. This personal order may portray other people, in contrast with a generally positive social order, as essentially "unreliable," "trustworthy," "accepting," and so on—the notion of "personal order" discussed in Chapter 2—as a result, perhaps, of your attachment style as discussed in Chapter 3.)

Listen in on Your Own Life

Make a list of types of stories that people tell you about their daily interactions with other people, especially in relationships. What is the structure of such accounts? How do such stories and accounts present the speaker as conforming to social order expectations about good behavior in relationships? How often do the stories make speakers look stupid, bad, or egotistical, as opposed to smart, decent, and generous or mistreated by other people?

Accounts are also, in the terms of Chapter 2, strongly *rhetorical*, in that they are intended to elicit support and to persuade the audience of the correctness and justifiability of ways of looking at other people and of being in relationships. Hence, accounts have to recognize the social order to which they are related. They play into the kinds of tales, narratives, and explanations that this social order recognizes as important or valuable. "I'm a bad friend," for example, is not just making a statement but is also implicitly referring to what a given society recognizes as making a friendship work, and how I have failed to perform those socially recognized requirements properly. The statement also invites the listener to deny it, contradict it, or forgive the mistake.

THE LANGUAGE OF RELATIONSHIPS FOR THE SOCIAL ORDER AND ITS GENERALIZED OTHERS

You constantly brush up against the social order in embodied physical and material ways by using language to other people/bodies who belong to it as well. You are not always clearly aware of the fact that your neighbors and friends are exerting influence by commenting upon ways to keep you within a social order. Nevertheless it is the case that they exert such influence on your personal relationships and even your sexual behavior (Chapter 5). So where does your social epistemic—your knowledge of the social order—come from? One way is precisely through your direct everyday communication with other people who represent society and know its rules. Another is based on rituals and norms, namely, the general rules within a culture that define examples of a particular kind of relationship and how it should be done, practiced, and celebrated.

Influence of Third Parties as Agents of Society

If you focus only on accounts, then an example of the strong influence of other people is provided by Baxter, Dun, and Sahlstein (2001). These researchers showed the ways in which network members help to consolidate and enforce knowledge of relational rules specifically. Membership in a network exposes people to the judgments of other people about how relationships should be conducted.

These judgments are embodied also by the social practice and the expectation of influence by others for carrying out certain practices in particular ways. People responded carefully to the judgments or rules stated by outsiders about personal relationships ("You should not date the former lover of a best friend," for example).

One example from Baxter et al. (2001) is "My friend Sue called me on the phone. We started talking about our mutual friend, Nan. I was telling her about the different guys Nan was dating. Sue said in a really snotty tone, 'I can't believe she dates all of those guys at once. She dates more guys than anyone I know.'" Such an apparently trivial story contains lessons, rules, and social judgments within a narrative such as often arises in everyday language use: Be monogamous, or other people will voice their disapproval.

Therefore, it is clear that people tune up reports about a relationship, partly because others in a network offer a commentary force. They also partly exert a practical influence on any activity that occurs between the two primary participants. Any reports about relational activity have to be consistent with what the other people want to hear. In other words, you might think that you have lots of freedom about what to do and say about relationships, and that they change and develop over time in your own mind. Actually, the power of public opinion (social order) exerts a force on how you give accounts and narratives of your relationships. If anyone were in any doubt that individuals do not have complete freedom of choice to conduct their personal relationships in any way that pleases them, then this is the proof. You can't just do what you want; other people out there will tell you what you can do and will comment directly or indirectly when you look like you are breaking the social order.

Gossip

One of the most powerful indirect effects of a social order is the power of gossip (Bergmann, 1993). Most people are careful, or even downright afraid, of being the objects of gossip and shape what they say or do to avoid being gossiped about as irresponsible, unfair, or selfish. Preferences about behaviors may be held in check if you don't want to be seen as "a bitch" or "a liar" or "a selfish relater" (Norwood, 2007). Speaking with other network members soon clarifies the existence of rules that will be applied to any relationship in that community. The enforcement of those rules in language, often gossip, unsolicited advice, or direct sanctioning is newsworthy. For example, it often occurs when politicians are discovered to have had affairs with their interns. Such public exposure and commentary serve to remind everyone that personal and intimate relationships are sustained, shaped, and permitted continuance by the social order.

DISCUSSION QUESTION

Have you ever been explicitly criticized by friends, acquaintances, or family for the conduct of your relationships? Have you ever offered critiques (or, more subtly, influential advice) about their conduct of relationships?

You cannot do whatever you like. You know that you must conform to some extent and are subject not only to vocal restraint but even physical enforcement as well. There are frequently stories in Western news outlets about "honor killings" by families in Asia who discovered that a daughter had been having a secret liaison with someone not approved by the family or had refused to marry the person chosen by her father.

Such stories are extreme and often represented as barbaric to a Western audience, but the mechanism is similar to the one used in the West. You are always aware of the fact that a generalized other—whether friends and acquaintances or people you don't even know who might see what you do—might comment on what you do and judge it good or bad. As a child, your talk may be monitored and directed by parents ("You must not say that to grown-ups," "Mind your language"), and even as an adult, you may be rebuked for bringing up topics in public or may choose not to talk about particular topics "in front of the children."

Given this, you have to ask a simple question: Is chat ever just chat, or does even private talk take you into embodied, material contact with the social order that judges what your relationships are like? Consider some other symbolic functions of talk and see what they do (because as you are recalling from earlier in the book, whenever a symbol is used/present, it carries overtones and can be evaluated by the social order).

The Rhetorical Situation

Consider the "rhetorical situation," where you materially shape and influence other people's views. The rhetorical situation refers to the circumstances in which speech is uttered, the way you need to adapt what you say for specific audiences, the required forms of address, or the appropriateness of formal or informal language (whether talking with your boss or your pals), among other things (i.e., situations where you rub up against the social order). You might want to think about whether it makes a difference that the private topics you want to discuss with your partner might be overheard by someone else.

DIFFERENT STROKES FOR DIFFERENT FOLKS

That is only part of what is meant by a rhetorical situation, where you adapt what you say because of your awareness of the audience that is present. The same information can be conveyed in dozens of different ways depending on whether one is, say, talking with children or adults, in a law court or in a bar, with friends or in a job interview. It is also true that people can describe their relationships differently in different circumstances and to different audiences.

That might not seem like a big point, but it means that any person in any relationship must have available multiple versions of the relationship that can be produced and reported somewhat differently as needed in the specific rhetorical situation. For example, you may want to conceal an affair from the rest of your family—one rhetorical situation—but at the same time, you keep telling your lover—a different rhetorical situation—just how much love you feel and how important the relationship is to you. Once you accept the key point that a person can have several simultaneous language forms for describing a single relationship, then you can move on to the second point: Both partners in the relationship can do that.

> **Questions to Ask Your Friends**
>
> Why do you and your friends talk about trivia? Do you say the same things in a public place as you do elsewhere, and what is the difference (if there is one)? What exactly do you change about your conversation if you think you can be overheard? Does it matter if the people who hear you are strangers? Why do drunk people not make this distinction in a loud bar? Do you and your friends ever talk about personal stuff on your cell phones while walking down the street? If so, ask your friends why they do that when other people can overhear.

DIFFERENT VIEWS AND REPORTS ON THE SAME RELATIONSHIP

The second issue that then arises is that the two partners in a relationship can each have different views of that relationship. What are you to make of it when, say, a husband and a wife give different reports of the intimacy of their relationship? You could declare that one or each of them is wrong, as judged against the objective tests of a scientist or the relatively independent views of a mutual friend. You could investigate how the two different views relate to other, systematic features of the relationship, such as satisfaction, amount of conflict, or the sex of the reporter.

In short, you could treat such discrepancies not only as errors or curiosities but also as meaningful information about the workings of that relationship or relationships in general. Indeed, differences in the way in which partners report a relationship could, in fact, *be* part of its history, as when people report a change in the way they started to see the relationship or the partner ("I didn't like him at first, but he grew on me"). You can also remind yourself that relationships are "unfinished business." Each new conversation or meeting continues the previous business, thus shaping the form of the later continuance of the relationship ("Our previous conversation patched up our fight and everything was fine the next time we met").

Given that there are different rhetorical situations, what forms of language are available to deal with them? Here we will look at metaphor and the hidden structure of stories about relationships. In the final chapter, I will show how these structures behind the social order affect the forms of relationship that people perform personally. I will not write about simple choices and emotions, but conclude that everyday speaking is all part of the larger machinery of the intersection of social and personal orders, and indeed is an embodiment of social rules.

Symbolic Structures in Talk: Metaphors in a Social Order

There are many ways in which you know what a social order judges as good or bad about relationships, but one of them is rather surprisingly connected to the language that applies to relationships. The *form* of utterance means something to the social order. Your social order materially exerts itself upon your thinking by the way in which it directs you toward certain *metaphors* about relationships that frame your experiences accordingly.

We normally think of metaphors as simply flowery and exaggerated ways of talking, for example when you describe a lover as "an angel" or a neighbor as "a teddy bear" or a workmate as "a pain," or you might live in an apartment that is "the pits." You talk metaphorically about all sorts of aspects of relationships: Your relationship was a roller coaster; you just burned with passion; I was head over heels in love, but he crushed me by ending it. These do, indeed, sound like merely flowery ways of describing your feelings, but because I have banged on (another metaphor) about epistemics, you are nervously expecting me to say that metaphors are epistemic, too, and you are right.

METAPHORS OF RELATIONSHIPS

One hidden result of metaphors is to create a recognized social order for relationships that generates predictability or shared understanding about their nature. Language serves to impose a structure on chaos, but a structure preferred in the social order. For example, you very often think about relationships in various metaphorical ways that create a sense out of the daily mix of experiences that you have in them: "The relationship just grew," "We're on a pathway to marriage," "The breakdown of marriage plays like a film shown in reverse." Examples such as "I got out of this relationship because it wasn't going anywhere" or "We lost our way" or "The relationship stopped in its tracks" are all part of a comfortable, structured *pathway* metaphor. Such a pathway metaphor gives you one "way to know" how relationships develop: They follow a path (for example, from courtship through engagement to marriage). The key point here, then, is that these metaphors structure your thinking, and so you should see them not as stylistic flourishes, but as epistemics and terministic screens.

> Many references to love use florid forms of speech, complex similes, or metaphors to convey the same emotion. "Shall I compare thee to a summer's day? Thou art more lovely and more temperate." "My love is like a red, red rose that's newly sprung in June." "You are my life." "Honey." "There was chemistry between us."

Metaphors as Thoughtways

Two linguists, Lakoff and Johnson (1980), were the first to propose that metaphors are not so much about language as about thought. Lakoff and Johnson viewed metaphors as *ways* of thought and structures for experience; or, in my terms, they are terministic screens that focus you on some aspects of experience and not others. Lakoff and Johnson called metaphors "thoughtways," but the idea is the same as the one that I am calling epistemics. The way that people choose their metaphors to describe their relationship represents the rhetorical vision of the relationship and may influence further talk about it.

For example, "I was smothered, trapped, caged" is much different from "The relationship just died." One metaphor suggests imprisonment by the partner and also points to an unwanted power of the partner over oneself. It also implies that one can get out of the prison if one can find a way of leaving the relationship. The implication is that the present prevention of self-expression or self-development can be escaped. The death metaphor suggests an *organic* failure of an independent entity (specifically, the death of the relationship). Essentially, the relationship acts independently of the actions, styles, or behaviors of the partners themselves and so cannot be reversed by anyone's action. In this case, the metaphor relieves the individuals from any personal responsibility for the relationship's end. Its life reached an end, and there was nothing they could do.

Metaphors as Hidden Values About a Relationship

The metaphors used by a person or social order therefore tell something interesting about the values and thoughts of the person or society: the epistemic. If I describe a relationship as a journey of discovery or as work ("Relationships take work," "We can work it out," "We tried hard to make it better"), or if I say that my partner and I were stuck on each other and just went on a wild ride, then I am thinking about the relationship in a particular sort of way that is different in each case.

Each metaphor presents a different way of experiencing it (knowing and performing it) but also presents a consequence of that way of knowing, an implication about how the relationship should be addressed. If society talks about the relationship as something you have to "work on," then it places responsibility for the relationship on some person rather than on chance. If you say that "the relationship is a wild ride," then you imply that you aren't taking responsibility. Instead, you are being driven about by exterior forces that other people familiar with the same social order can recognize as relevant to understanding your reported relationship experience. If you claim to be "stuck on" someone, then you are telling your social order audience that there are irresistible attractions and forces that keep you together, whatever you try to do about it.

Metaphors as Symbols of Relationships

We can thus see that the metaphors used in a social order to present relationships use a symbolic form that implicitly offers an explanation for experience. This is a deep point about language usage: Metaphors help you to explain and understand what is otherwise hard to understand, and they do that by referring to something that you understand quite well. This helps you to connect an unknown idea to a known idea. But they also contain implicit overtones or explanations.

You can get some helpful idea of how the mind works by thinking of the brain as a computer, or some understanding of relationships by seeing them as *connections, bonds, ties* of affection or *couples* (all of which are metaphors based on the material world) or seeing that love is like a turkey sandwich (I'm kidding, but you could probably find a way to hold the relational mayo).

In each case, the way you would account for, or attempt to fix, the relationship if it were to go wrong would follow from the metaphor used. Broken bonds need to be reconnected, torn ties need to be mended, uninteresting turkey sandwiches need to be spiced up. Even if you call your lover "honey" or "sweetie" or "hot lips," or you talk about "a burning passion," then you are using metaphors of food and fire. When you say "Our relationship went over a cliff," you are using a metaphor suggestive of no turning back, or that reclaiming it is possible only with much effort devoted to "climbing back to where you were."

DISCUSSION QUESTION

What do you think are the primary and most commonly used metaphors about relationships? Work? Journey of discovery? Lack of control? Make a list of the metaphors of relationships that you can think of.

METAPHORS AND TERMINISTIC SCREENS

If metaphors are ways of thinking, and epistemics are ways of knowing, then the metaphors you use are symbolic actions that have implications for the ways you perform relating. You could see relationships as accomplishments, performed and sustained in talk. Now recall from Chapter 2 what Burke said about terministic screens and the ways in which motives are explained in the forms of language that you use.

The grammar of motives is not simply a pattern for describing events but a system of symbolic forms through which experience is created (constituted) and approached. Hence, metaphors are really a form of social action for framing performance and understanding (Kovecses, 1991). Metaphors about relationships therefore present shared knowledge in a society about the ways to frame relationships. They shape the epistemics about the manner in which relationships operate.

Of course, that also gives you a way to judge them and explain how to deal with problems that arise. If the relationship is "hard work," is the amount of work too hard? If you "fall head over heels in love," are you too much out of control? If you "burn with passion" for someone, should you be judged as dangerous to others and yourself? If the relationship falls apart, was it because you didn't work hard enough to keep it together?

METAPHORS AND SOCIAL ORDER JUDGMENTS

Metaphors are not interesting just because they represent material frames of thought for individuals but because they also represent implicit frames of judgment in a language that presents you with reference points in the social order. A relationship that is a "bond," "couple," or "connection" can also be a "prison," "ball-and-chain," or "bind." You need to see that when you choose your metaphors, you are also implicitly judging the relationship just as a generalized other would do within your social order.

So when you use a language that has built-in metaphors, you are sharing a common way of understanding the ways in which relationships can be described and judged. Metaphors therefore represent a subtle imposition of social order on your ways of knowing and being in relationships (epistemic). They also remind you that all your personal relationships are social and public activities that a society judges as good or bad. So when you report on your relationships, you place them in a frame of reference that calls upon the social order and invites its judgment. When you give accounts or narratives of relationships in a particular way, you are doing so with full awareness that you have an implied audience.

As noted previously, awareness of the existence of the generalized other stops or checks your behavior ("What would the neighbors think?" "How on earth am I going to explain this to my mom if I get caught?"). The essence of the generalized other then depends on an *attitude of reflection,* where you realize by reflection that you are a social object perceived and judged by other people, just as you perceive and may judge them.

As I've written about it here, moral accountability to the social order is translatable into these terms: that an attitude of reflection creates awareness of a generalized other that steers your connection to the social order. You may not have first thought of a metaphor as a mechanism of the generalized other or social order, but in fact, metaphors present a frame for relationships. Judgments about the stories that you tell about your relationships depend on their appreciation or evaluation by the social order as appropriate or not.

Stories About Relationships in the Social Order

Epistemics are a way of organizing knowledge and can show up in various ways, from metaphors to social orders, that prescribe the format for revealing personal orders with a hope that shared meaning will be the pot of gold at the end. Remember from Chapter 1 where the widow talked about her feelings? It was an epistemic, but also a story or a narrative.

THE STRUCTURE OF STORIES/NARRATIVES

Stories are particularly interesting formal ways in which you organize talk and knowledge. They indicate a clear connection between relationships and social knowledge. Stories formally organize meaning while also serving relational purposes, so they contain *a scene or setting* where the action took place, *characters,* a *plot,* a specific *sequence of events,* and a *reason or moral.* In this case, the moral may serve a relational purpose in identifying someone who was to blame for the breakup or otherwise casting doubt on the character of another individual. From the structure of reports, listeners learn more about the placement of the "facts" in the person's evaluative meaning system. Thus, you learn a lot about events but also about the narrator when someone tells a story.

You have lots of stories in your lives, and many of them concern relationships, but all share the feature of organizing your thinking and understanding about the nature of the life and experience that you have had. Stories put events and characters into a systematic plot, making sense of what characters do and giving a rationalized explanation of what happens to them—at best, "systematic," "sense," "rationalized" within your social order.

Stories organize events into epistemic orders that make sense within the prevailing social order. There are, for example, many cultural stories about relationships that tell you something about the values of society, whether these are about Cinderella, the ugly sisters, and the redeeming Prince Charming, or stories about celebrities in *People* magazine that indicate who's doing what with whom and whether or not they should be doing it. When telling their stories, people play into those social superstories.

> I know where I'm goin'
> and I know who's goin' with me
> I know who I love
> and my dear knows who I'll marry.
> [English folk song]

ORIGIN STORIES

Relationships typically have a story about origin, the story of "how we met." Societies as a whole have such stories that are called *origin myths*. They describe how the society originated, usually from some contact with a god, the society's place in that god's order, and the physical structure of the world the society inhabits. This tells a society where it came from, where it went, and what its future holds in store. Island cultures in the Pacific usually talk about where the people came from beyond the horizon, and the Bible starts with a vivid description of the origin of the physical world and the placing of humans in it, along with an account of how humankind failed to get it right. In this case, God evidently didn't just wipe the slate and start over, so the sequence and moral accounting in the story are used to explain why humans still suffer quite a lot.

Several researchers have noted that people's close relationships develop "origin stories" about the ways in which the relationship came into being and what they set in place. Family stories are key ways of representing not only events but also the *values* that the family espouses (Huisman, 2008; Koenig Kellas, 2005). Such stories tend to be idealized or creative even if based on real events. But that is because they serve to encapsulate the themes that the couple or family wants to stress in the relationship that conform with the social order expectations. It is not exactly that people willfully make events fit their epistemic, but that a part of the social epistemic involves making sense of life and people.

This perfectly normal human enterprise involves the folding of events into a place that explains what people are doing and why. The story is a symbolic presentation of their way of knowing the world of their relationship. The stories serve a function for the people and connect to their present feelings and the social order, rather than to strict representation of historical truth.

NARRATIVES AS EPISTEMIC

Origin stories about relationships are actually not true or false, but they identify points that a narrator believes to be crucial to explain something about the relationship to others in the same social order. Social order expects consistency, and so personal stories consolidate beliefs about the earlier relationship with what you know about the relationship *now*. So if you're in a relationship that is experienced in a turbulent kind of way, then you need a socially acceptable origin myth that says it has always been a crazy kind of relationship with a crazy atmosphere where crazy stuff happens, and now it is still crazy.

The form of those stories itself communicates to other people the key elements of a relationship as well as the social order basis for that relationship. For example, Western stories usually emphasize love, friendship, support, common fate, and many other reasons. When people tell stories about the relationship, they are also communicating something to the social order that connects themselves, the nature of the relationship, and its structure to social expectations. For example, their story could emphasize the companionable aspects to the relationship, its basis in common experience, or the ties of loyalty and connection that bind it.

People basically try to derive the present characteristics of the relationship from the way it started. But they do it backwards and say, "This is how it looks now, and so that must be where it came from." Thus do narratives make experience epistemically consistent with the present. Equally acceptable would be a story based on deep soulmate love. Only Lady GaGa can produce a story based on selfish instrumentality: "You get yours; I get mine."

Life is more complicated than the stories told about it. Relationships have their ups and downs, and everything that goes on in relationships can be interpreted more than one way. People are thus faced with the problem of making sense of chaos, or making sense out of a variety of material experiences. You make sense out of the events by forcing sequence onto them even though the events were chaotic at the time. Stories omit detail and inconsistency as they strive to present coherence from chaos.

> People sometimes change their stories of the origin of their relationship, or partners may disagree about it.

So a social order expects accounts that explain a sequence of circumstances in a way that makes a certain kind of sense to it and its presuppositions.

NARRATIVES THAT SIMPLIFY RELATIONSHIPS

Sociologist Diane Felmlee (1995) looked at people in long-term relationships that had broken down and asked them to say what they thought of the whole relationship altogether. It is very unlikely that you have *never* had any relationship that has gone bad. Whenever you are in that position (where, for some of the time, the relationship was going positively and you enjoyed it but then it switched to a negative experience), then you have some explaining do.

Diane Felmlee wanted to find out how people change their stories of relationships, and she found that people give the same sequence of events or the same features of the partner as being responsible for both the beginning of the relationship and the end of it much later. People would say, "I met him and he was really exciting and there was always something happening with lots of new ideas and wonderful new suggestions for places to see and new ideas that were full of excitement." When it comes to the ending of the relationship, however, they say, "There were so many new ideas that I never knew where I was, and it was totally confusing that we were constantly going to different places, and doing different things and it became really hard to deal with." So people give a different interpretation to the positive side in terms of excitement and variability and having lots of new ideas, but then they say that this began to produce too much stress.

The same happens with a person who is liked because she was always completely reliable, and the story switches to say that eventually everything became so absolutely predictable that it was boring: never early, never late, but always predictably on time. What this comes down to is describing the same events then giving a different interpretation, first positive and subsequently negative.

But of course you do not—and could not—get away with telling just any old good story or making up any old switcheroo like this. The story has to fit with the major themes in the social order in which it is told, and a culture that needs heroes wants a story with a hero and a villain. It assumes that the hero should be decisive and independent, like a starship commander, and should uphold traditions of good treatment of other people while being fearlessly and decisively ruthless with the bad guys.

So, given the social order language background and expectations for the linguistic and material forces acting on people's narratives, how do they talk about the positive and negative elements of relationships when they come together face to face? What happens when your relationship might threaten the assumptions of the social order?

BREAKUP AND THE DISRUPTION OF SOCIAL ORDER

Relationships are supposed to be good things that proceed nicely and pleasantly, but (metaphorically) hit occasional bumps in the road.

Social Assumptions About Relational Civility

A typical assumption is that partners are nice to each other; will feel guilty about hurting partners' feelings; will control outbursts of crappy feelings; will be decent when the time comes for breakup; and will handle it in a straightforward, fair-minded, defused, and socially packaged way. They are, after all, respectable human beings and know how to behave.

Believe that or not, everyone wants to avoid, and struggles to prevent, public demonstrations of annoyance with a partner or disaffection with a spouse. It is bad to be negative or to make derogatory remarks about people, especially partners. When you break up with someone, you are under a lot of pressure from a social order that wants you to tell stories about the breakup that makes relationships in general appear to be a good thing for society.

Within that context, you must appear to be decent, strong, sensible, and fair-minded rather than rude, uncivil, a poor loser, or really nasty—whether you really *feel* you want to be rude and uncivil and nasty or not.

Giving Order to the Breakup

Even so, the breakup of a relationship is not a single, far less a simple, event. Indeed, at the time it is all happening, the partners may not even be breaking up, but merely see themselves as going through a rough patch. Later, as it turns out looking back, that rough patch was actually part of the ending of the relationship.

In many cases, the breakup of a truly committed relationship is really painful for both partners and something they do reluctantly and with a great deal of uncertainty and wavering, ambivalence, or doubt. False reconciliations are quite common in the endings of close relationships.

A key point to note here, then, is that because the social order prefers couples, marriage, and long-term pairings (Chapter 5), the breakup must disrupt that social order even though it is happening at a personal level. One of the complicating factors of breakup stories, therefore, is that the social order requires the ending not just of affection but of other things when romantic relationships go bad. One of these is a social order rearrangement, one is a material adjustment, and the third is a personal order issue.

What Is Broken in a Breakup?

There are many reasons for this, but they have not previously been understood from the new perspective that I am offering. For a long time, researchers (Hagestad & Smyer, 1982) have claimed that the breakup of close relationships is not simply the ending of an *emotional* attachment to someone (personal order issue). In fact, there are material, performative, and embodied elements also.

The partners do, of course, have to separate from one another emotionally, but they also have to separate from the social order idea of *being a couple*. In a social order where the idea that people go around in couples is very deeply rooted, not having a partner is regarded as a negative situation and one to be soon corrected.

Performatively, materially, and in embodied form, the partners have to separate from the routines and habits that they established as a couple (for example, the way that they used to structure the day—dinner is always at 6:45, and Friday evenings are always date nights that the couple spends together enjoying one another's company).

So, in case anyone was under the illusion that breaking up is *not* hard to do, or is just about emotion and choice rather than materiality, think again.

Every aspect is hard to do in and of itself, but the parts add up to a very complicated package for people to handle as they violate the expectations of social order for stability and commitment. From my perspective, language and its forms work differently at different points of breakup because the whole darn process is an extended realignment of epistemic viewpoints.

STORIES AND THE BREAKDOWN OF RELATIONSHIPS

Your understanding of the world can be upset by negative relationships (involuntary, pain-in-the-butt relationships [Kirkpatrick, Duck, & Foley, 2006] or breakup of good ones [Rollie & Duck, 2006]). In these cases, the relationship experiences deconstruct and dilapidate your social world—a process that creates a threat to your *personal* orders while also destabilizing institutional expectations in the *social* order.

Part of the negativity of such relationship turmoils and woes is not just due to the fact that they challenge your worldview and your view of yourself, but that you have to justify yourself to the social order. The processes should be understood as being about that as well as about emotion and the rest.

Making Sense to Self and Others

When your relationships turn bad, they disturb your epistemic and personal order. For that reason, people tend to turn private, to conceal infidelity, loneliness, conflict, or hidden interpersonal violence. But all of that needs to be explained in terms that other people can understand and will comprehend in terms of the social order.

Narratives have to make sense to other people, even if you yourself do not understand what happened. You need them to put some sense on it for public consumption, and that's where the social order plays a big part in the breakdown of relationships.

Face Management

An important aspect of the narratives of relationship breakdown consists of the management of the face of the person telling the story. Everyone wants to tell a story about relationship breakdown where he or she comes out either as the injured party or as the person who handled everything maturely and sensibly.

Of course, this story, like the process of relationship breakdown itself, has many parts and phases, from your own private thoughts about it to the public gravestone that gets erected over the tomb of the relationship after all else is said and done. That gravestone tells an important story for the social order.

PROCESSES OF BREAKUP

Intrapsychic Processes

Accordingly, humans clearly carry on much of their relational lives without communicating every syllable of it to other people; indeed, much relational activity is carried out inside the head, where people plan, enjoy, consider, evolve feelings, replay memories, or create expectations. If you are willing to write off a partner's careless word or thoughtless action as insignificant, unintentional, or excusable, then the effect of such words or deeds will be negligible.

Thus, although your partner's actions can create negative feelings in you, it is ultimately your own thoughts or reactions that start the process of relational termination if you are the one who begins to get bored, resentful, or displeased. This is the intrapsychic process of Figure 7.1. Until your personal order is imbalanced by some action that would look bad in the *social* order, you have no reasonable grounds for breaking up—or at least no grounds that others would accept as reasonable. You can churn, grumble, and feel negative whether or not you tell anyone about it, until the grumbling comes up with a set of reasons that will be convincing to others.

Dyadic Processes

However, when you do decide to voice any concerns, then you start to get into the sort of conversation with your partner that presents difficult problems (dyadic process). This involves not only facing up to an angry, surprised, and hurt partner, but perhaps also outraged or disapproving friends and relatives, or negative reactions from other people who liked your partner more than they liked you or from social or religious groups who disapprove of what has happened. (Many social orders disapprove of divorce, for example.) You also may want to nurse your wounds for the ended relationship and withdraw from social contact, or alternatively, you may want to get back on the horse and start up new relationships as soon as possible. In all of these cases, you have to step outside of your own head and re-engage the social world. Such confrontation with the thoughts of other people involves you in a lengthy process of readjustment that can make relationship dissolution not only terribly painful but also terribly extended.

Social Processes

The social processes start the process of going truly public about the relationship troubles. Both partners consult their friends, family, and other people in order to discuss the problem and seek advice or support. Once this public line is crossed, the matter is taken into the social order directly and will be judged, so that accounts are no longer personal but for your audience also. In social processes, people spend a certain amount of time criticizing the partner to other people and attempting to receive support and validation for their critique (their epistemic personal order).

Grave Dressing Processes

Next comes a grave dressing process. After the relationship has died, people need to distribute a potted history of the relationship from birth to death. The two needs here relative to the social order are

1. to make such a history plausible, and

2. to present yourself in such a way that the social order judges you as suitable for new relationships.

Resurrection

The final process, resurrection, involves preparing oneself to reenter the social order in a new form: an available, acceptable, desirable social partner.

In all of these processes, the structure of the narratives used for each audience must reflect awareness of the relative rhetorical situation. Each phase must follow the general social order rules for accounts and narratives as well as being accompanied by performative actions that are consistent with what is being said.

As Figure 7.1 indicates, different kinds of communication occur as different processes take charge of the breakup, with an individual withdrawing from society at the intrapsychic process, consulting only with the partner and no others at the dyadic process, breaking out into multiple conversations in the social network in the social process and grave dressing process, and once again constructing a "time to open a clean page" story about self in the resurrection process. As also indicated in Figure 7.1, the topics of communication are different in the different phases of the process, with complaints, confrontations, and narratives all taking a larger part as the process itself continues.

Figure 7.1   Breakdown Process Model

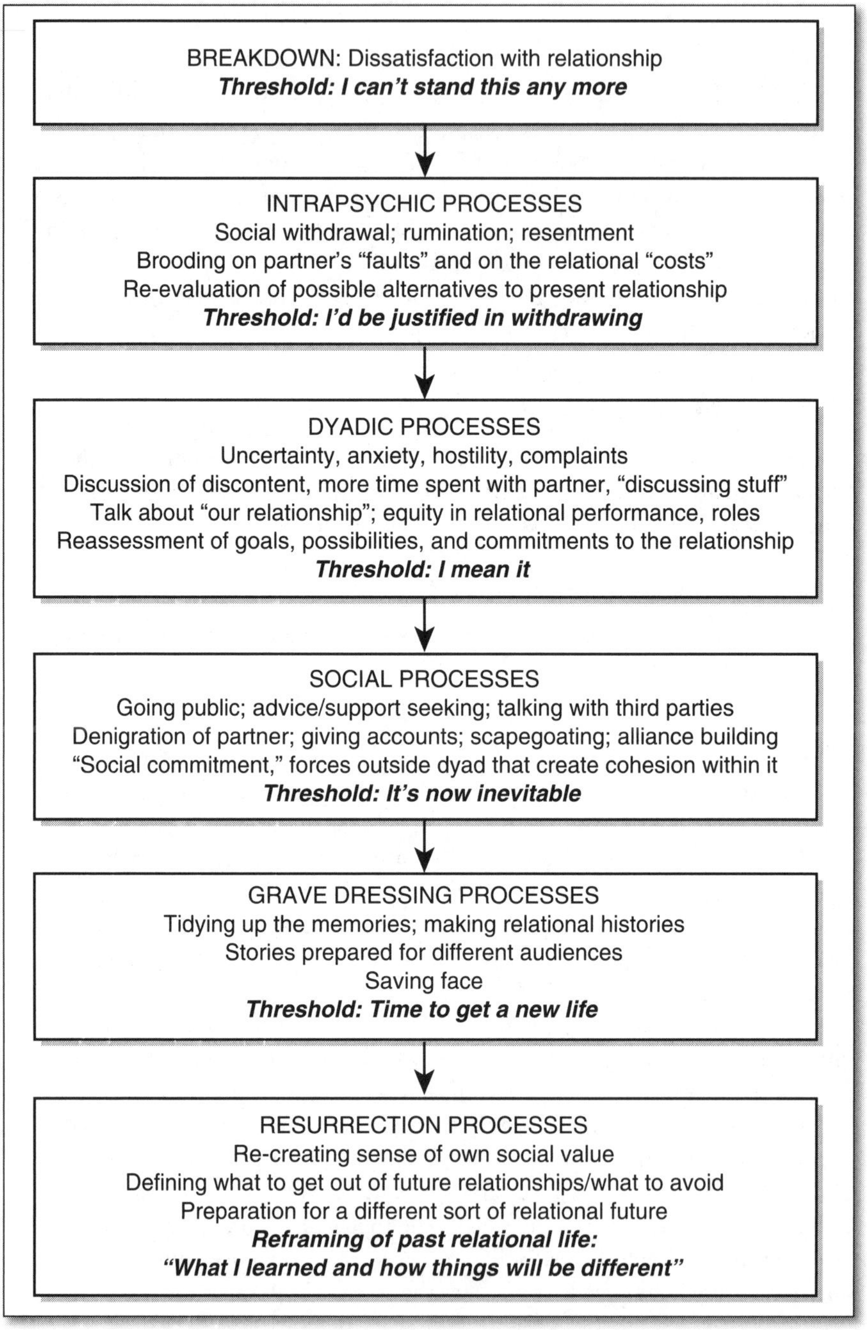

BREAKDOWN: Dissatisfaction with relationship
Threshold: I can't stand this any more

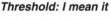

INTRAPSYCHIC PROCESSES
Social withdrawal; rumination; resentment
Brooding on partner's "faults" and on the relational "costs"
Re-evaluation of possible alternatives to present relationship
Threshold: I'd be justified in withdrawing

DYADIC PROCESSES
Uncertainty, anxiety, hostility, complaints
Discussion of discontent, more time spent with partner, "discussing stuff"
Talk about "our relationship"; equity in relational performance, roles
Reassessment of goals, possibilities, and commitments to the relationship
Threshold: I mean it

SOCIAL PROCESSES
Going public; advice/support seeking; talking with third parties
Denigration of partner; giving accounts; scapegoating; alliance building
"Social commitment," forces outside dyad that create cohesion within it
Threshold: It's now inevitable

GRAVE DRESSING PROCESSES
Tidying up the memories; making relational histories
Stories prepared for different audiences
Saving face
Threshold: Time to get a new life

RESURRECTION PROCESSES
Re-creating sense of own social value
Defining what to get out of future relationships/what to avoid
Preparation for a different sort of relational future
Reframing of past relational life:
"What I learned and how things will be different"

Source: Duck, S. W. (2007). *Human relationships* (4th ed.). London: Sage.

Connection to the Next Chapter

This chapter has emphasized the high level, untouchable, and immaterial social order in contrast to the previous chapters. Its focus has been on language and the styles and linguistic structures in a social order in the abstract.

Previous chapters have stressed that everything abstract has a material manifestation. The following chapter deals with these issues with some insights into the ways in which talk and speaking in all the preceding material and embodied contexts carry the burden of such connection.

Language is nothing without people speaking it and recognizing the social order that lies behind it. Stories are nothing until there is a teller or a reader. Therefore, people make the abstraction of stories and language into something material and real through their everyday conversations.

The forms of talk, the way self is reported to others, and the explanations given for relational success or failure are nevertheless always delivered from one person to another against the background of a social order. The discovery of someone's personality involves action and speaking to disclose it. These performances deliver a presentation of the self.

The final chapter, while looking at all of these performances of abstract ideals, will also consider why the previous discussion of the material influences on abstractions such as emotion are important to the consideration of the future of the field of study of personal relationships.

PEDAGOGICAL ISSUES

EXERCISES

Write the contents list for a book titled *My Friendship With X*. The book should have nine chapters. Write the contents list for another book titled *Why My Friendship With Y Went Wrong*. Again, there should be nine chapters. Now examine the metaphors that are used in the chapter titles.

ETHICAL ISSUES

Is it wrong to tell different stories about a relationship to different audiences?

MEDIA ISSUES

Listen for the metaphors that are used in the tabloid press and popular magazines like *People* and *Us* to describe the romantic lives of celebrities. What moral lessons do you think we are supposed to draw from these descriptions?

References

Baxter, L. A., Dun, T. D., & Sahlstein, E. M. (2001). Rules for relating communicated among social network members. *Journal of Social and Personal Relationships, 18,* 173–200.

Bergmann, J. R. (1993). *Discreet indiscretions: The social organization of gossip.* New York: Aldine de Gruyter.

Duck, S. W. (2007). *Human relationships* (4th ed.). London: Sage.

Felmlee, D. H. (1995). Fatal attractions: Affection and disaffection in intimate relationships. *Journal of Social and Personal Relationships, 12,* 295–311.

Hagestad, G. O., & Smyer, M. A. (1982). Dissolving long-term relationships: Patterns of divorcing in middle age. In S. Duck (Ed.), *Personal relationships 4: Dissolving personal relationships* (pp. 155–187). London: Academic Press.

Huisman, D. (2008). *Intergenerational family storytelling* (Unpublished doctoral dissertation). University of Iowa, Iowa City.

Kirkpatrick, C. D., Duck , S. W., & Foley, M. K. (Eds.). (2006). *Relating difficulty: The processes of constructing and managing difficult interaction.* Mahwah, NJ: Lawrence Erlbaum.

Koenig Kellas, J. (2005). Family ties: Communicating identity through jointly told family stories. *Communication Monographs, 72*(4), 365–389.

Kovecses, Z. (1991). A linguist's quest for love. *Journal of Social and Personal Relationships, 8,* 77–98.

Lakoff, G., & Johnson, M. (1980). *Metaphors you live by.* Chicago: University of Chicago Press.

Norwood, K. M. (2007). *Gendered conflict? The "cattiness" of women on* Flavor of Love. Paper presented at the Organization for the Study of Communication, Language, and Gender, Omaha, NE.

Rollie, S. S., & Duck, S. W. (2006). Stage theories of marital breakdown. In J. H. Harvey & M. A. Fine (Eds.), *Handbook of divorce and dissolution of romantic relationships* (pp. 176–193). Mahwah, NJ: Lawrence Erlbaum.

Weiss, R. S. (1974). The provisions of social relationships. In Z. Rubin (Ed.), *Doing unto others* (pp. 17–26). Englewood Cliffs, NJ: Prentice-Hall.

8

Talk and Speaking
Personal Orders

The previous chapter dealt with the ways in which language itself shapes
and represents a social order's expectations about relationships. This
background is present during all personal interchanges between people in all
sorts of relationships, from the distant social relationships of strangers to the
intimate personal conversations of lovers. However, in these conversations, the
partners are also expressing their personal orders, the exploration of which is
a large part of the process of getting to know someone.

Language is an abstraction, but one that is used on occasion by minds and
persons who have a material being. It is not useful, especially in the field of personal relationships, to write about language or discourse in the abstract without considering the bodies that produce it and the ways in which talking and
speaking are performances. The critical difference between language as an
abstracted system not subject to change by individuals, on one hand, and
speaking as a performance of a personal order version of that abstract system,
on the other hand, is not to be overlooked. I will keep using my favored terms
of *social order* and *personal order,* but in the context of the *performance* of language in conversation, it is important to consider the broader ways in which
the two are different. Language is, of course, a resource that is used by speakers, and they cannot change it because it is a social order. Although it guides
their thoughts and speaking, language is different from the occasions of its performance in conversation. Here, partners adapt, choose, and select the forms of
speaking that best suit their individual purposes at the time, and this occasion
offers speakers the chance to rub their personal order up against the social
order, and hence to contest or conform with it. Let's see how it works and why
that matters.

The Surroundings of Conversation

I have stressed that relationships are unfinished business and need to be directed or continued, often by apparently trivial means. We have learned the *presentational* nature of communication about relationships, but also that language and its use in everyday communication actually shape and even create relationships. People can give a meaning to their relationships through an organized *narrative* that does not necessarily reflect their varying experiences at the time described. Having a straightened-out, narrative-shaped story, and especially one about a relationship, is essential to people's sense of relationship continuity and indeed to their sense of their own continuous identity (Duck & McMahan, 2010).

This all complicates the process of getting to *know* someone, which most people agree is what acquaintance, attraction, falling in love, and the development of friendship are all about. However, the point of view of this book is that these processes involve an exposure of personal orders against the background of the social order. We can therefore take a new look at some familiar processes.

TALKING PRESENTS A SELF

From all this, it follows that getting to know people involves more than simply listening to them express the inner core of truth about themselves. As we have seen in previous chapters, such truth can be described from many different points of view in many different rhetorical situations.

Any personal declarations are, at the very least, surrounded by the social order, of which we are so often unaware that it surprises us to have it exposed. We can no longer defend the view that personality or self is simply revealed by communication, exposed layer by layer, unless we ignore completely the situation in which an individual does such declaration and revelation. Although it has been true that previous research has often ignored such circumstances, one of the points of this book is that to do so is a major error.

The self is actually constructed in part from material circumstances, communication, and social order expectations about suitable descriptive terms for self and mental templates of how to relate to others. From this arise one's personal feelings of security and the social order's rhetorical visions about the expression of inner life to others. Because everyday talk is structured action—symbolic, embodied, and performed in a way that simple recitation of words from a dictionary is not—it therefore involves meaning and presentation of a preferred way of being perceived. Everyday speaking conveys symbolic hypertext to others and is shrouded in metaphors that reveal states of mind about relationships to the broader society.

Everyday speaking is also performative (stories are *told* and storytelling is often an *occasion*) and embodied in the physical characteristics, mannerisms, and material representation of the speaker. Talking about one's self is therefore not in the least a simple process but a highly compounded and contextualized one. It presents a personal order, but does so in a bounded context provided by the social order of the expectations of others.

For all these reasons, we can expect that everyday talk plays a central role in relationships that is much more complex than simply peeling the layers of an onion. Talking involves interconnected mechanisms richer than simple exposure of thought, as if layers of skin were peeled away from a central (and, by implication, more important) core. Rather, the situation is more dramatic, like that being presented by an actor in a public theater with a purpose: to make an audience laugh or cry; to mock or pity a character; or to interpret a character's motivation, indecision, or self-destruction by giving an edge to the way in which words are spoken.

> The word *personality* is derived from the Latin word *persona*, which is the word for a mask worn by an actor. Such masks served not only to represent the character being played by the actor but also were designed with funnels around the mouth to project the voice in an age before microphones and digital technology.

In real life, performances have repeated effects on the assessment of individuals as potential relational partners, as the unfinished business of the relationship unfolds. These effects are brought about by the fact that language itself is not the only message of an embodied performance that conforms to the rituals and expectations of a given social order. The words themselves are not the only point. Messages are shaped by the way words are spoken, performed, and embodied or accompanied by nonverbal communication.

CONTEXT

Context helps us to interpret talk and makes some of it more relevant to our understanding of each other than other parts do. We glean something also from the positioning of the talk in the social order, the taken-for-granted, and the unsaid. An audience becomes part of the performance because it has the same set of understandings and shared beliefs that characterize the speaker and the teller of stories, as discussed in the previous chapter.

Without such a set of shared and taken-for-granted material, the stories that individuals tell about their lives would lose some of their central meaning. They would be merely idiosyncratic and lacking in the connection to the larger social order that is necessary for their interpretation. However, audiences are also critical listeners who do not buy into any old cock-and-bull story about someone's experiences. Audiences question, probe, evaluate, and make judgments. In effect, they act as agents of the social order.

The previous chapters have also shown that historical and even present-day materiality seriously influences the way in which people see relationships in a social order. The nature of relationships as simple and emotional connections has not been merely carried through from one century to the next without stylistic and material transformation. Although we are as unaware of our positioning in a material history as previous generations have been in theirs, we are nevertheless surrounded by the expectations of the historical social order that puts speech and talking about oneself into a particular context.

For example, even within the past 50 years, it has become much more acceptable for people to open their hearts and disclose themselves freely to their partners and to others as the therapeutic value of a transparent self has been exposed by some clinicians (Jourard, 1971). Thus, whereas our great-grandparents would have stonily endured the pains and anguish of unhappy marriages, the present historical context encourages people to tell it all. Indeed, many celebrities and politicians can make money by revealing selective secrets of their personal lives.

CONVERSATION IS MORE THAN SIMPLE EXPRESSION

When I reinterpreted personality as a way of knowing and suggested that personality can be based on physical experience, I deferred discussion of the role of everyday conversation in relationships as a means through which we learn about one another.

One (naïve) way to look at speaking is as a simple expression of facts and feelings through language. But there is more. It's almost too obvious to mention that face-to-face talk brings two bodies into close proximity. The physical materiality of those bodies also contributes something to the conversation, whether physical attractiveness, a nice fragrance, beautiful eyes, or a generally agitated nonverbal style. Therefore, we need to continue to distinguish *language* as an abstraction in a social order from *speaking*, where talk embodies the performance of expression.

This chapter will focus on talk/speech and the materiality of speaking in everyday talk. I will look at speaking as the embodiment of the expression of language, often accompanied by a rich array of nonverbal and other material signals. Here, we will look at talk as the symbolic way of referring to everything that gets done in speaking—everything that is an expression of a personal order in a setting that recognizes and reflects the social order. How does your talk—its structure and form as well as its contents—continue to vibrate and resonate with your material understanding of the world as you perform your self and your relationships? For example, we saw in the previous chapter what happens to your talk when your understanding of the world is disrupted in relationship breakdown. There are alterations to both your patterns of speech in your social network and your topics of conversation as different processes command the unfolding stories.

CONTINUING RELATIONSHIPS IN TALK

To consider deeper connections between talk, speaking, and relationships, it is essential once again to recognize that relationships are unfinished business, conducted more often in the idle chatter where you report on activities day by day than in star moments of intimate revelation. So if relationships are unfinished business, they engage you constantly doing, performing, and talking them into being. This occurs through the performance of relating in routines. Momentary changes in form and style of talk can change the relationship. Reciprocally, each changes the other into a modified form of being and knowing.

> One message of Chapters 4 to 7, however, is that talk is not equivalent to language or spoken text. Talk comes out of bodies, engages other bodies, and is a physical performance, not just a disembodied playing of a tape recorder. People are not walking megaphones playing computer-generated voice output.

Part of the impact of what people say comes from who they are, how they look, how they say what they say, what sort of performance they give, and whether their nonverbal communication is consistent with their verbal reports. Part comes from the material circumstances of the occasion of speaking; the audience to whom a person is speaking; and the historical times, culture, and circumstances of the utterance (rhetorical situation). "Veni, vidi, vici," said by Julius Caesar when reporting his conquests, was a punning but serious message to friends and foes alike concerning his invincibility. Said today by anyone, it is merely a historical reference, a joke, or a display of general knowledge. "I will," said in a magistrate's office in the material circumstances labeled "marriage ceremony," means more than it does as a response to a roommate's request to do the dishes.

SPEAKING: TALK STYLE AND CONTEXT

Speaking, then, is not just words; it involves the whole body, its material form, and context. For example, even without understanding the words, you can learn from tone, pitch, rhythm, and pacing of the voice the speaker's age or sex, and perhaps whether or not there is an argument going on, a joke being told, or comfort being offered, whether the people are strangers or friends. When you are more informed about context, the meaning is fuller. Sometimes, you talk with a partner about your experiences (catch-up talk at the end of the day maintains the relationship). Sometimes, you talk about each other and your relationship ("our relationship" talks define a relational future). Sometimes, you take care of tasks (routine talk takes care of business). Sometimes, any of those items can affect the future of the relationship (all talk exposes rhetorical visions to a reflective audience).

Such talk is not simply giving people a chance to mouth off about their personal opinions and their days, and to expose, disclose, or display their ideas. It is actually serving a much more important and much deeper *symbolic* function for the relationship, including one that connects to the very nature of the relationships that are tolerated in a given society.

Style and Intimacy

First, the *style* of communication in close relationships (for example, loose, rambling, anything goes) conveys a symbolic message about the intimacy of the relationship. All the same, it does so only within a symbolic framework of a social order that regards *that* as the way to do/perform intimacy. When you chat with friends, you do so in casual surroundings (a material physical environment), whatever the topic of discussion, and you do it informally and in a friendly way, as defined by your society.

Content and Intimacy

Second, the *content* of your chat is symbolic when it is unrestricted like this. The fact that you can talk about almost anything is symbolic of your level of comfort with the other person as someone who shares the same orders of belief about relationships and many other matters.

Personal Hypertext and Intimacy

Third, people in close relationships develop their own ways of talking about themselves and to themselves. For example, partners develop a private language that refers to significant moments in their relationship, their nicknames for each other, or cues for activity. These "personal idioms" (Hopper, Knapp, & Scott, 1981) could be such phrases as "Have you brought the yarmulke for the cabbage patch kid?" which might turn out to be a coded way of asking if the partner has a condom handy. In a particular relationship, to say "Beetlejuice!" may be a code for "You are so weird!" or "Nih!" could serve as code for "OK, that's enough of that; let's change the subject."

There are almost as many personal idioms as there are people, and you can produce your own examples of nicknames and code words that you use only with certain other friends and partners. Although you play out these sorts of language usage rather often in close relationships, you may overlook the symbolism of the process. The use of private language not only signals intimacy, but is a subtle way of excluding other people and drawing a symbolic boundary around the relationship. You and your partner have knowledge that other people do not. You keep other people out by having a talking "passport" that lets in only those people who understand your personal symbolic codes. You keep the relationship private and intimate by this speaking form.

Form and Intimacy

Fourth, as we saw in Chapter 7, language has a form and structure to it, most often a narrative form that involves characters, plot lines, outcomes, and the connection of events in predictable and systematic ways. Talk, therefore, is not a random collection of words but a formally constructed one performed within a social order about what constitutes a meaningful report and how such a report should be constructed.

It isn't good enough, then, to suppose that talk between people is doing nothing more active than giving the mind a microphone for revelation or discovery of personalities or attitudes. We must take account of all the material, embodied, and performative aspects of the social order as previous chapters have shown. Speaking makes relationships happen or *talks them into material being* through performance in a social order. If relationships are ways of knowing (epistemic), and because, by definition, they involve more than one person (i.e., more than one personal [epistemic] order), then something has to be *shared* between the two ways of knowing for the two people to communicate in the first place. But what?

Listen in on Your Own Life

How easy do you find it to tell from the way two people are talking with one another whether or not they know one another or are strangers?

Forms of Talk and Speaking

Chapter 7 dealt with forms of language and inspected language, metaphor, narrative, and the structure of the social order. When two people talk, they perform the social order and also present their own personal orders in that context. It is therefore appropriate to ask, What are you *doing* when you talk in a relationship?

A conversation is not just talk but also an event. The occurrence of such events has symbolic meaning. Indeed, people often report how much they miss speaking with an absent friend, even though they will admit equally frequently that when a conversation does take place, it is invariably not about very much that is important.

In relationships, you talk in ways that accomplish much at once. You can send information (data) in a way that is friendly (relational). You can say something casually that indicates comfort in the other person's presence (which is a relational message that *talks informality into being*) as well as answering the questions that they put to you (which is the "content" of the message), and so on. Thus, speaking can perform a relationship "quality" while also acting to transmit information. Within the general observation that talk always conveys both content and a relational message (Watzlawick, Bavelas, & Jackson, 1967), there are other functions of speaking. These follow the analysis that I have given in previous chapters on embodiment, performance, and the social order.

SOME SYMBOLIC FUNCTIONS OF SPEAKING

The several different possibilities that talk serves are not mutually exclusive; a single act can achieve different goals simultaneously. For example, you can ask a friend for a favor in a way that not only indicates the strength of your need but also stresses the strength of relationship as part of the persuasion attempt ("You are my friend and I really need your help on this") (Sahlstein, 2000).

Furthermore, the occurrence of just a single utterance in any conversation is extremely rare. For the most part, conversations last a while and meander across a variety of topics and issues. The looseness of this form of speaking in itself indicates relaxation and intimacy. Thus, when I am discussing "speaking," I don't normally mean single utterances but rather the whole context of conversation. Indeed, more than that, I mean the whole series and sequences of conversations that have happened before in that relationship and that set an important context for what someone says in a particular comment. You know what partners mean and why it is important to them because they have a history of concern about a particular topic, for example (Duck, 2002).

Given this, three forms can be differentiated in the material structure of speaking and talk: indexing, instrumentalism, and essentializing (Duck & Pond, 1989).

Indexing

This is something that you do all the time and that comes up in everyday chitchat: you indicate, by your speaking, the kind of relationship you have with the person to whom you're talking. Strangers can listen to tapes of conversation and are able to tell the level of relationship between the two people, whether it's a close relationship or not (Planalp & Benson, 1992).

The cues have to do with what people say, what they take for granted without further explanation, and the shared knowledge that they have and assume self-evidently in the conversation. There are many indexes like this in a conversation. For example, if I say, "I met Jack yesterday, and he said . . .," the fact that I don't explain who Jack is indicates that the two of us know the person and something about him. "We went to Maddux yesterday and had a cappuccino." "What did you think of the party last night?" These might be the sorts of talk that people who know one other would say. Contrast this with "Jack—that's my husband—and I went to Maddux—that's a small town south of here—and had a cappuccino at a little cafe down there that is a hotspot romantic place for lovers to go. We wanted to re-light the magic in our relationship."

> Research has been done on ways in which nonverbal communication indexes aspects of talk by emphasizing through bodily action the way in which a person feels as he or she speaks. The talk itself can contain many indexes of closeness and distance such as immediacy in the form of talk that is employed.

An important finding of one study is that talk can be accurately differentiated by observers as occurring between friends or acquaintances (Planalp & Garvin-Doxas, 1994). Features about the talk of friends and acquaintances follow social order codes of relational activity but personalize the performance to convey indications to outsiders that the partners are performing a particular social form recognized by the social order.

This is not a trivial observation: The fact that relationship forms are encoded in speech permits judgment of whether people are acting appropriately to their relationship or assessment of whether your partner is speaking to you in a form that is merited by your relationship. The fact also allows one to observe—and perhaps celebrate or bemoan—changes in the form of relationship that are conveyed indirectly by means of expression. When a relationship grows or declines, people's speaking changes, and conversation either occurs less frequently or is more distant in tone.

Another sort of index in relationship is that people do not watch their language or their manners as carefully when they're talking with intimates as they do when talking with higher status people, for example. Even interruptions mean something different according to whether speakers know one another well or not (Dindia, 1987); intimate friends tend to interrupt one another more often than do formal, distant acquaintances.

So, from the way people interrupt and how they do it, you can tell whether they know one another well. When people know one another well, the flow of conversation is much less stilted and deliberate than it is between strangers. When people are in a formal situation, then such interruptions are offensive and cause difficulty. You are not supposed to interrupt people who are talking in a formal setting, such as a lecture or a business presentation.

People who know one another will also use more inclusive pronouns ("we," "us") or other indications of togetherness and partnership, like creating plans that include both parties. For example, servers use it to get more money (tips). This element of talk is referred to technically as "immediacy" in language (Mehrabian, 1971). An immediate form, including also the use of nicknames and informal tones, indexes a sense of closeness that is not conveyed by stricter and more tightly grammatical forms of speech.

Other researchers from a different background have noted that such tonal aspects of speaking can be changed in the course of an interaction (Giles & Coupland, 1991): A parent might start out saying, "Jill, honey, please tidy up your room," and after several unsuccessful attempts might switch to a more formal tone: "Ms. Weinstock, your room is a mess. Get it tidied up!" Each tone and style of communication represents a relational statement. Therefore, different relational meanings can be picked and used in the course of the same interaction. This is an important indication that one of the roles of speaking is to index (changes in) the tone of the relationship during the course of an interaction. As the form of talk changes, so the relationship performance is minutely adjusted for the moment, and aspects such as power are stressed and exerted in place of casual intimacy.

Instrumentalism

An important job of speaking is to sustain but also to change relationships directly. For example, if I ask you out on a date or propose marriage or invite you to my home, then I'm using talk instrumentally to bring about a specific relational experience. Talk is used to create a new form of relationship or bring about a desired relational outcome or change. If you see relationships as unfinished business, then people can just change a relationship instrumentally by the form of their talking about it, whether negatively or positively.

Once a relationship has been changed instrumentally in this way, it can also be indexed differently, and after an acceptance of a marriage proposal, the couple may adopt different forms of address or a more relaxed and informal tone. The key difference between instrumentalism and indexing is that the first *causes* a change or state in a relationship and the second *reflects* the state of a relationship and any changes in it.

Epistemic shifts follow the way the relationship is talked into being, although relationship definitions also need to have a certain and significant level of agreement between the partners. That is, they

> **Question to Ask Your Friends**
>
> How long can you address one another in formal language, using titles and last names, before one of you finds it too awkward to carry on?

don't work as relationships unless the partners share a definition. For example, two people must agree that they are intimate for intimate forms of speaking to work, other than as a joke. Also for one person to perform a style of relationship that is "inappropriate" in the other person's eyes is to provoke a dispute about the nature of the relationship.

Essentializing

If two people present a relationship as having a particular form, then it *becomes* that in some sense, because it doesn't work as a relationship unless the partners share a definition. What that tells you is that the talkers' epistemic about their relationship is essentially a personalized structure through which to understand what relationship behavior means and how it should be interpreted and reacted to. Partners in a relationship create an understanding of what the relationship should look like and what the norms and rules are for them personally. They decide what counts as positive and negative. This personal order is created in the context of their own relationship, even if there are larger social guidelines. Everyone's experience is different, but members of the same social order share certain commonalities of understanding. Every personal order occurs within a larger social order without being exactly the same as it. When your rhetorical visions of the world are put out there on display in conversation, other people can accept, reject, or challenge them. Acceptance personalizes intimacy.

THE MEANINGS OF SPEAKING

People can argue whether a comment is indexical or instrumental and so essentialize the relationship differently because the rhetorical vision they are presenting makes the relationship in a particular form. "I love you" could be news, a routine at the end of the phone call, a shocking revelation, or the first conversational step on a pathway to a deeper relationship.

Speaking to Reduce Uncertainty or Create Definition

People are not always sure what they're doing in relationships and do not always know where they are going. The open-ended nature of relationships thus makes the essentializing of a relationship ambiguous. Sometimes you know what you want to do in a relationship and sometimes you don't. Sometimes you're just looking to see how it turns out. Sometimes you will raise questions about a relationship to decide what the other person thinks and what his or her intentions may be. If someone says "I love you" and the other person says nothing back, then that lack of response can itself have significant meaning.

In everyday speaking, then, you index, define, essentialize, and present friendship. The range of talk on a particular occasion helps to essentialize the fact that two people have a particular sort of relationship whether this is mere acquaintance or a deep, close friendship. From time to time, especially as a relationship develops, you are able to move to deeper topics and a wider range of them also, and so you essentialize the development of the relationship. A friendship that does not move on to new and more extensive topics is not really going anywhere. The structure of speaking essentializes the relationship in a specific material or symbolic form.

Speaking and Change

Speaking on particular occasions tells you about the ways in which two people are thinking about a relationship only at that particular time. Talk topics can change and so the relationship changes; it is not simply that people describe differently something that has an *inherent* nature. As with all social items, the description, the performance, and the tonality of interaction *is* the relationship, because a change in mind about a relationship described to a partner *is* a change in the relationship.

You can end a relationship just by *saying* "This one is over" or "I want to be friends and not lovers from here on." In this sense, the form of speaking essentializes the relationship, and people talk relationships into being. However, they do so in relation to the social order. We have already seen how membership of networks and social orders changes your personal orders and is another way in which people talk relationships into being.

Getting to Know You:
Unscrambling Another Person's World of Meaning

The basic process of getting to know someone is therefore a process of the serial, sequential, and persistent construction and reconstruction of a map of their meaning system or personal order. The first sketch map is improved and becomes more accurate the more you speak with a person. Because relationships and personality are both, in their own ways, forms of knowing, the connection of personality to relationship development works through the same channel. Both are about ways of knowing. When you get to relate to someone, it is because you are getting to know about his or her ways of knowing and you are telling him or her about your ways of knowing.

There are actually four different ways in which you can know about someone else and his or her experience. Each one involves a deeper understanding of the connection between the events that have occurred in someone's life, and his or her broad understanding, categorizing, and evaluating of those events, which makes them into meaningful experiences, as distinguished in Chapter 4 (experience as an event versus experience as what you make of something or how you understand it).

When you first meet someone, it is quite likely that that person has a number of event experiences in common with you that you do not yet know are shared. Most people you meet socially are predominantly from your own social class, religious group, and racial or ethnic background, and such similarities are good bases for the first sketch map. Not all of them, but the vast majority.

This makes one of the tasks of getting acquainted the job of digging out specific commonalities. You do this for a variety of reasons, most of which have to do with the comfort that you get from finding that someone else has had the same background as you have had, which makes you feel a basic connection to him or her. However, it also arises because similarity of background actually helps you to communicate, not only because you have a lot of shared topics but because similar people tend to communicate similarly. It is a whole lot easier to talk to someone who gets your jokes, understands what you are referring or alluding to, and does not need everything perpetually explained. They *get* it. They get *you*. So what is the process of "getting to know you" all about?

Commonality of Experience

In the most superficial cases, people have a simple *commonality of experience*. They have had a similar event occur in their lives, but they don't know it yet because they have not had time to tell one another much about themselves. I might distrust my mother's manipulativeness and her need to control, and so I might become suspicious of all powerful women as a result. You may have the same sorts of views about *your* mother, too, but we have not talked about our childhoods or our views of our parents, so at the start of a relationship, we do not yet know about our feelings about our respective mothers.

Mutuality of Experience

Once a particular topic (mothers, in this case) comes into the conversation, the two people may become aware that they have had the same events occur in their lives (both had controlling mothers). At this point, that is all they know: that the same experience happened to them. They do not know what it meant to each of them or what they made of it, they just know it happened. Hence, the second part of getting to know someone is *mutuality of experience*. You both know that you had these same experiences in the past or that you have equivalent knowledge about some experience, place, event, or topic.

In itself, knowing that you both had this mutuality of experience is not useful except as a springboard for further conversation. One of you may have dealt with the experience well and never thought of it again, whereas the other may have been scarred for life. The difference in what two people made of an event will be reflected in their respective personal orders, and the mere existence of the same event in their past is not predictive of how they experienced it or how it is constructed in their personal order. Therefore, it is important that each party to the conversation gets to know what each person made of his or her experience or his or her knowledge about a topic.

Equivalence of Meaning

In order to understand a person's personal order, it is meaningful to get to know how he or she evaluated events in his or her past. You both went to Alaska and loved it; both had controlling mothers and hated the resulting sense of powerlessness; both studied psychology and thought that social psychology was fascinating but the stuff about rat learning theories was utterly boring. This third process is therefore labeled *equivalence of meaning*. You both evaluated your separate experiences in much the same way and hence are entirely on the same page when you talk about those experiences and what they meant to you. Your personal orders both begin to look to each of you as if they are similar with respect to that particular topic at any rate.

Shared Meaning: Overlap of Personal Orders

The fourth part of the process of recognizing overlap of personal orders is where it really starts to cook as an emotional experience. You begin to find out that the particular topic referenced in equivalence of meaning is an element of a wider scheme of understanding that also matches your own. You start to find out that within the broad scheme, the other person places the equivalent meaning of the topic within a broader arrangement of meanings that mirrors yours, too. For example, you both feel that the trip to Alaska was an epiphany and a defining experience for you, that having a controlling mother steered your whole life, and that studying psychology was a time of fundamental change and growth in your attitudes to the world. In short, you discover in this fourth process that you have *shared meaning*. You've had the same event in your past, you both know you've had it, you've experienced and evaluated it in the same ways, and you agree about how it fits into your whole scheme of understanding (personal order).

Not only is there shared meaning, but also shared sensemaking in your personal orders. Hence, shared meaning is a good basis for assuming that there is more similarity under the surface that has not yet been explored. You both have similar ways of thinking about this one item, so you probably have similar ways of thinking about a lot of other matters as yet unexplored. As the future unfolds in the relationship, you will discover either that this inference is correct and the relationship will develop, or that it is incorrect. In fact, equivalence of meaning about one particular topic does not generalize to shared meaning about other topics, and so you will abort the relationship. Otherwise, that recognition of shared meaning systems is when the relational fuse gets lit and the relationship can really begin to take off. Both of you now believe that your personal orders of meaning are broadly comparable and you think it is worth spending a lot of time finding out.

This ultimate discovery of the underlying value system of someone's personal order is powerful when it is securely based; the social order creates rules and templates for it to happen (such as the polite questions that one may ask a new acquaintance). Stories and metaphors are powerful blueprints from which greater detailing of someone else's personal order can be built.

Talk and Change for the Better

In keeping with the rest of the book, talk about improving relationships or developing them to a new level is about epistemic overlap and how it increases. The process of acquaintance is the process of sharing your world of meaning with someone else. The greater the overlap in both extent and depth, the stronger the relationship, so you can see that metaphors are at work here, too.

Personality, we have learned, is epistemic—a set of organized ways of knowing the world and the people in it. Personality is manifested or performed in a number of ways (such as your patterns of behavior or your styles of speech or your ways of behaving in social settings), but all of these represent the person's way of knowing. I've also said that personality support from other people (Weiss's seventh provision) actually serves to support and match these ways of understanding. Of course, the way that works is through talk and what you are doing in it. You get support from talking to other people.

I hypothesized in Chapter 1 that you might think of relationships as based on similarity of personality or attitudes, but I can now restate that thought differently. *Getting to know someone is getting to know his or her personal order.* This process of acquaintance opens the way people think and understand the world, including their understanding of how relationships work with other people—whether, for example, they expect relationships to be loose affiliations or close attachments.

Of course, you never get to know all of a person's ways of knowing the world in one shot; people are extremely complex. The processes of getting to know them are likewise long, complex, and probably an eternally open-ended endeavor ("unfinished business"). Some of these processes happen in speaking, as you exchange views of the world with one another. Some of them happen as you observe what other people do. Some result from hearing information about them from other people and also when you observe them interacting with others. People can always surprise you, even when you think you know them well, and in fact, that is part of the pleasure (and sometimes the pain) of knowing them, that they can make life more interesting by being relatively unpredictable at times!

The New Look at Relationships

I started the book by assuming that you had particular beliefs about the way in which relationships operate. My speculation was that you considered them to be made from choice and emotion. I have spent the rest of this book attempting to demonstrate the effects of talk, social order, performance, embodiment, materiality, and the oversight by the social order of private activity, whether explicitly by law or implicitly. Does this commit me to the view that we are all doomed to be puppets of the social order, deprived of choice and free will? No. The surprising reason is precisely because we talk to one another using our personal orders, but let me get there by first walking through the thicket of "performativity" introduced earlier and giving it another spin.

For those who hear now, as in the second paragraph of the chapter, the echoes of Judith Butler and the associated dead French guys who amorously arose in Chapter 5 (on sexuality), let me point out that language is (in their terms) "an iterative system" (i.e., a system that necessarily is used repeatedly and has an imposing force about it, as we saw in the previous chapter). That fact could, but should not, be seen as inducing iterative, repetitive performativity. In shorter words, it could be seen as creating a kind of mechanical repetitiveness to our conversations that would show how we are all dominated by unseen powerful forces, perpetually doomed to the rat race/treadmill of running round and round, thinking we are getting somewhere when, in fact, the system constrains us to stay at the bottom of the wheel.

Speaking and everyday chitchat are when persons, minds, and agents escape this paranoid trap of iteration, because we do not make the mistake of confusing iteration/repetition/limits on resources with temporality or occasion (or rhetorical situation). Each occasion of *speaking* is always different, as Heraclitus pointed out way before the French guys forgot it. What is iterated is done afresh at another time and in a different set of circumstances and requires agency (or personal orders) for it to recur, even though it may require the same toolbox of language. Likewise, Bourdieu's concept of *habitus* (a kind of set of habitual behaviors, customs, styles, rituals, and habits that people use in a society) does not swat the human tendency to invent, through curiosity and change, new ways of performing old behaviors.

Personal orders may or may not replicate a social order. Merely using social order tools, such as language, does not commit everyone to the same thoughts, conclusions, or actions. That is why everyday chitchat about life's experiences can modify the parties' personal orders (attitude change does happen!) and eventually lead to change in the social order itself as personal orders pile up for change.

THE ROLE OF SOCIAL ORDER IN RELATIONSHIPS

A social order oversees personal behavior by obvious mechanisms such as direct observation and regulation of public behavior, but it also does so less obviously through formal regulation of private behavior (like sex, Chapter 5). In even more subtle ways, it does so by use of belief systems that define "appropriateness" in culture (Chapter 3); metaphors that contain people's thoughts along desired lines (Chapter 7); and conventions that are imported into people's minds and then reinforced (usually unnoticed) by education, the media, and conversation with others. Casual chatter is thus a more significant influence on the individual's beliefs, criteria, and choices about friends, acquaintances, and partners than first appears.

Groupings Within a Social Order

My new approach to relationships is to regard them as essentially the projection of rhetorical visions into a shared, socially ordered world where they are either accepted or rejected by other people. Personal visions can accept or contest the social order, and people who share common visions will, as other comments in the book suggest, tend to cluster together in groups that either support or contest, resist, and attempt to change the social order. Conservatives cluster with conservatives; LGBT people talk of themselves as belonging to "a community" and attempt to change societal views about their human value. Only rarely does the lion lie down with the lamb.

Thus, the groupings that are observed in society and have been seen as the basis for relationships are not so much sociological predeterminants of choice (Kerckhoff, 1974) as material influences on the way in which people's personal orders are shaped by those around them. Within that context, the process of acquaintance is now seen as one by which two individuals become more closely aware of each other's broad psychological structure, system of values, personal orders, and evaluative judgments against the background provided by social order.

Everyday Talk as an Instrument of Relationships

I have briefly demonstrated in the previous chapter the way in which language is a particularly symbolic force in the breakdown of relationships as well as in their everyday conduct, but this present chapter has continued the theme to show its influence on the growth of relationships also. The point in both cases is that everyday talk is the instrument through which social order is played by different mouthpieces. The construction of a grave dressing story to avoid negative judgments during the breakdown of relationships is a person's way of adjusting the perception by others in conformity with the social order expectations for relational outcomes. The unveiling of another person's personal order and its iterative comparisons with one's own are the basis for growth of understanding and relationship.

I have also shown the ways in which other people influence an individual's personal order. The individual per se is not the only influence on the personal orders that he or she manifests to the world. Other people, even innocent friends, partners, and acquaintances, are acting as agents of society and reinforcing the social order through their commentaries and judgments—real or imagined—on the individual's behavior or expressed attitudes. Therefore, it is not similarity of attitudes per se that is attractive, but the discovery of a similarity and the projection of it beyond a particular instance to a larger systemic overlap that gives comfort in a potentially judgmental world.

This more complicated view of relationships does not, of course, in any way affect the way in which they are carried out. Part of its point, however, has been to demonstrate precisely that the way in which relationships are carried out is more complex than the old way research has suggested. In offering a new way of understanding what is happening when relationships occur, and, more pointedly, demonstrating that they occur persistently through everyday chitchat and not only at moments of expression of affection, the new approach points us to some old thoughts in a new light.

It points to the fact that many of the long-term aspects of relationships are carried out through performance and symbolic linguistic forms that are overlooked in a research agenda that focuses solely on emotion or the role of "preformed personality." It points to the fact that any study of commitment must examine the social order to define the context in which commitment is understood. It points to the fact that we have for too long ignored material forces that subsequently turned early attachments from psychological determinant forces into adapters and backgrounds for the *interpretation* of experience. Finally, the new way points us toward some taken-for-granted activities in human experience that have not been sufficiently unpicked, examined, or deprived of their force as commonsense characteristics.

When I have taught courses from this point of view, students are rarely shocked but some do feel that the new perspective gives some insights into everyday behavior that they had never noticed, had noticed but not understood, or had understood but not seen in a broader context. In particular, the students have rarely thought about material aspects of relationships, the symbolism of gifts, or the provisions of relationships. Not all are convinced that relationships are about epistemics, but the epistemic perspective is usually challenging and valuable even so.

PRACTICAL IMPLICATIONS OF THE NEW WAY

There is more than an eye-opener for relaters and researchers here, though. The new vantage point has some practical implications.

Relationships and Everyday Practices

Understanding how relationships are constructed by persons steered by, but capable of modifying, the social order in the personal order can be helpful, I think, in allowing us to understand existential truths about what we face in making relationships. In particular, it is illuminating when dealing with forms of relationship that have been outlawed in the past but have become more acceptable or with relationships that have found clever ways to resist society and a prevailing wartime rhetoric.

For example, Queer Theory has been developed to understand the ways in which certain bodies are marked and differentiated materially from the prevailing social order as different and "unacceptable" for relational and other purposes (Bennett, 2009). It has also been used to show how heteronormativity is being destabilized with new gendered/sexed enactments of relationships, because these upset the normal expectations within the social order (Manning, personal communication, April 2010). Furthermore, West (2007) has examined the experiences of women's resistance of 1970s "appropriately feminine" relationship forms, and indeed, the Vietnam War itself, by analyzing a maternal pacifist group named La WISP. This group created and marketed cookbooks in order to raise funds for women's pacifist politics. The cookbooks enabled the women to use everyday practices in order to redefine issues of war and peace in international rather than national terms. By this simple relational technique, they were able to argue for a universal humanity based on a larger social order of identification and cooperation, beyond nationalistic social orders.

Relationships as Agents of Social Change

When personal orders are resisting a social order—whether it is the Marquis de Sade and his Gnostic views of sexuality, the "make love not war" campaign of the 1960s and 1970s, student hookups in the first decade of the

21st century, or Facebook disclosures that exceed what occurs face-to-face—everyday relationship practices are brought to bear on the nature of society rather than vice versa. There is a material connection between the way in which the letter of the law is propounded by society and how it becomes malleable and bendable as personal orders take on resistance of the social order.

The issue of gay marriage is a continuation of, rather than a deviation from, the various uses that have been made of new relational forms in order to bring about social change. Issues such as deadbeat dads or whether children can divorce their parents do not gain traction in political discussion until they have gained traction in interpersonal chitchat. Once the public in its everyday form discusses these momentous matters, then they become issues of social policy debate. They are rarely imposed from above. Social change is a bottom-up process.

Is the Future of Relationships to Be Found in Technology?

Yes and no. It is obvious that relationships will be conducted through technology because this has always been true of the technologies available to any historical material age. As developing technologies become available to a wider public, so their use becomes relational whether through literacy and writing or telephones. Most technical and technological advances have been used in the conduct of relationships eventually, whether it be the motorcar, with its backseat; the computer, with its possibilities for boundless personal exposure; or the mobile phone, which gives us constant connection and availability to our nearest and dearest (and some others). All of these forms embody some of the symbolic acts that we would otherwise carry out face-to-face or by other means and so may equally be seen positively or negatively by our partners or potential partners. Sometimes, it takes a while for people to work out the protocol; it took about 3 years for an etiquette to develop against the ending of relationships by text message, for example. The recent movie *Up in the Air* works through the ways in which it is likewise ultimately unacceptable to fire people in a videoconference. And so the world turns.

The future of relationships is so much about what we know about others and how we display it, often electronically. Intimacy is not dead because technology is thriving. The warm hand on the shoulder, the loving embrace, will still be better than blankets or animatronic sex. However, perpetual connection to partners and the availability of alternatives on the Internet has altered expectations about the nature of commitment and relationship appropriateness. Concepts of commitment that were developed in the 1980s (Reis & Shaver, 1988) are no longer suited to present-day experience. In fact, much of the classic research that was done 25 years ago or less has been based too much on the material circumstances of two decades ago.

Now that we understand the importance of material circumstances upon thought, it is clear that our research agenda in the field of relationships must change. We need to know more about the mechanisms through which the larger views of a social order are filtered, used, resisted, and projected by personal orders based on . . . everyday chatter.

References

Bennett, J. A. (2009). *Banning queer blood: Rhetorics of citizenship, contagion, and resistance.* Tuscaloosa: University of Alabama Press.

Dindia, K. (1987). The effects of sex of subject and sex of partner on interruptions. *Human Communication Research, 13,* 345–371.

Duck, S. W. (2002). Hypertext in the key of G: Three types of "history" as influences on conversational structure and flow. *Communication Theory, 12*(1), 41–62.

Duck, S. W., & McMahan, D. T. (2010). *Communication in everyday life.* Thousand Oaks, CA: Sage.

Duck, S. W., & Pond, K. (1989). Friends, Romans, countrymen, lend me your retrospective data: Rhetoric and reality in personal relationships. In C. Hendrick (Ed.), *Close relationships* (Vol. 10, pp. 17–38). Newbury Park, CA: Sage.

Giles, H., & Coupland, N. (1991). *Language in social context.* Milton Keynes, UK: Open University Press.

Hopper, R., Knapp, M. L., & Scott, L. (1981). Couples' personal idioms: Exploring intimate talk. *Journal of Communication, 31,* 23–33.

Jourard, S. M. (1971). *Self-disclosure.* New York: Wiley.

Kerckhoff, A. C. (1974). The social context of interpersonal attraction. In T. L. Huston (Ed.), *Foundations of interpersonal attraction* (pp. 61–77). New York: Academic Press.

Mehrabian, A. (1971). *Silent messages.* Belmont, CA: Wadsworth.

Planalp, S., & Benson, A. (1992). Friends' and acquaintances' conversations I: Observed differences. *Journal of Social and Personal Relationships, 9,* 483–506.

Planalp, S., & Garvin-Doxas, K. (1994). Using mutual knowledge in conversation: Friends as experts on each other. In S. W. Duck (Ed.), *Dynamics of relationships* (pp. 1–26). Thousand Oaks, CA: Sage.

Reis, H. T., & Shaver, P. R. (1988). Intimacy as an interpersonal process. In S. W. Duck (Ed.), *Handbook of personal relationships: Theory, research and interventions* (pp. 367–390). New York: Wiley.

Sahlstein, E. M. (2000). *Relational rhetorics and RRTs (Relational Rhetorical Terms).* Unpublished manuscript, Iowa City, IA.

Watzlawick, P., Bavelas, J. B., & Jackson, D. D. (1967). *Pragmatics of human communication: A study of interactional patterns, pathologies, and paradoxes.* New York: Norton.

West, I. (2007). Performing resistance in/from the kitchen: The practice of maternal pacifist politics and La WISP's cookbooks. *Women's Studies in Communication, 30*(3), 358–383.

Index

About the Author

Steve Duck is the Daniel and Amy Starch Distinguished Research Chair and a College Administrative Fellow in the College of Liberal Arts and Sciences at the University of Iowa. He has served as Departmental Executive Officer for the Department of Communication Studies and the Department of Rhetoric at the University of Iowa. He was trained in the United Kingdom at Oxford (BA, MA) and Sheffield Universities (PhD) and taught in Scotland and England for 13 years before moving to Iowa. He founded, and edited for 15 years, the *Journal of Social and Personal Relationships* and has written or edited more than 50 books on relationships, television, research methods, social support, and a history of social psychology. His two most recent publications are with David McMahan and are *Basics of Communication* (2009) and *Communication in Everyday Life* (2010), both textbooks published by Sage. In April 2010, he was awarded the College of Liberal Arts and Sciences' Helen Kechriotis Nelson Teaching Award "for a lifetime of commitment to, and excellence in, teaching." He was elected to the National Communication Association's highest honor, Distinguished Scholar, in 2010. He reads Latin for pleasure and is interested in history, especially Roman military history and Tudor England. Latin and the history of Tudor England have come in handy as he traced his family tree back to 1550. He loves the music of Ralph Vaughan Williams, Kate Bush, and Gerry Rafferty; does bird-watching; and has a website where you can find out the rest, such as the fact that he always wears two watches and carries a Swiss Army Knife: http://myweb.uiowa.edu/blastd.

Supporting researchers for more than 40 years

Research methods have always been at the core of SAGE's publishing program. Founder Sara Miller McCune published SAGE's first methods book, *Public Policy Evaluation*, in 1970. Soon after, she launched the *Quantitative Applications in the Social Sciences* series—affectionately known as the "little green books."

Always at the forefront of developing and supporting new approaches in methods, SAGE published early groundbreaking texts and journals in the fields of qualitative methods and evaluation.

Today, more than 40 years and two million little green books later, SAGE continues to push the boundaries with a growing list of more than 1,200 research methods books, journals, and reference works across the social, behavioral, and health sciences. Its imprints—Pine Forge Press, home of innovative textbooks in sociology, and Corwin, publisher of PreK–12 resources for teachers and administrators—broaden SAGE's range of offerings in methods. SAGE further extended its impact in 2008 when it acquired CQ Press and its best-selling and highly respected political science research methods list.

From qualitative, quantitative, and mixed methods to evaluation, SAGE is the essential resource for academics and practitioners looking for the latest methods by leading scholars.

For more information, visit **www.sagepub.com**.